THE HALAKAH OF JESUS OF NAZARETH ACCORDING TO THE GOSPEL OF MATTHEW

Phillip Sigal

UNIVERSITY
PRESS OF
AMERICA

Lanham • New York • London

Copyright © 1986 by

Lillian Sigal

University Press of America,® Inc.

4720 Boston Way
Lanham, MD 20706

3 Henrietta Street
London WC2E 8LU England

Printed in the United States of America

Library of Congress Cataloging in Publication Data

Sigal, Phillip.
    The halakah of Jesus of Nazareth according to the
Gospel of Matthew.

    Bibliography: p .
    1. Jesus Christ—Teachings.   2. Divorce—Biblical
teaching.   3. Sabbath—Biblical teaching.   4. Bible.
N.T. Matthew—Criticism, interpretation, etc.
5. Jewish law.   6. Jesus Christ—Attitute towards
Jewish law.   I. Title.
BS2415.S55   1986   226'.206   85-29432
ISBN 0-8191-5210-2 (alk. paper)
ISBN 0-8191-5211-0 (pbk. : alk. paper)

All University Press of America books are produced on acid-free
paper which exceeds the minimum standards set by the National
Historical Publications and Records Commission.

Preface

My interest in Jesus and the New Testament began many years ago. It was influenced by a variety of factors. Among these were an undergraduate course at the University of Toronto, intensive interfaith activities in the ministry, and an interest in dual covenant theology. Having specialized in rabbinic-talmudic studies and engaged in a work on the origin of the halakhah, I perceived that the halakhah of the New Testament is an integral part of the sequence from the Old Testament to the Mishnah. A fresh examination of well-trod ground seemed to be a desideratum in order to arrive at a new understanding of Jesus' role in first-century Judaism and the role of first-century Judaism in the shaping of Christianity.

One of the pertinent themes related to this dissertation, the identity of the Pharisaioi, still requires an independent monogram. Furthermore, the halakhah in the Sermon on the Mount and the rest of Matthew, that in Mark and Luke as well as that reflected in John, Paul and James, all has to be examined from fresh perspectives. This dissertation is only an effort to begin to find understanding. I hope it will stimulate others to join in a search for a clearer perception of the authentic role that Jesus can play in the history of Judaism, and that Judaism plays in the Early Church, with consequent flowering of significant theological dialogue.

Those who have encouraged me in my work are here acknowledged. I am thankful to my major adviser, Professor Douglas R. A. Hare of the Pittsburgh Theological Seminary, for graciously accepting me as his student and then as an Assistant in New Testament studies. My thanks go to Professor Ulrich Mauser of the Pittsburgh Theological Seminary who also accepted me as an Assistant in New Testament studies; and to the other members of the committee, Professors Donald Gowan of the Pittsburgh Theological Seminary, and Harry C. Avery and Bernard Goldstein of the University of Pittsburgh.

My appreciation for unfailing courtesy is extended to Dikran V. Hadidian, Director of the Clifford Barbour Library of the Pittsburgh Theological Seminary, and to all of the members of his staff. I thank the typist of my first draft, Pamela C. Flinn, who labored at two of my manuscripts simultaneously, hard pressed to meet constant deadlines, and to Roberta M. Cadman for this final typing.

Concluding words of gratitude go to my wife, Lillian, and to my daughters, Sharon and Sabrina, whose unselfish love for me and regard for my work allowed me to leave full-time employment in 1975 in order to undertake my doctoral studies.

TABLE OF CONTENTS

Page
PREFACE iii
ABBREVIATIONS viii
  I. INTRODUCTION 1
     A. THESIS 1
     B. ASPECTS OF EARLIER SCHOLARSHIP 9
        1. HOW SOME SCHOLARS SEE MATTHEW'S
           PERSPECTIVE ON JESUS 9
        2. UNDERSTANDING "THE LAW" 12
        3. THE LOVE COMMAND FACTOR 17
        4. THE MEANING OF MATTHEW 5:17-20 19
     C. RECAPITULATION AND PROJECTION 23
        1. RECAPITULATION 23
        2. PROJECTION 23
           a. PREMISES 23
           b. SOURCES 24
           c. METHODOLOGY 24
     D. THE CHAPTER SEQUENCE 25
 II. STAGES IN THE FORMATION OF RABBINIC HALAKHAH 28
     A. PRE-EXILIC ORIGINS 28
     B. PRE-EXILIC DIVERSITY AND POST-EXILIC
        RETRENCHMENT TO THE HASMONEAN ERA . . . 29
        1. 587 B.C. TO THE NEHEMIAN REFORMATION . 29
        2. FROM EZRA-NEHEMIAH TO THE KNOWN
           PROTO-RABBIS 31
        3. THE GREAT ASSEMBLY 32
        4. THE SECOND CENTURY B.C. 34
     C. FROM EARLIEST PROTO-RABBIS TO THE
        ERA OF JESUS 37
        1. THE EARLY FATHERS 37
        2. AN HISTORICAL RESUME 42
III. PROTO-RABBINIC HALAKHIC ACTIVITY 47
     A. FACTORS IN REINTERPRETATION AND
        INNOVATION OF HALAKHAH 47
        1. PROTO-RABBINIC AUTHORITY 47
        2. ON DATING RABBINIC TEXTS 51
     B. A PROFILE OF PROTO-RABBINIC HALAKHIC
        PREMISES 54
        1. RELIGIO-HUMANITARIAN CONCERNS IN
           HALAKHAH 54
        2. THE HISTORICAL FACTOR 58
        3. HERMENEUTICS AND EXEGESIS 60
        4. THE TENDENCY TOWARD LENIENCY 69
        5. THE PRINCIPLE OF LIFNIM MESHURAT HADIN 74
 IV. THE MATTHEAN JESUS AND THE HALAKHAH OF
     DIVORCE 83
     A. A GENERAL OVERVIEW 83

B. MATTHEW 5:32 and 19:9 AND THE MEANING
   OF PORNEIA 94
C. MATTHEW 5:17-19 AND THE DIVORCE PERICOPAE 102
D. DIVORCE IN POST-PENTATEUCHAL SOURCES . . 104
   1. ELEPHANTINE 104
   2. EZRA AND NEHEMIAH 105
   3. THE APOCRYPHA AND PSEUDEPIGRAPHA . . 106
   4. PHILO 107
   5. QUMRAN 111
V. THE MATTHEAN JESUS AND THE SABBATH HALAKHAH 119
A. A GENERAL OVERVIEW 119
B. PLUCKING, PICKING AND/OR RUBBING GRAIN
   ON THE SABBATH 128
C. HEALING ON THE SABBATH 136
D. PENTATEUCHAL AND EXTRA-PENTATEUCHAL
   SABBATH HALAKHAH 142
   1. THE PENTATEUCH 142
   2. THE PROPHETS 143
   3. THE WRITINGS 143
   4. THE BOOK OF JUBILEES 145
   5. PHILO 146
   6. QUMRAN; THE ZADOKITE FRAGMENT 149
VI. SUMMARY AND CONCLUSIONS 154
A. SUMMARY 154
B. CONCLUSIONS 157
NOTES 160
BIBLIOGRAPHY 250

ABBREVIATIONS

(Note: All the works of the Old and New Testaments and the Talmud are listed. Otherwise only the books cited are listed.)

The Old Testament
(The Order According to Masoretic Text)

O.T.	– Old Testament	Mic.	– Micah
Gen.	– Genesis	Nah.	– Nahum
Ex.	– Exodus	Hab.	– Habakuk
Lev.	– Leviticus	Zeph.	– Zephaniah
Num.	– Numbers	Hag.	– Haggai
Deut.	– Deuteronomy	Zekh.	– Zekhariah
Josh.	– Joshua	Mal.	– Malakhi
Judg.	– Judges	Ps.	– Psalms
I Sam.	– I Samuel	Prov.	– Proverbs
II Sam.	– II Samuel	Job	– Job
I Ki.	– I Kings	S of S	– Song of Songs
II Ki.	– II Kings	Ruth	– Ruth
Is.	– Isaiah	Lam.	– Lamentations
Jer.	– Jeremiah	Ecc.	– Ecclesiastes
Ez.	– Ezekiel	Est.	– Esther
Hos.	– Hosea	Dan.	– Daniel
Joel	– Joel	Ezra	– Ezra
Am.	– Amos	Neh.	– Nehemiah
Ob.	– Obadiah	I Chron.	– I Chronicles
Jon.	– Jonah	II Chron.	– II Chronicles

The Translations

LXX	– Septuagint	P. Targ	– Palestinian Targum
Onk.	– Targum Onkelos		

Apocrypha and Pseudepigrapha

Bar.	– Baruch
Ben Sira	– The Wisdom of Sirach
I En.	– I Enoch
Jub.	– Jubilees
I, II, IV Macc.	– I, II and IV Maccabees
Test. Benj.	– Testament of Benjamin
Test. Dan	– Testament of Dan
Test. Gad	– Testament of Gad
Test. Iss.	– Testament of Issachar
Test. Jos.	– Testament of Joseph
Test. Jud.	– Testament of Judah
Test. Reub.	– Testament of Reuben
Test. Zeb.	– Testament of Zebulon

The Dead Sea Scrolls

C D C	– Zadokite Document
I Q S	– Manual of Discipline
I Q M	– Scroll of the War

The New Testament

N.T.	– New Testament	I Tim.	– I Timothy
Mt.	– Matthew	II Tim.	– II Timothy
Mk.	– Mark	Tit.	– Titus
Lk.	– Luke	Phm.	– Philemon
Jn.	– John	Heb.	– Hebrews
Acts	– Acts	James	– James
Rom.	– Romans	I Pet.	– I Peter
I Cor.	– I Corinthians	II Pet.	– II Peter
II Cor.	– II Corinthians	I Jn.	– I John
Gal.	– Galatians	II Jn.	– II John
Eph.	– Ephesians	III Jn.	– III John
Phil.	– Philippians	Jude	– Jude
Col.	– Colossians	Rev.	– Revelation
I Thess.	– I Thessalonians		
II Thess.	– II Thessalonians		

Josephus

Ag. Ap.	– Against Apion
Ant.	– Jewish Antiquities
Vita	– The Life
War	– The Jewish War

Philo

Abr.	– On Abraham
Alleg. Int.	– Allegorical Interpretation
Dec.	– On the Decalogue
Hyp.	– Hypothetica
Mig. Ab.	– On the Migration of Abraham
Q E	– Questions and Answers, Exodus
Q G	– Questions and Answers, Genesis
Spec. Laws	– On the Special Laws

The Talmud

(M or T before the name of a tractate signifies Mishnah and Tosefta, respectively; B or P before the name of a tractate signifies Babylonian and Palestinian Talmud, respectively; R preceding a name signifies Rabbi.)

Ab.	Abot	Men.	Menahot
Ab.de.R.N.	Abot de Rabbi Nathan	Mid.	Middot
		Mik.	Mikvaot
Ahal.	Ahalot	M.K.	Moed Katan
Ar.	Arakhin	Naz.	Nazir
A.Z.	Abodah Zarah	Ned.	Nedarim
B.B.	Baba Batra	Neg.	Negaim
Bekh.	Bekhorot	Nid.	Niddah
Ber.	Berakhot	Or.	Orlah
Bez.	Bezah	Par.	Parah
Bik.	Bikkurim	Peah	Peah
B.K.	Baba Kama	Pes.	Pesahim
B.M.	Baba Mezia	R.H.	Rosh Hashanah
Dem.	Demai	San.	Sanhedrin
Ed.	Eduyot	Sem.	Semahot
Er.	Erubin	Shab.	Shabbat
Git.	Gittin	Shebi.	Sheviit
Hag.	Hagigah	Sheb.	Shebuot
Hal.	Halah	Shek.	Shekalim
Hor.	Horayot	Sot.	Sotah
Hul.	Hulin	Suk.	Sukkah
Kel.	Kelim	Taan.	Taanit
Ker.	Keritot	Tam.	Tamid
Ket.	Ketubot	Tem.	Temurah
Kid.	Kiddushin	Ter.	Terumot
Kil.	Kilayim	Tah.	Taharot
Kin.	Kinnim	Teb. Y.	Tebul Yom
Maas.	Maasrot	Uk.	Ukzin
Maas. Sh.	Maaser Sheni	Yad.	Yadayim
Mak.	Makkot	Yeb.	Yebamot
Makh.	Makhshirin	Yom.	Yoma
Meg.	Megilah	Zab.	Zabim
Meil.	Meilah	Zeb.	Zebahim

Midrashim

Gen. R.	-	Genesis Rabbah (Note: Each volume of Midrash Rabbah is cited in this manner: The biblical book followed by R.)
Mekh.	-	Mekhilta de R. Ishrael to Exodus
P.K.	-	Pesikta de R. Kahana
PRE	-	Pirke de Rabbi Eliezer
Sifra	-	Sifra to Leviticus
Sif	-	Sifre to Numbers and Deuteronomy

Other

ddd	-	dină demalkhută dină
EJ	-	Encyclopedia Judaica
JE	-	The Jewish Encyclopedia
TDNT	-	Theological Dictionary of the New Testament
TWNT	-	Theologisches Worterbuch zum Neuer Testament

Periodicals

BA	– Biblical Archaeologist
BJRL	– Bulletin of John Rylands Library
BSOAS	– Bulletin, School of Oriental and African Studies
CBQ	– Catholic Biblical Quarterly
ETR	– Études Théologiques et Religieuses
HTR	– Harvard Theological Review
HUCA	– Hebrew Union College Annual
JBL	– Journal of Biblical Literature
JES	– Journal of Ecumenical Studies
JJS	– Journal of Jewish Studies
JQR	– Jewish Quarterly Review
MTZ	– Munchener Theologische Zeitschrift
NKZ	– Neue kirchliche Zeitschrift
NTS	– New Testament Studies
PIJSL	– Papers of the Institute of Jewish Studies, London
SJT	– Scottish Journal of Theology
ZAW	– Zeitschrift für die Alttestamenthiche Wissenschaft
ZNW	– Zeitschrift für die Neutestamenthiche Wissenschaft
ZTK	– Zeitschrift für Theologie und Kirche

I. INTRODUCTION
A. Thesis

The objective of this study is to examine two specific themes of the _halakhah_ of Jesus of Nazareth, namely Sabbath and Divorce, which will serve as paradigms in an effort to place Matthew's Jesus in a chain of tradition stretching from Ezra and Nehemiah to the Mishnah.

This dissertation proceeds on the premise that the canonical text of Matthew contains an authentic presentation of what the redactor of Matthew believed to be the views of Jesus. Out of considerations of space and cohesiveness I take no side in the complex controversy surrounding the synoptic problem. There is also no effort here to uncover a category one may term "dominical sayings" through a cumbersome effort of form or redaction criticism. This work has already been done by many able scholars who have failed to reach unanimity as to what precisely are the words of Jesus and what are the interpolations and expansions of the redactors.[1] In a real sense this study leans toward some of the views expressed by what has been called the "Scandinavian school," which is somewhat wary of the exaggerated claims of form criticism. I can endorse what W. D. Davies has indicated, that H. Riesenfeld and B. Gerhardsson:

> have made it far more historically probable and reasonably credible, over against the skepticism of much form-criticism, that in the Gospels we are within hearing of the authentic voice and within the sight of the authentic activity of Jesus of Nazareth...[2]

The question of the relationship between Matthew and rabbinic literature, whether to affirm or deny rabbinism to Jesus, or as some have expressed it, the question of "Jesus and the Law," has also been examined by a wide variety of modern scholars.[3] It would be impossible and impractical here exhaustively to survey these writings and offer a critique of them in order to justify one more study of the same problem. Recent works be Asher Finkel,[4] Robert Banks[5] and John Meier[6] succinctly review many older studies and embody the results of more recent scholarship.

1

There are, however, certain deficiencies in past studies dealing with "Jesus and the Law," which result from four presuppositions. One or more of these presuppositions pervade the writings of both Christian and Jewish scholars, with rare exceptions.[7]

1. The first presupposition is that the _Pharisaioi_, the persons in controversy with Jesus in many gospel narratives, constitute the predecessors of the later rabbis, and thus by extension represented rabbinic Judaism. So-called "Pharisaism" is thus generally equated with rabbinic Judaism.[8] From this position I know of no dissenting voice until very recently.[9] This almost universal opinion is largely based on the testimony of Josephus who devotes a good deal of attention to the _Pharisaioi_. Because he describes the "Pharisees" as the most important of the leading religious parties (e.g., _Ant._ XVIII, 1.2(11)-5(23); _War_, II, 8.14(162)) it was only natural that scholars should seek to connect this group with that movement which later dominated the Jewish religious scene, viz., rabbinic Judaism. There were, indeed, a number of features in Josephus' narrative which appeared to support this identification. For a number of reasons, however, this traditional view must now be challenged.

It should be noticed, in the first place, that not once does Josephus connect the Pharisees with rabbis or rabbinic Judaism. He does indeed describe them as people who "excel the rest of the nation in observance of religion and as _exact_ [my italics] exponents of the laws,"[10] but these words need not be taken as a description of the rabbis of Josephus' literary period or of the proto-rabbis who preceded them before 70 A.D. They can just as well, indeed better, describe the pietistic _perushim_ who are mentioned in the Tannaitic literature (M. Hag. 2:7, T. Yad. 2:20). That is to say, Josephus and the tannaitic sources use similar terms to describe people who are rigorists in their interpretation and practice of the halakhah, whereas, as we shall see, the proto-rabbis and their successors were in fact opposed to such rigorism. On the other hand, there are many times when Josephus describes individuals in terms which remind us of the rabbis, and in no case does he identify these persons as _Pharisaioi_. He refers to them as _logiōtatoi_ (most learned), _exēgētai tōn patriōn nomōn_ (exegetes of the norms of the fathers), _sophistai_ (the Greek equivalent of _hakhamim_) and

<u>punthanomenoi</u> (people who learn by inquiry, scholars, the equivalent of Hebrew <u>darshanim</u>).[11] Some of these, at least, may well have been proto-rabbis. Thus he writes, the:

> ...<u>logiōtatoi</u>, [the most learned] of the Jews and unrivalled <u>exēgētai tōn patriōn nomōn</u>, [interpreters of ancestral norms] and men especially dear to the people because they educated the youth, for all those who made an effort to acquire virtue used to spend time with them day after day. When these <u>punthanomenoi</u> [scholars]... (Ant. XVII. 6.2 (149f)).

There are occasions when Josephus explicitly refers to individuals as Essenes of <u>Pharisaioi</u>, as in the case of "Pollion the Pharisee" (ibid. IV. 1.1 (3)) or Manaēmos [Menahem] the Essene (ibid. XV.10.5 (373)), to offer only two examples. It is therefore possible to propose that when he speaks of scholars and lecturers without employing such epithets he has in mind persons I refer to as proto-rabbis.

Another example of this is conceivably found in his discussion of the "Sons of Baba" (<u>Ant</u>. XV.7.10 (260-266)). Identification of these persons is very difficult, but the names Baba b. Buta and Judah b. Baba occur in rabbinic literature (M. Ker. 6:3; Yeb. 16:7). The former is connected with Herod (B.B.B. 3b-4a) and the latter is a major first-century scholar who may have been a scion of the same family. Again it must be noticed that Josephus does not refer to them as <u>Pharisaioi</u>, despite the fact that he tells us they were of "a high position and great influence with the masses" (<u>Ant</u>. XV.7.10 (263f)).

When Josephus refers to <u>Pharisaioi</u>, on the other hand, he identifies them as stringent in their interpretations of halakhah, and very precise, meticulous and zealous in their observance. Not proto-rabbis, but pietistic rigorists are described by Josephus' statement, "The Pharisees simplify their standard of living, making no concession to luxury... They show respect and deference to their elders, nor do they rashly presume to contradict their proposals..."[12] Similarly, throughout the New Testament we find that "Pharisees" are meticulous and fastidious about ritualism.

One of the unfortunate results of the traditional identification of the <u>Pharisaioi</u> of Josephus and the New Testatment with the predecessors of the rabbis is the misdirected effort to rehabilitate the former for the sake of the latter. "Pharisaism" is presented as a noble spiritual movement, and its deficiencies are neglected, out of a desire to defend rabbinic Judaism.[13] But if the initial error of identifying so-called "Pharisaism" with rabbinic Judaism had not been made, this defense would not be required.

Although this proposal cannot be fully pursued within the scope of this work, the study will proceed on the assumption that it is legitimate to conjecture that the <u>Pharisaioi</u> of the New Testament represent a complex, incohate mass of pietists and separatists.[14] Some of these may have been in organized societies such as those of Qumran and the Essenes, while others remained unorganized pietistic <u>hasidim</u>. These people, as will be elucidated in the relevant sections below, were rigid in their halakhah, "strict constructionists" in their hermeneutics and exegesis, and were therefore at serious odds with Jesus. Some proto-rabbis, those pre-Yabnean scholars of the halakhah, experts in the <u>nomos</u> (<u>nomikos</u>,[15] <u>nomodidaskalos</u>[16]), by inclination or upbringing may have indulged in some aspects of <u>perushit</u>, so as to be taken as such occasionally in colloquial idiom, but they were sufficiently relaxed in their piety as to find <u>perushim</u> distasteful and never to refer to themselves by that rubric.[17] Thus it is possible for Luke (Acts 5:34) to refer to Gamaliel the Elder as a "pharisee," but he immeidately identifies him also as a <u>nomodidaskalos</u>,[18] a teacher of the <u>nomos</u>. Luke is conscious that to identify Gamaliel as a "pharisee" alone is to be inaccurate concerning Gamaliel. Luke places him in proper perspective as a proto-rabbi, indicating also that he knew that as a proto-rabbi Gamaliel would find little to give battle with in the teaching of Jesus now being propagated by Peter and the others. And indeed, Gamaliel's statement to the Sanhedrin,

> ...because if of men is this scheme and this activity it will be destroyed. But if it is indeed from God you will not be able to destroy them, but you might find yourselves

> fighting against God (Acts 5:38b,
> 39)[19]

if authentic, constitutes an historic challenge to Judaism to examine the survival of Christianity.

Further support for this working hypothesis will be provided by a closer examination of the Sabbath and Divorce halakhah which will make manifest that it is not the teachers of "rabbinic Judaism" after 70 who are in controversy with Jesus. The halakhah of those delineated <u>Pharisaioi</u> in the gospel will be shown to be closer to the halakhah of Jubilees and the Dead Sea Scrolls than to that of emergent rabbinic Judaism. The "strict constructionism" placed upon the halakhah in the heyday of retrenchment and separatism after the missions of Ezra and Nehemiah was deepened by the pietists who dissented from the Hasmonean usurpers of the Zadokite priesthood and Davidic throne.

The acrimony expressed in controversies between Jesus and <u>perushim</u> is analogous in modern times to the acrimony that obtains toward the Conservative Movement in Judaism on the part of the Orthodox. On the premise that more people can be "led astray" by the Conservative Movement's "appearance" of traditionalism than by the Reform Movement's frank disavowal of talmudic authority, the Orthodox oppose the Conservative Movement more vigorously. Thus Jesus' demands are severe in his preaching, and his halakhah is frequently stricter than that of the <u>perushim</u>, but on the other hand, he is no consolation to them and constitutes a threat to them when he manifestly rejects their elitist "elect" system, sometimes disregards their strict halakhic norms, and denies the need for an organized monastic society. Their objections to him become of cumulative benefit to the priests and their supporters, the Sadducees.[20] The latter groups are concerned, as was Antipas over John, that Jesus constitutes a real source of potential insurrection. His messianic preaching could not but hearten the Zealots and <u>sicarii</u> and frighten the Establishment. The priests could broaden the base of their anti-Jesus conspiracy by appealing to the interests of the <u>perushim</u> while really being frightened of the messianic fervor exhibited by the Zealots and <u>sicarii</u>. They had, however, no doctrinal basis for putting him to death, and the only way to achieve this was by using Roman authority to suppress potential insurrection.

2. The second presupposition is that, beginning with the time of Ezra and Nehemiah, Judaism became a hopelessly "legalistic" system. It is commonly held that the controversies in the New Testament reflect the attempt on the part of Jesus and his followers to transcend what is regarded as a perversion of prophetic religion. The conception of Judaism as "legalism" even extends to interpretations of its soteriology, it being commonly maintained that Judaism offers salvation only by "works," and that this interplay of works and salvation reinforces the rigid legalism. The scope of this dissertation does not permit a close examination of this proposition, but it requires mention here because it is one of the elements responsible for the failure to assess correctly the halakhah of Jesus in relation to that of rabbinic Judaism.[21] Basically we are weighted down by what E. P. Sanders [22] has summarized as the Weber--Schürer--Bousset tradition, fueled by the theological ingenuity of Rudolf Bultmann, sustained by what has become a surrogate for authentic rabbinnic literature, viz. the Strack-Billerbeck <u>Kommentar</u>, and perpetuated by Gerhard Kittel's Wörterbuch.[23] Sanders[24] has written a devastating critique of this long-standing conception, building upon some earlier work by George Foote Moore.[25] Even if part of Sanders' specific critique of individual scholars is modified, his contribution toward helping us surmount this traditional premise can help us understand Jesus in his capacity of proto-rabbinic halakhist as well as charismatic prophet and thus bring us closer to a proper evaluation of the matrix out of which Christianity emerged.[26]

3. The third presupposition is the conviction that Christianity was separated from Judaism owing to the irreconcilable conflict in theology and halakhah between it and later rabbinic Judaism and that this had its origin in the bitter conflict between Jesus and the Pharisees (understood as "rabbis"). In light of the foregoing, however, it should be emphasized that it was not this branch of Judaism which was in controversy with Jesus. Rather what is to us an unknown group of pietists are the protagonists in the controversy narratives, and these were not the precursors of the rabbis. Sadducean priestly antagonism won the support of non-Establishment priestly circles to whom Jesus also appeared to be a danger, and his crucifixion came about as a result of

political concerns.[27] The new baptist and messianic movements of John and Jesus had appeal to the same kind of person as the Qumran and Essene fellowships and monasteries, but the latter lacked the open-ended brotherhood of the former. Those Jews who adopted faith in Jesus as the Messiah after the crucifixion in effect became enemies of Zealots, _sicarii_, and _perushim_, all of whom despised the Christian notion of a non-political Messiah. The Christian Jews abstained from the Roman war. The survivors who achieved power after 70 A.D. were those around Yoḥanan b. Zakkai and his peace party. After 80 A.D. the survivors of the Jerusalem Establishment reassumed power in concert with Rome which was forever seeking to pacify unruly provinces without war, if possible. Like the Christians, Yoḥanan's peace party was shunted aside and with apparant obtuseness Rome recognized the patriarchate in Palestine. The latter would yet again test Roman patience and power in the debacle of the Bar Kokhba rebellion.[28] The new Jewish Establishment in post-Yoḥanan Yabneh now set about to break the Christian Jewish faction in what was bidding to become a near-monolithic Judaism for the first time in centuries. This is rabbinic Judaism. The schools of Hillel and Shammai were gone, the priesthood was gone, organized Essenes and Qumranites and the whole assortment of Zealots and _sicarii_ were decimated. The rabbis (the title "rabbi" assumed by the new sacerdotal class upon ordination within a system devised by Yoḥanan at Yabneh) set about to gain unilateral authority.[29] That this bid for monolithic ecclesiastical authority never succeeded is a matter for separate discussion. Beyond our purview is the quest for total authority on the part of the rabbis who therefore sought to suppress Christianity. This latter effort undoubtedly went through a lengthy process into the second century. We may assume that it had the support of the masses because of a strong antipathy against the Christians for disassociating themselves from the war of 66-70. It was neither doctrinal nor halakhic issues that made for the isolation of Christians by the _birkhat hāminim_ and perhaps by letters of expulsion of Christians from the synagogues.

Thus it was not that the supposed antinomian or anti-halakhic posture of Christianity, or the Christology, was incompatible with "Pharisaic Judaism" which led to the separation of faiths. The premise that underlies this work is that at no time during the

7

first five decades after the crucifixion were Christian Judaism and pre-rabbinic Judaism wholly incompatible. Post-70 Jews were antagonistic to the returned Christians at Jerusalem and to the expansion and success of their movement. This success implied a growing anti-national trend among Palestinian Jews and thus a shrinking reservoir of population available for a future war of messianic liberation. It was undoubtedly with broad-based support of the nationalist elements that Gamaliel II and his circle were able to supersede Yohanan and his peace circle at Yabneh. The suppression, isolation and separation of Christianity followed.[30]

What concerns us, however, is that just as at the end of the century it was neither theology nor halakhah that finalized the schism between rabbinic Judaism and Christian Judaism, so at the year 30 neither theology nor halakhah brought about the crucifixion. And because neither theology nor halakhah were at stake, the proto-rabbis who were the leading non-Establishment spiritual leaders were not in controversy with Jesus. They were not the "Pharisees" of the New Testament. They were brothers under the skin to Jesus. What made their successors, the rabbis of Yabneh, antagonists to Jesus' successors was not theology nor halakhah but national and political complications, including accomodation with militant circles. This view of the separation of Christianity is therefore profoundly related to the thesis of this work in retrospect, and this thesis reinforces the view. For halakhah of Jesus of Nazarath according to the Gospel of Matthew places Jesus in the line of proto-rabbinic teachers. He is sometimes stricter because, as we will see, he insists upon norms of piety that go beyond the minimum halakhah just as sometimes the school of Hillel did and sometimes the school of Shammai did. His approach to the halakhah is manifestly similar to that of proto-rabbinnic and rabbinic Judaism.

4. The fourth presupposition which contributes to obscuring a correct understanding of the halakhah of Jesus of Nazareth is the tendency on the part of many scholars to seek to understand Jesus of Nazareth in the light of incarnation theology. This compels scholars to labor at proving the uniqueness of Jesus. The doctrine of incarnation impels the assessment that Jesus could not be "merely" a proto-rabbi since he was God incarnate.[31] This study seeks to examine the

halakhah of Jesus as that of the man from Nazareth who, in rabbinic terms, had to be a Torah which speaks in "the language of humans."[32] As a human, living and functioning in the social environment of his day, he appeared as a prophetic proto-rabbi. The Gospel of John, as significant as its prologue is to Christology, is a gospel written in retrospect. The people around Jesus did not know of or speak of incarnation in regard to him. They knew him as the man of Nazareth. The halakhah of Jesus of Nazareth should be studied in the light of his humanity and not his divinity.

Summary

The working hypothesis of this dissertation is that the <u>Pharisaioi</u> in controversy with Jesus in Matthew are <u>perushim</u>, pietistic sectarian Jews of various circles whose identity is still not clear to us. While Jesus often made demands that were stricter than the proto-rabbinic norms, he acted on principles that were not acceptable to <u>perushim</u> but were either already part of or destined to become part of proto-rabbinic and rabbinic Judaism. He was therefore an early proto-rabbi of the tannaitic era and taught halakhah accordingly. He was neither a Sadducee nor a Pharisee, neither a Hillelite nor a Shammaite. He employed freedom of interpretation and authority in conformity with the fashion of proto-rabbinic Judaism. As will become manifest, he applied principles that overcame certain hardships of the halakhah. In such cases he waived the halakhah. At other times he applied principles that made severe demands that would test the mettle of one who sought to enter the Kingdom of Heaven.

B. Aspects of Earlier Scholarship

1. How Some Scholars See Matthew's Perspective on Jesus

Previous scholars have debated several questions which relate to the subject matter of this dissertation.

The first is whether the redactor of Matthew was a Jew or a gentile. Scholars have extensively and minutely examined the antitheses of the Sermon on the Mount, the crucial verses Mt. 5:17-20, and each of the references in the synoptic gospels and in the Gospel of John to the questions of divorce, the Sabbath, and other halakhic issues raised by the New Testament text. No purpose can be served by reviewing all of the manifold works and views at this time. It is but necessary to cite recent conclusions.

W. D. Davies[33] and R. Hummel[34] argued that the redactor of Matthew was a Christian Jew. K. Stendahl's[35] view was that Matthew was a redactor of a work that took shape in a Qumran type community. G. Strecker believed he was a gentile.[36] O. Lamar Cope, more recently argued that he was a Christian Jew, familiar with the Old Testament and an expert in the contemporary Judaic interpretations of it.[37] J. P. Meier evinced a degree of ambivalence, but finally concluded that Matthew was a Gentile Christian.[38]

The second question that has occasioned much debate is whether Jesus abrogated the Law.[39] Some modern scholars have argued that Jesus did not abrogate the Law, but rather penetrated to its inner spirit.[40] Others argued that Jesus abrogated the Law.[41] A modern proponent of this view is T. W. Manson, who has incorporated it in his various writings that apply to the halakhah of the New Testament.[42] There were those who did not argue abrogation, but insisted that Jesus had done something that came close to that. This they referred to as "radicalization," a condition in which Jesus' interpretation of the Law had such implications that it made for a toally new approach, tantamount to abrogation.[43]

There are several other approaches to how Jesus handled the Law. Some take the view that one need not compare Jesus' words with those of the Old Testament, seeking the answer to the question whether or not he abrogated it. For example, H. J. Schoeps takes the view that since Jesus was regarded by his followers as speaking the divine word, the very content of the Old Testament has to be tested against his injunction.[44] Others have seen Jesus' attitude as "fulfilling" the Law, a term that begs much definition.[45] His attitude can be interpreted ultimately as predicting the abrogation of the Law with the advent of the Kingdom, or as having the Law remaining effective through faith in Jesus whose death is its fulfillment. There are those again who see in Jesus' teachings an exposition

10

of Moses' commands.[46]

Related to this second question is a third: how precisely Matthew deals with the Law. Matthew has been described as a "catholic" evangelist whose work contains both strict and lenient attitudes.[47] Others see him as highly nomistic.[48] And yet a third group of scholars looks upon him as having emancipated the church from the Mosaic law.[49] Of the latter group, some see the Gospel as reflecting Petrine Christianity and others Hellenistic Christianity.[50]

Some scholars have attempted to explain Matthew's departures from rabbinic halakhic material as deriving from his thesis that for Jesus the love command stood at the heart of the interpretation of the Torah. Nevertheless, they concede that Matthew preserves Christian Jewish elements in his effort to formulate a new Christian halakhah.[51] Arguing against this "rabbinic-type" Matthew are those who are exemplified by G. Strecker[52] who makes the point that Matthew's redactional activity stressed emancipation from the rabbinic emphasis on halakhah, and that such elements are no longer valid or vital in his church.

In this dissertation I am examining aspects of Jesus' halakhah as seen in Matthew's finished product. It is appropriate to take note of attempts by others to see precisely what it was that Matthew thought Jesus himself taught.[53] It is not my task here to come to grips with whether or not they have succeeded. The foregoing is only intended to place the question in perspective. Under the headings of divorce and Sabbath halakhah in Chapters Four and Five I will more comprehensively survey the views and conclusions of a variety of scholars as they affect the precise understanding of the halakhah of Jesus as presented in Matthew. There it will become evident that I regard Matthew as a Christian Jew, faithful to the fundamental Judaic concept that loyalty to an interpretive halakhah is as vital as fidelity to the Torah, and that this was the message of Jesus. But Matthew presented Jesus in terms of a proto-rabbi who offered alternative halakhah and for whom even abrogation of specific halakhot was not a problem.

What none of the above-mentioned studies attempts to do is to assess the halakhah attributed to Jesus as part of the evolution of halakhic understanding that was an ongoing process from Mosaic times. This was to

11

some extent presented by Asher Finkel.[54] But his account requires correction on several grounds which will become clear in the process of subsequent chapters. Otherwise the scholars who have engaged in the quest for the halakhah of Jesus have been "negative" in the sense of finding discrepancies in Matthew, arguing that he was ambivalent, or that he did not have Jesus say the same things in private as in public.[55] This study intends to be "positive" insofar as it undertakes to explicate how Jesus, as presented by Matthew, stood in the historical sequence of Torah and halakhah. We will see that Jesus was not a deviant Pharisee,[56] as Finkel proposes, but simply an individual teacher applying his inherited hermeneutic as well as any revelation granted him, to the exposition of Torah, the innovation of new custom or the abrogation of old practices.

2. Understanding "the Law"

Biblical principles and institutions were sometimes "forever," but the detailed forms were not. Essence and form are two separate aspects of a whole. Together they constitute religion, consisting of theology and halakhah or doctrine and practice respectively. We can see this exemplified in several institutions of Judaism. The essence of the Sabbath is commemoration of Creation or the Exodus, the theological affirmation of God as Creator and Redeemer. The form is how to observe a Sabbath. The essence of marriage is the union of male and female in accordance with the will of God at creation in order that the blessing of Creation be fulfilled (Gen. 2:24, 1:28). The institution of marriage is the form which makes it a social reality; divorce is the form through which this is dissolved.

We may illustrate this further with circumcision. Circumcision is the sign of the covenant (Gen. 17:9-14): theologically conceived as a sacrificial offering, its blood a redemptive remembrance before God.[58] The particulars of the practice of circumcision as surgical act and as liturgical process constitute the forms. Circumcision is declared to be "for their generations," "a sign of the covenant" (Gen. 17:9, 11). The halakhah or form is minimal in the Torah. The male child is to be circumcised on the eighth day; this applies to one born to the family or purchased as slave from an outsider (Gen. 17:12; Lev. 12:3). It is clear, nonetheless, that many halakhot are required: the instrument to use, whether it is to be a private rite or performed in community, the type of excision, and the liturgy. It is not our task here to review the anthropological details of where, how, and at what age circumcision was performed on males and females in a wide variety of ancient societies.[59] Our concern is merely to point out that while the Torah declares an institution of profound theological import to be "for their generations," "an eternal covenant," (Gen. 17:33) and threatens expulsion from God's elect community for non-compliance (v. 14), it hardly provides sufficient guidance on how to practice it.

Similarly the Sabbath is considered a "covenant sign" and is declared to be "for your generations" (Ex. 31:12-15). It is pronounced "an eternal covenant for their generations," "an eternal sign" of the creation (Ex. 31:16-17).[60] Nevertheless, there is scanty reference in the Pentateuch to the form, a matter we will take up more fully in Chapter Five. All that need be remarked at this juncture is that we have before us a major permanent institution of Judaism, but how to observe it is left undetermined.

Divorce is nowhere mentioned in the Pentateuch in any serious way. It is presupposed. It is an old institution, known throughout the ancient Near East among both semitic and non-semitic people.[61] There are provisions in Babylonian and Assyrian laws that have minimal points of contact with biblical divorce practice. Biblical Israel apparently did not produce as highly developed a legislation as her neighbors.[62] It is my conjecture that the reason for this is that biblical Israel looked down upon divorce. The few provisions in the Pentateuch allowing for, or forbidding divorce imply that there was a broad area for innovation and development, both toward easier or harder divorce, and toward no divorce.[63] We must recognize this as allowing for the freedom which Hillel or his school took in the face of Shammai or his school's stricter construction, and for the ultimate freedom Jesus took to prohibit the dissolution of almost any marriage.

From the foregoing we see that in both cases, where an institution is permanent and where it is merely a presupposed cultural inheritance, there was need for the conceptualized framework to be fleshed out with forms. In the light of this, scholars who see Judaism as "a body of rules" or "system"[64] mislead the unwary as to the nature and function of midrash, and the consequent possibilities of repeated change in halakhah. The "system" is not the individual halakhot by which people live. Rather it consists of hermeneutical rules and motivating principles that all combine to evolve halakhic forms out of theological essence. I will come back to this in Chapter Three. This must be borne in mind when considering the activity of Jesus.

It is all the more surprising, therefore, that scholars miss this obvious point even when they correctly interpret "Torah" as signifying "instruction" rather than "law," and correctly see nomos as more than mere "legal custom," incorporating as well "ethical maxims" and "social virtues."[65]

Banks understands that there is a limitation to the extent of Torah and that this required much expansion at the hands of halakhists in all areas, from personal and social morality, through economic and political life to individual and corporate worship and rite, making for a "flexibility in application."[66] And yet he stands so bound by former presuppositions that he is led to pronounce the phrase torah hazot ("this Torah") as signifying an absolutist requirement.[67] But a cursory examination of the usage of that phrase in the precise contexts referred to by Banks reveals the opposite.[68] As a matter of fact the term "Torah" used in that context emay come exceedingly close to a fascinating mingling of the three commonly used terms in New Testament studies: kerygma, didache, and parainesis, a mixture of proclamation, halakhic teaching and moral and ethical exhortation. Throughout Deuteronomy, Moses links the observance of hatorah hazot with the mighty deeds of God for Israel, and the content of hatorah hazot is consistently narrative along with halakhah.

Banks thus manages to reverse himself from the moment of promise in which the Torah-halakhah spectrum can be understood and therefore Jesus' role in it appreciated, back to the Weber-Bousset line of reasoning which finds legal absolutism where it is not, and finds the villains of the piece to be not only Sadducees,[69] ammei haárez,[70] and fringe sectarians,[71] but pre-eminently the so-called Pharisees. These are equated with "rabbis"[72] for whom "...Law not only moves into the central position, it

14

becomes almost the sole object of concentration."[73] And again: "Great emphasis is laid upon ritual requirements, especially those concerning defilement and the Sabbath, and the few Old Testament provisions are multiplied into a complex network of regulations...All legal requirements come to be considered as of equal importance, at least from the viewpoint of obedience..."[74]

Banks uses loaded language whose meaning is unsubstantiated. "Law...becomes almost the sole object of concentration...all legal requirements come to be considered as of equal importance..." Banks here neglects the problem of àb and toldah in melakhah, the primary and derivative form of an activity, and the subdivision of major and minor mizvot. He ignores the wide diversity of first century halakhah in this regard and the internal complaints within rabbinic literature of the problems that attach to Sabbath halakhah as flimsily founded.[75] The point is that much of the material upon which Banks builds is well-founded. His inclusions and interpretations are damaged by his presuppositions. His objective is to declare Jesus "different" from the "rabbis" (="Pharisees") and all interpretation heads toward that preconception. His terminology for the Pharisaic-rabbinic activity is always "Law," "legislation," "legal structure," "legal fiction."[76] The judgment made is polemical. Although at times Banks reflects a more moderate understanding of rabbinic flexibility even to the assumption of the right to annul halakhah of the past, he takes away with his other hand what the first is willing to give.[77] He echoes the type of intellectual abuse of rabbinism that was prevalent in the sixteenth and seventeenth centuries,[78] that in turn reverted to the polemics of the Church Fathers and pointed forward to the Weber-Bousset tradition referred to by Sanders. One has a right not to expect this from Banks. In any event, Banks writes that all this legal activity displays "...that loss of perspective in religious matters that the Gospel portraits so frequently attest..."[79]

This dissertation is studiously avoiding polemics and apologetics. It is not my interest to show the "Pharisees" or "rabbis" in a good light or to refute the tradition to which Banks is bound. But it is essential to understand properly the rabbinic texts. We will look at one or two cited by Banks. The

15

Mishnah records a change of liturgy (M. Ber. 9:5). Because certain minim[80] denied a "World to come," "they" (anonymous) enacted a new wording in praise-formulae to refer to God as the God of two worlds. Banks says, "The principle upon which these alterations were validated is exemplified in Ber. 9:5..."[81] What is that principle? R. Nathan phrases it quite succinctly: "'They have violated your Torah' (Ps. 119:126b) because 'it is a time to act for the Lord'" (Ps. 119:126a). R. Nathan expresses the proto-rabbinic conviction that when one must act for the Lord annulment of provisions is allowed. He maintains this in reference to either Torah, the written or the interpretive. (The latter is usually simply referred to as "oral," which, since some of it is written in notes, is a misnomer). In other words, R. Nathan enunciates the view that no "law" is absolute. What stands above all is the will of God. This application of the will of God through a series of hermeneutical and ethical devices will be pursued further in Chapter Three. This is not "legal fiction." It is precisely the type of thing we encounter in the New Testament: the setting aside of legalistic considerations in order to transcend them and meet the will of the Father.

Similarly Hillel's prozbol[82] referred to by Banks is not the product of legal fictionalizing. It is the utilzation of one verse in scripture in order to annul another, the application of an ethical norm to radicalize the halakhah and prevent an unethical result. The prozbol, attributed to Hillel, was instituted to prevent the violation of Deut. 15:7-11 which forbids the refusal to lend money to the needy. This pericope is ethically pregnant. But economic conditions of Graeco-Roman society made it impractical to lend money if the debt will be voided in the release year (Deut. 15:1-3). Thus proto-rabbinic schools activated Deut. 15:7-11 against Deut. 15:1-3, a process with which Jesus was well acquainted and which he himself utilized in order to radicalize the halakhah with ethical objectives. The point is that in each case cited by Banks the reason for change or annulment of Torah may be different, and cannot be lumped together. Similar reasons can be found in the teachings of Jesus. The prozbol literally, and by no circumlocution, nullifies Deut. 15:1-3 in its wording, "I can collect whenever I please." (M. Sheḅi. 10:4). This matter will be further elucidated in Chapter Three.

16

3. The Love Command Factor[83]

Banks maintains that the love command pericope places Jesus in a controversy with people Banks regards as proto-rabbis.[84] Banks sees nothing wrong with the term "lawyer" as a translation of nomikos at Mt. 22:35. It must be objected that nomikos more correctly signifies an "expert in the nomos," while the English term "lawyer" has a professional nuance that is not applicable to the nomikos of the New Testament. The latter is more of a law school professor and at times a jurist. In any event we are not certain that nomikos ought to be in the text.[85] Omitting this word, we read that the Pharisaioi, having heard that Jesus maintains a doctrine of resurrection, gathered for one of their many "testings" of his halakhic views, possibly always hoping that he will fall into their camp. These Pharisaioi are reminiscent of the perushim who had no principal command. For them each halakhah had equal validity and none could be elevated as a greater mizvah. That even "You shall love your fellow-human (or fellow-Israelite)" (Lev. 19:18) or "You shall love the Lord your God" (Deut. 6:5) took no precedence was clear to strict constructionists from the Torah itself. Both statements are embedded without fanfare in a larger mass. This is also true in the Damascus Document (6:20), a product of people we may well name perushim. Jesus disappoints them again. Even if, with Luke, we retain the reading nomikos we get the same result. Among the perushim there were proto-rabbis. One of them put the question to Jesus simply because the others would defer to the scholar in their midst. The nomikos obviously does not challenge Jesus.

If the next passage (Mt. 22:41-26), has any relationship to the context our point is strengthened. Jesus, having first scored against the Sadducees, satisfied the nomikos in whose presence the other perushim are reluctant to debate. He now turns the tables upon the perushim. One might imagine that while the nomikos nodded his head in agreement with Jesus' answer, some of the perushim muttered under their breath. Jesus then challenges them on the very heart of the current agitation: the messianic question. Jesus' question essentially echoes a denial of the consensus view that the Messiah is to be a national-political liberator and restorer of the

Davidic throne. The implication is that the Messiah brings a Kingdom "not of this world" (or is brought by the arrival of the Kingdom).[86]

Banks misses the point when he labors at showing the love command episode as a "controversy" and in which there is great disparity between Jesus and the rabbis. There may be disparity between Jesus and the perushim of the Damascus Document, who use the term "brother" (CDC 6:20) in place of "fellow" (Lev. 19:18), certainly narrowing its scope. But it is more important to settle another matter. Banks claims the rabbis never negate "the principle of the equivalence of commandments."[87] Here Banks misunderstands the rabbinic texts. One text (M.Ab. 2:1) reads "be as anxious about a light mizvah," one that takes little effort and has seemingly little consequence, as for a "difficult one" which involves much more effort and has graver consequences, because one knows not the reward of mizvot. We read again (ibid. 4:2) in the name of Ben 'Azzai, a first-century teacher, "Be as hasty to do a light mizvah as a difficult one...for one mizvah brings another in its train...for the reward of a mizvah is a mizvah..." This is not the assertion of equivalence. It is merely pious advice that when a mizvah comes to hand one should not disdain it because it is "light." This suggests a very obvious consciousness of a lack of equivalence, of the existence of "greater" and "lesser" precepts. Jesus does not deny that; he merely sets the love command as a significant criterion by which to make a choice when options are available. The rabbi par excellence of the first century, Akiba, far from denying that the love command is a significant criterion by which all action should be measured, insisted upon it.[88] To think that there would be a controversy between Jesus and proto-rabbis on this question is to unreasonably deny that this tradition was maintained prior to 300 A.D. in the face of apocryphal testimony and rabbinic attributions of the "golden rule" to Hillel.[89]

This is not the place to enter the debate as to whether Jesus expanded the obligation to fulfill the love command from one that applied to one's fellow-Jew to an obligation equally applicable to all fellow-humans. If it was more narrowly conceived at the time Leviticus was written and even by the proto-rabbis, there is nothing in the gospel accounts to say that Jesus regarded the obligation any

18

differently from the nomikos. To both is attributed the term plēsion by which to identify the object of one's love. In the Testaments of the Twelve Patriarchs and in Philo we find a broader construction.[90] In the New Testament we find a narrow construction.[91] Qumran texts indicate that at least one segment of perushim did not particularly use the love command as a criterion of behavior. In their halakhah one encounters a rigor that would hardly allow for bending a requirement or seeking a loophole. Neither Mark (12:28-34), nor Luke (10:25-28), have the Pharisaioi in their accounts of the love command teaching. Mark reports a scribe in full agreement with Jesus. Luke has a nomikos posing the question to Jesus of what he must do to inherit eternal life. The nomikos answers his own question by citing the love command upon being prompted by Jesus, and Jesus agrees. The nomikos is apparently a proto-rabbi. The scribe in Mark may also be a proto-rabbi. The text in Matthew (22:35) can be taken either as a controversy or as a simple testing by persons, who at this point have no quarrel with Jesus. In any event it seems likely that the Pharisaioi of Mt. 22:34 are perushim, i.e., Qumranites or other like-minded separatist-pietists. This is suggested at Mt. 5:43, where Jesus apparently quotes them as contrasting love of plēsion with hate of enemy (IQS 1:10).

4. The Meaning of Mt. 5:17-20

The problem of understanding the law and the relationship of the love command to its development is affected by the meaning we attribute to Mt. 5:17-20. It is not my purpose here to review the massive work already done on these four complex verses.[92] Here it will suffice to say that I agree with Banks that where Jesus says, "Do not think I have come katalysai" (v.17), something much stronger is signified than some scholars attribute to the word. A. Merx sees in it no more significance than in the rabbinic term matir (tountie, permit, allow), but there are sufficient examples of its usage to justify ascribing to it the strong meaning of "abolish."[93]

Another problem in the pericope is the term pleroō (to fulfill, complete). Many scholars[94] have dealt with this and have imparted a legacy of little clarity. Although there is much debate about it, Meier[95] points out that either of two Hebrew or Aramaic terms may be behind it. These are milê and kum, to fulfill or carry out, which are often interchanged in targums, and signify to fulfill a requirement or a religious obligation. He therefore aptly relates the opposite, batel, to nullify, to the term katalyō, as in the Maccabean literature, signifying the drastic act of annulment of the totality. Although the details of redaction criticism will not delay us here, the conclusion Meier reaches[96] after working his way through Matthew's redaction to what he considers the original saying of Jesus, is quite supportive of the notion that the end-result of Jesus' teaching is not to abandon actual practice of the Torah's precepts. He conjectures that the original words atributed to Jesus were ouk ēlthon katalysai ton nomon alla poiein (or tērein) "I have not come to annul the nomos but to observe it." While Meier does not see the idea of observing or carrying out the nomos in practice as the meaning of pleroō, arriving at a rather fuzzy conclusion that it has the sense of fulfilled prophecy,[97] he has really made out a case for the sense of "fulfilling" it in the sense of living according to it. A paraphrased meaning of the saying at Mt. 5:17, as I see it, would be, "Do not think that I have come to annul (or abrogate) the extant corpus of Judaism (the nomos and prophetic sayings). I have not come to abolish it but to fulfill it." That is to say, what he is about to teach (vv. 21-48) is the correct interpretation for those aspiring to enter the Kingdom. Even if the statement is Matthew's, not Jesus', there is no reason to deny that Matthew taught that that was what Jesus meant. Redaction criticism only provides us with Matthew's midrash on Jesus, and one has no way to attribute to Jesus any other meaning. In any event we are examining Jesus' halakhah as presented by Matthew. And as presented by Matthew, Jesus called for a form of fulfillment of Torah and the prophetic demand that Israel live up to Torah. That does not preclude the possibility of change in particulars of halakhah.

As I read the Sermon on the Mount I see no break in continuity between 5:16 and 17; 5:1-16 is ăgadah, the non-halakhic preliminaries of a sermon, which, as can be seen in midrashic collections, was constituted of both halakhic and ăgadic segments. At v. 17 Jesus switches from the ăgadic to the halakhic. For the light of the disciples to shine (v. 16) they must abide by unprecedented virtue (v. 20). Examples of what this entails is given at vv. 21-48, but lest anyone fear or suspect that this signals a program to abolish the extant, canonical corpus, he offers the assurance of 17-19. He is not referring to any specific individual practice or doctrine but to the whole, <u>ton nomon ē tous prophētas</u>, the <u>nomos</u> and prophetic works. But this assurance that what he wants is fulfillment or observance, albeit on his terms, does not preclude changing individual items, precisely in order to have these particulars meet his terms. The <u>nomos</u> is an archaeological tell possessing a variety of strata. Ezekiel's departures from Leviticus do not abolish Leviticus. Jesus' soon-to-be pronounced departures from older norms are declared similarly as not intended to signal an abolition of the extant corpus (vv. 17-19).

The redactor informs us that in his tradition it is recorded that Jesus climaxed that assurance by anticipating and responding to a further concern in the light of v. 16. Since he was soon to urge norms of conduct (halakhah) that were significantly more difficult than those of both the written Torah and the oral interpretive torah, he anticipated both inevitable protest and neutral inquiry as to why. He therefore insists that those who hope to enter the approaching Kingdom of Heaven must be more worthy than "scribes and Pharisees." Here v. 16 points to v. 20. The <u>perushim</u> of Qumran prided themselves on their rigorous pietism and on their intensively observed purificatory rituals. Jesus warns aspiring "Kingdomers" that their <u>dikaiosynē</u> (virtuousness) must go beyond these norms (v. 20).

The so-called antitheses (vv. 21-48) follow. These are only some examples of the higher standards. We have no way of knowing how many other norms Jesus taught. The matters taken up in Mt. 6-7 also contain variations from known Judaic norms. Whatever the variations of antitheses that Jesus introduces, they are not intended to abolish the extant corpus, only to carry forward the teaching already implicit in it. Thus, Mt. 5:17-20 is not a "programmatic statement on the Law," in terms of setting forth a "philosophy." Nor is v. 20 alone, or the whole unit, an introduction to the antitheses only.[98] Mt. 5:17-20, in effect, is in its entirety an introduction to at least 5:21-6:18, with 6:19-7:27 possibly representing other agadic and halakhic discourse material collected from various preaching occasions and placed in this context as representing the basic teaching of Jesus.

The above appears to me to overcome all of the problems perceived by the many scholars who have struggled with this pericope and have confessed their utter bewilderment.[99] There is no discrepancy between the affirmation of Torah at 5:18-19 and the antitheses of 5:21-48. Therefore, both the scholars who attempt to harmonize the alleged discrepancy[100] and those who feel all attempts at harmonization are "hopeless"[101] labor in vain. There is no need to understand the Sitz im Leben of 5:18 and 5:19 as "two different groups or two different stages of development in a Jewish-Christian community...allowing the moderate position to triumph,"[102] with 5:17 as "a solemn introduction to the thesis and its conclusions."[103] There is also no need for the elaborate structure erected by J. P. Meier[104] to reconstruct Matthew's theology of the Law in order to establish that Matthew was not confused. Meier argues that for Matthew the Law is valid until all the Old Testament prophecies are fulfilled. The criterion he proposes in the name of Matthew as signalling the passing away of the Law is "the eschatological passing away of heaven and earth which signals the new age."[105] Meier takes the death-resurrection of Jesus as that apocalyptic terminus. Yet that is a rather arbitrary decision to make. Although we have insufficient data it would appear that Palestinian Christian Judaism between 30-70 abided by much Judaism in conformity with both Judaic tradition and Mt. 28:20, and did not see "the Law" as having passed away, for it did not see heaven and earth as having passed away. After 70, Christianity was as free as other segments of Judaism to arrange for post-70 rite and doctrine to meet the needs of the new age. This cleared the way for the hegemony of gentile Christianity as it did for that of rabbinic Judaism in their respective spheres of influence. Meier's elaborate structure is built upon the faulty presuppositions discussed above,[106] as revealed in his statement that the dikaisynē Jesus demands "far transcends the legalism, externalism, minimalism, lovelessness and hypocrisy of the scribes and Pharisees."[107] He thus exposes the normative bugaboo of "legalism," as having played a role in his anlysis, cancels any likelihood that the love command served as a proto-rabbinic criterion of piety, makes a value judgement (lovelessness, hypocrisy), and overlooks the fact that "minimalism" was closely related to proto-rabbinnic psychology and even the love command.[108] Meier evinces no recognition that those in controversy with Jesus may have been perushim and not proto-rabbis, and that their "externalism" may have been as objectionable to other segments of Judaism as it was to that segment of Judaism which followed Jesus. To this extent, however, Meier is correct: that Matthew has done a masterful job of redaction in 5:17-20 which "makes a rich and profound statement on the Law, addresses the pastoral needs of his church, and introduces the all-important antitheses."[109]

C. Recapitulation and Projection

1. Recapitulation

The foregoing has placed in perspective aspects of problems encountered in the effort to understand the halakhah of Jesus of Nazareth as expressed by Matthew. It has been emphasized that certain presuppositions have been at the root of the failure to assess correctly the relationship of Jesus to the historic unfolding of the halakhah. As scholars have attempted to grasp this difficult matter, many have centered their attention on the Gospel of Matthew and have given special consideration to the antitheses of the Sermon on the Mount. This study seeks to set aside those presuppositions and place in a new context the love command and Mt. 5:17-20, both of which are treated as especially significant in scholarly research into the subject of what is frequently called "Jesus and the Law."

2. Projection

a. Premises. In order to ascertain the correct relationship of Jesus to the halakhah it is proposed here that one must place him in the historic sequence between the Old Testament and the Mishnah. This involves working with several premises. The first is that Matthew is a Christian Jewish redactor who correctly transmits the recorded oral and written tradition concerning Jesus and aspects of the halakhah. The second is that even if in the antitheses we have the abrogation of specific precepts of written Torah, this is not unusual for Jesus' milieu. The third is that Mt. 5:17-20 is not a mystery, but rather a straightforward statement in the name of Jesus calling upon the disciples to fulfill all that the two torahs require of them, not necessarily as proto-rabbinic or perushite or priestly circles would require, but in

23

the light of Mt. 28:20 and in accord with Mt. 5:20.

b. <u>Sources</u>. The two themes, Sabbath observance and divorce practice, are selected paradigms. It will be shown that Jesus, as seen by Matthew, approached these two questions in the light of halakhic methodology current in proto-rabbinic Judaism. The halakhah of divorce is not as clearly an evolving institution as that of the Sabbath, but its development is ascertainable. When what is called post-exilic Judaism[110] gets underway the halakhah to be presumed as operative is that of the Old Testament. Soon thereafter, new elements enter as we can detect in Nehemiah and Jubilees. The Dead Sea Scrolls reveal further development. The synoptic tradition comes upon the scene at that juncture. Proto-rabbinic Judaism is developing its halakhah simultaneously with that of Qumran, and with that which is reflected in Jubilees. For our purposes, therefore, we will examine the relevant halakhah of these four literary sources: the Old Testament, the Aprocrypha, the Dead Sea Scrolls, and the Gospel of Matthew. We will then seek to clarify the affinities between an example of contemporary diaspora halkhah, that of Philo, and our Palestinian sources. We will also examine the rabbinic sources in order to determine the precise Sabbath and divorce halakhah found therein, as compared to that represented as the view of Jesus. Our assumption will be that neither the halakhah of Jesus nor that of the early first-century proto-rabbis can be given unquestioned chronological priority. They enjoy a degree of simultaneity.

c. <u>Methodology</u>. The examination of the two themes, Sabbath and divorce, will be undertaken from the standpoint of proto-rabbinic method. This includes a resume of those factors that motivated the scholars in their departures from extant halakhah and their innovation of new halakhah.[111] The objective is to indicate how Jesus applied this halakhic method current in his milieu to the questions of Sabbath and divorce. This will also include those hermeneutical rules which Jesus clearly used and that were in evidence in proto-rabbinic Judaism.

In addition to the explication of the motivating factors in the development of halakhah and to the indication of traditional hermeneutical rules utilized by the Matthean Jesus, I will indicate that other halakhic principles are involved in how the Matthean

24

Jesus worked with the halakhah. The first is the tendency toward leniency which begins with Yosi ben Yoezer (ca. 170 B.C.), and the second is the principle of lifnim meshurat hadin, requiring standards beyond the norms of the Torah. While on the surface these two principles appear contradictory, they are not. "Leniency" in the tendency referred to, is not a matter of minimalizing, but of considering human and social need. Requiring the "super-norm" is not a matter of being thoughtless and strict, but of expecting a high degree of piety expressed in human and social concern. Thus it may be said that both principles derive ultimately from the love command.

The relevant pericopes (Sabbath: Mt. 12:1-8; 9-13; Divorce: 5:31-32; 19:3-9) will be examined in the light of these approaches and compared to the halakhah of the proto-rabbis, Philo, Qumran, Jubilees and the Old Testament. The result should indicate where the Matthean Jesus stood in the halakhic sequence between the Torah and the Mishnah. We should then be able to answer the question as to whether he abolished, refined, revised or innovated, whether he was proto-rabbinic or Qumranic, a strict constructionist or a liberal, or perhaps wholly unique in his halakhah.

D. The Chapter Sequence

Following this general introduction to the subject, the remainder of the dissertation is to proceed along the following lines.

1. Chapter Two will trace the development of the halakhic process from the Pentateuchal era to the first century. This will survey the functionaries who interpreted and taught what they believed to be the word of God as well as transmitted traditions they knew to be of human origin. Such functionaries will include the sofer (II Ki. 22:8ff), the zaken (Ez. 8:1; 20:1),[112] the hakham (Jer. 18:18), in addition to the often described kohen and nabi, the priestly and prophetic teachers and preachers. We will then note the evolution of the proto-rabbi out of the early hellenistic sages.[113] It is this proto-rabbi who takes center stage during the first century but does not gain hegemony until after 70 A.D., which is beyond the period of our immediate concern.

25

2.   Chapter Three will survey the halakhic methodology current in the milieu of Jesus of Nazareth.

3.   Chapter Four will discuss in detail the pertinent Matthean pericopes concerning the divorce halakhah. This discussion will not enter into form or redaction critical work but will be based upon the Aland Greek New Testament text. The halakhic findings in these passages will be compared to the Old Testament, Jubilees, Philo and the Qumran texts.

4.   Chapter Five will undertake to deal similarly with the halakhah of the Sabbath as presented by Matthew at 12:1-8, 9-13.

5.   In Chapter Six I will gather together the conclusions reached on the basis of the previous chapters. These conclusions will flow from the following findings: a) by the first century a rather extensive corpus of halakhah already existed in varying forms; b) the proto-rabbinic halakhah was conceived in a humanitarian and socially conscious framework, and sought to establish lenient forms while simultaneously allowing for, but not encouraging, going beyond the minimal norms; c) Jesus insisted upon maximizing the requirements at some points, but at others stressed the looser construction that would make the burden of observance more lenient; d) there were significant points of contact between the methodology of proto-rabbis and that of Jesus; e) there were no halakhic grounds in the teaching of Jesus that could lead to the crucifixion or to the expulsion of Christian Jews from the synagogues and from legitimacy in Judaism; f) that if the Christian Jews had not been expelled after 90 A.D. for political reasons Jesus could have been considered a proto-rabbi within Judaism. It should be emphasized in connection with the last point that although formal ordination is traced to post-70 A.D. at Yabneh (B. San. 5a-b, 13b; P. San. 19a), and there are therefore grounds to declare the title of "rabbi" used for persons prior to 70 in the New Testament an anachronism, this requires reconsideration. For one thing, preservation of the term in the New Testament (Mt. 23:7-8), points to its informal usage as a title of respect and honor for certain individuals prior to 70. In rabbinic literature we find a similar anachronism when R. Meiasha is called "rabbi" (M. Peah 2:6). Jesus' own negative view of the title (Mt. 23:7-8), does not

prevent his disciples from paying the courtesy to him (Mt. 26:25, Mk. 14:45). The historic probability is thus enhanced that he was considered a proto-rabbi in his day, for not only Judas but also Peter addresses Jesus as a rabbi (Mk. 11:21), and he was not the only proto-rabbi who was negative to the use of the title and its perquisites.[114]

II.   STAGES IN THE FORMATION OF RABBINIC HALAKHAH

A.   Pre-Exilic Origins

"Rabbinic Judaism" is a full-grown product depicted in the Mishnah,[1] Tosefta[2] and the various tannaitic midrashim,[3] and then expanded in the talmudic[4] literature. A continuing challenge is to identify its origins and to determine whether it is rabbinic Judaism that is under fire in the New Testament[5]. It may be easily retorted that rabbinic Judaism is not under fire in the New Testament because "rabbinic Judaism," in a technical sense, does not emerge until after 70 A.D., well after the emergence of Christianity.[6] But then one becomes embroiled in the problem of the dating of the New Testament writings, especially the Gospels. Are they earlier than 70 A.D. and therefore unable to be in conflict with rabbinic Judaism?[7] Are they later than 70 A.D., representing the early church in conflict with rabbinic Judaism, rather than the conflicts of Jesus with certain segments of Judaism who opposed him?

The view taken in this dissertation is that, although the rabbinic texts are post-70 in the form in which we have them, in many instances they represent older, pre-70 traditions.[8] Therefore, the dating of the New Testament is not an indispensible factor in our concerns. Whether the New Testament texts are early or late they represent the conflict of Jesus with segments of contemporary Judaism. The premise here is that just as post-70 rabbinic texts often reflect pre-70 and pre-first century tradition, New Testament texts reflect early traditions that have their roots in the years 30-60.[9] The departure I make, however, is to attribute the views of the Pharisaioi of the New Testament to Judaic elements other than those who adhered to rabbinic Judaism. In the light of the remarks made earlier about the title "rabbi" it is of curious significance that the Pharisees are generally not identified as rabbis, that Jesus is, and that Jesus attacks "rabbis" only once (Mt. 23:7-8). But in this regard it is worth considering that Mt. 23 tells us more about Matthew and his church than it does about Jesus.[10] Furthermore, the term "rabbi" in this context may be the Greek writer's post-70 rendering with a more familiar term of the pre-70 Palestinian Aramaic mari. Perhaps the translator used it in place of abba, a term used to address sages. These terms all had about

28

the same significance, just as <u>kyrios</u> denoted "sir" when not ascribed to God.[11] This would support the view that the formal title, appointment, office of "rabbi" did not exist before 70 A.D. Be that as it may, in order to ascertain the emergence of those elements we refer to as "rabbinic Judaism," it becomes necessary to provide a brief historical sketch.

B. Pre-Exilic Diversity and Post-Exilic Retrenchment to the Hasmonean Era

1. <u>587 B.C. to the Nehemian Reformation</u>[12]

The scope of this chapter does not allow for more than a brief mention of the sources of doctrine and practice in pre-exilic Israelite and Judean religion. It is clear from our sources that there were three types of schools or three agencies through which to convey religion and knowledge in pre-exilic Judah. The <u>kohen</u>, the <u>nabi</u>, and the <u>hakham</u> are all referred to at Jer. 18:18.[13] Each dispensed his form of instruction, counsel and doctrine. The priests had their schools (II Ki. 12:13), the prophets received seekers after the word at their homes (II Ki. 4:23; Ez. 8:1; 14:1; 20:1); the <u>hakhamim</u> conducted schools (Prov. 22:17; 25:1); Ben Sira offers a description of the sagacity, learning, piety and versatility of the <u>hakham</u> or <u>sofer</u> (39:1-15).

During the last days of the First Commonwealth, however, the <u>sofer</u> emerged out of the royal court context.[14] This functionary become the major post-exilic figure as the <u>nabi</u> goes into decline and the <u>kohen</u> loses credibility. The figure of the <u>sofer</u> cannot be understood unless we recognize him as more than a "scribe" or a "secretary." He is a scholastic, the learned scholar-researcher, as we can tell with the description given Ezra the Sofer (Ezra 7:6, 10f). Although priests still offer instruction (Hag. 2:10-14), the last prophets already give their own halakhic interpretations (Zekh. 7:1-14; 8:16-17). One might receive the impression that the great anonymous prophet only cited extant halakhah (Is. 58:13-14) but did not decide it, or that Malakhi reflects an anti-divorce posture (Mal. 2:14-16) but does not create new halakhah. It would be naive, however, to think that these prophets of God who uttered the <u>dabar</u> of God (Jer. 18:18)[15] did not teach halakhah to their immediate disciples and wider circles, just as Jesus

29

does in the New Testament. That the nebiim⁷ were
regarded historically as transmitters of torah (and
for me this term, uncapitalized, includes oral
interpretive torah or halakhah) is evident at
M. Abot. 1:1.16

There is no certainty about who constituted the
religious leadership and teachers of religion in
Jerusalem and Judah during the period from 587 B.C. to
458 B.C. There is no greater clarity concerning who
served in these capacities in Egypt and Babylonia, the
two major diaspora centers. We discern from Old
Testament sources that the same kind of syncretistic
religion as obtained in both Israel and Judah prior to
722 B.C. and 587 B.C. respectively, continued into the
fifth century B.C. in post-exilic Palestine,
Babylonia, and Egypt.17 But if our source is correct
(Jer. 41:5), it is evident that the sacrificial cult
continued in Jerusalem after the destruction of the
Temple, and so presumably priests continued as
religious authorities. There also appears to have
been the rise of a temple in Babylonia (Ezra 8:17)
where again priests must have been active. From
Ezekiel sitting and receiving consultations, as noted
earlier, and from the activity of Haggai, Zekhariah
and Malakhi, it is evident that prophets continued in
their role as charismatic preachers and teachers. The
evidence is clear that there was a temple at
Elephantine, Egypt, as early as the 6th Century B.C.
where priests continued to serve in the same capacity
as they had in Palestine.18

Nevertheless, the continued ministry of Priests
and Prophets between 587-458 B.C. did not avert the
continuation of the syncretistic cults in Palestine.
This condition evoked the severe denunciations found
in Ezekiel, Isaiah 56-66, Zekhariah and Malakhi.19

The permission granted by Cyrus for the exiles in
Babylonia to rebuild the Temple in Jerusalem
(Ezra 1:14, 6:3ff) and the execution of this task
under Zerubbabel and Joshua the High Priest with the
encouragement of Haggai and Zekhariah the prophets
(Ezra 5-6) did not immediately issue forth in a
religious reformation. Malakhi's stern denunciation
of the priests must have been uttered before 458 B.C.
and helps explain the mission of Ezra.20 With Ezra's
arrival and his important work, and the
successor-labors of Nehemiah, the sofer rises to
temporary preeminence in Judaic religious

leadership.[21]   Although we have little information
concerning the fourth century it is clear that by a
process of evolution, the rapidity or gradualness of
which is not known, the sofer comes to be identified
with the man of wisdom, the hakham. This, rather than
sofer, is the title used of the pre-Hasmonean
spiritual leaders and continues so down into rabbinic
times. But it was Nehemiah, who was neither kohen nor
sofer, but a secular leader, wielding the power of a
Persian governor, who apparently enforced the
reformation of Ezra in matters related to the Temple,
the Sabbath, and mixed marriages (Neh. 13:4-14, 15-22,
23-27). This is significant. It bears out the
historic fact that only when governmental power was
applied in the interests of one given faction of
Judaism did a semblance of an "orthodoxy" arise.
Otherwise there was manifest consistent diversity.
Nehemiah used verbal excoriation and physical force to
put an end to mixed marriages (Neh. 13:25). In the
process he went beyond the limitations of Ex. 34:16
and Deut. 7:3-4, shedding light on another aspect of
Judaism pertinent to our thesis, that the norms of the
Torah (the Pentateuch) can be superseded, even without
a new revelation.

2.   From Ezra-Nehemiah to the Known Proto-Rabbis

Ezra's importance is in his intensification of
the religious life of Jerusalem and Judah. A period
of retrenchment and consolidation, of religious
conservatism, was introduced and enforced by the state
power exercised by Nehemiah. The fourth century is
obscure. It is difficult to ascertain the lines of
spiritual development after Ezra and Nehemiah.
Nehemiah had asserted his secular power over the
priests in Jerusalem, and it is difficult to know
whether the Zadokite priesthood ever regained autonomy
in the Temple. Although there continued to be
prophets (Neh. 6:7, 10, 12, 14), we have no names of
prophets or of sofrim after Malakhi and Ezra. None of
the apocalyptists are named for us, and only when we
encounter Ben Sira and Simon the Righteous are we able
to identify proto-rabbis by name.[22]

That a vigorous religious life must have
continued throughout the fourth and third centuries is
evident from the large amount of scriptural material
that is generally dated to that era, and from the work
of Ben Sira on the eve of the Hasmonean period. Our
knowledge of religious life during the Ptolemaic

control of Palestine (302-198 B.C.) is meager. But the great watershed had been reached. Hellenism was introduced into Palestine, and we are aware retrospectively that three major points of view asserted themselves. There were those who argued for, and participated in, a process of acculturation. There were those who insisted upon loyalty to the separatist and pietist arrangements covenanted by Ezra and Nehemiah. And there was a third more radical group that ultimately went over to apostasy. But more important is that this era is the time of the growth of the synagogue into a major religious institution and the emergence of the non-hereditary, sometimes charismatic spiritual leader, the proto-rabbi.

From Ben Sira's description of the ideal <u>sofer</u> ca. 200 B.C. (39:1-11) we receive our first description of the emergent proto-rabbi, a scholar and teacher who engages in prayer, and welcomes students without fees. He gives instruction, counsels, pours forth wisdom, investigates obscure things, all without benefit of the kind of direct revelation common in bygone generations. He seems to already foreshadow or fulfill the programmatic suggestions for the rabbi.[23] More, he anticipates the rabbininc halakhah in which all of scripture and all of the interpretive torah receive the authority and status of revelation. This is clear in Ben Sira's great hymn to pre-existent Wisdom which he identifies with the Torah.[24]

When Ben Sira is shown to have literary affinities with Euripides, Theognis and Aesop, it is clear that it is wrong to compartmentalize Hellenistic and Palestinian Judaism.[25] Ben Sira becomes the first known representative of Palestinian Judaism who functioned in both cultures and helps us see more clearly the Hellenistic influences in proto-rabbinic Palestinian Judaism which reach their climax in Paul.[26]

3. <u>The Great Assembly</u>

We have arrived in our brief sketch at what marks the beginning of rabbinic Judaism's self-identity, the chain of tradition transmitted from the pre-proto-rabbinic age of prophecy, to Simon the Righteous who inaugurates the proto-rabbinic age (M. Ab. 1:1f.).[27] We are told that Simon was of the last remaining members of a "great assembly" (ibid. 1:2). This term, <u>keneset hagedolah</u>, "great assembly,"

32

causes much mischief. There is no extant primary source which is able to tell us what is meant by it. But later rabbinic sources attribute to it a wide variety of religious, especially liturgical developments, in Judaism.[28] In effect the rabbinic authorities of the second and thrid centuries attributed the origin of much that was post-biblical rabbinical Judaism to this "great assembly," an amorphous body that sat somewhere from the time of Ezra to that of Simon the Righteous.

We know of a series of major or "great" assemblies held during this period. More than one is depicted in Jerusalem in the time of Nehemiah (Neh. 5:7; 8-10). The likelihood, therefore, is that while there was not such a one-time synod that made so many innovations in Judaism, the "great assembly" was also not a fictional figment of later imagination. For example it is well-attested that such a synagōgē megalē or "great assembly" occurred around 142 B.C. to establish the union of the Hasmonean priesthood and principate into one person (I Macc. 14:25-49). It is indecisive whether ekklēsia megalē (I Macc. 5:15f.) would point to the same type of religious synod or a purely political assembly. Be that as it may, the evidence indicates that at times, of which we have only several examples, great assemblies were called to deliberate on and ratify significant innovations or covenantal arrangements. For example, an ekklēsia Israel declared the festival of Hanukah in 164 B.C. (I Macc. 4:59).[29]

What must be said, then at a very minimum, is that at certain crucial juntures synods were called, and the burden of radical innovation was laid at their doorstep. But while such sporadic efforts in post-exilic Judaism at functioning as a "covenanted" community are likely, and a more fixed and permanent communal assembly did operate at Qumran and among the Essenes, there is no evidence whatever that such great assemblies were called to decide proto-rabbinic halakhic developments in the first century B.C. or first century A.D. The meeting of the year 65 A.D. is no exception to this statement.[30] Finkel's conclusion that "...the vehicle of tradition [i.e., the process of conducting religious affairs]..." into the Hasmonean era was regulated by a general assembly is unwarranted by the evidence.[31] The very fact that there were so many undecided issues between the schools on the eve of the war of 66-73 indicates they

were not accustomed to issuing halakhah out of a great
assembly which would or could enforce uniformity.
Each school deliberated in its own session and each
school had its own loyal following. There was no
"great assembly," no central authority, and no
"orthodoxy" in the face of which Jesus or Paul would
be antithetical. From the Dead Sea Scrolls we know
that Qumran had a single vehicle through which it
exercised governance, but Judaism as a whole did not.
Furthermore, contrary to Finkel it was not the
"scribes" who were responsible for religious
activities.[32] Priests continued to govern formal
religious life in Jerusalem, and scribes could have
been both priestly and non-priestly, just as in later
times they were rabbinic and non-rabbiinic. Not all
hakhamim (sages, proto-rabbis) were sofrim (scribes)
and not all sofrim were hakhamim. It is with caution
that we will use a post-70 rabbi as an example, but
the example is instructive for the pre-70 period. R.
Meier is spoken of highly as a scribe, and the very
fact that he is pinpointed as a librarius, a
professional scribe, "an especially good copyist"
indicates that not all rabbis were such.[33] The rabbis
speak of sofrim consistently as a specific profession
distinct from their own, even if, as in the case of R.
Meier, some rabbis were sofrim. It is important to
see these distinctions and to use the terms with
precision in order to better understand the New
Testament references to "scribes."[34]

Although R. Meier takes us beyond our period, it
is important to note that the very fact that rabbinic
literature speaks of sofer in a special professional
sense leads us to a better perspective on the term
"scribe" in the New Testament. The old Ezraic
scholastic sofer has become the hakham, the
proto-rabbi, but somebody else is not the
sofer-"scribe." The sofer becomes a teacher
(P. Ḥag. 76c) and a custodian of the archives or
repository of traditions (M. Peah. 2:6) as well as a
copyist and writer of documents (M. Git. 8:8). Each
group, priests, perushim, Sadducees, Essenes, etc.
would have its own sofrim.

4. The Second Century B.C.

Our previous discussion has brought us to the
time of the early proto-rabbis. Aside from the
ambiguity surrounding Ben Sira, Simon the Righteous
was believed to be the first of the proto-rabbis known

by name. Whether this is a historically authentic tradition is not relevant to rabbinic Judaism since no halakhah is given in his name. The significant thing is that the history of tradition is traced from him to the rabbis through links with whom we are more familiar, the "pairs."[35] The exception to this is the immediate disciple of Simon, Antigonus of Socho (M. Ab.1:3), of whom we know nothing. It appears from the text of Abot that an older list once ended here, for in 1:4 the two Yosis are said to have received the tradition "from them," and the antecedent in 1:3 is only Antigonus. It is therefore reasonable to conclude that 1:1 - 1:3 constituted an older list later attached to a more recent list beginning with the Yosis who are said to have received "from them," meaning the men of the great assembly of 1:1.[36] The later list beginning with the Yosis as having received the tradition from the great assembly simply incorporated the shoftim, Eli, Samuel, Ḥaggai, Zekhariah and Malakhi into elders and prophets, and tacked on the Yosis after Antigonus. Some copyists did not notice the incongruity of leaving "from them" (1:4) in the older text, with only Antigonus as antecedent. Others did notice this and as a result some texts read "from him,"[37] suggesting that the Yosis received the tradition from Antigonus.

The reason for an older list leaving off with Antigonus might be that the proto-rabbinic circle sought to emphasize the legitimacy of their tradition as derived from Sinai and coming in unbroken sequence into the hellenistic period, an era alluded to in the Greek name. They resume the list with scholars dating from the time of the severance of hakhamic-proto-rabbinic religious interpretation from Hasmonean priestly Judaism, the era of the Yosis. The later list beginning with the Yosis and proceeding to R. Simon ben Gamaliel I (M. Ab. 1:18), the last pre-Yabneh figure of note, omited Simon the Righteous and Antigonus because the post-Yabneh editors sought to exclude all high priestly and hellenistic connections from the chain of tradition.[38] Much later, when the priestly question was no longer of great moment and the patriarchate itself engaged in much hellenistic academic pursuit, even preferring Greek over Syriac, these names could be reinstated (B. Sot. 49b). In sum, the final redaction of the Mishnah seeks to establish legitimate tradition from God through the prophetic line, including only the one priestly connection, Simon the Righteous, who was of special quality and was even accompanied by the incarnate deity in the Holy of Holies (Lev. R. 21:12). The rabbinic implication is that the priesthood has legitimacy but only if it is reinstated through the Zadokite line which ended with Simon the Righteous.

Even if the foregoing reconstruction of the beginning of the chain of tradition which seeks to establish the legitimacy of rabbinic Judaism is not accurate in every detail, we have before us an important statement. The table of succession provided at M.Aḃ.1:1-16, from Moses to Gamaliel brings us to the period contemporary with Jesus. The redactors of the Mishnah are informing us that the interpretive torah to which they attribute authority almost equal with that of the Torah of Moses is the product of continuous transmission from biblical <u>kohen,</u> <u>nabi</u> and <u>hakham,</u> all of whom were represented among the "men of the Great Assembly" among whom also sat Simon the Righteous. The fact that this chronology is historically impossible is not our concern. Our interest is in what the first century scholars believed. What they believed relevant to this question of the transmission of tradition is enshrined at M.Aḃ. 1:1-3. Halakhic statements that constitute traditions of scholars known by name begin only with the Yosis of Aḃ. 1:3 and their legitimization had therefore to be accounted for. It was originally accounted for by having them receive the tradition directly from "the men of the Great Assembly," and later from Antigonus and Simon. Why was it necessary to reinstate Simon and Antigonus?

Simon was reinstated, as noted earlier, to reaffirm the legitimacy of a true Zadokite priesthood. Antigonus was reinstated to give greater credibility and support to the view of R. Judah haNasi who favored Greek over Syriac or Aramaic as an alternative language to Hebrew to be used in Palestine (B.Sot.49b). Furthermore, the saying of Antigonus (M.Aḃ.1:3) that one must serve God without thought of reward reinforced anti-Christian polemic. It must be remembered that discussion with Christians did not cease with the earliest period of debate 35-65 (Paul)[39] or the post-war polemics between Yaḃneh and the early church leading to the expulsion of Christians from the synagogues (75-95 or 100),[40] but continued on through the second century as we see from Justin's <u>Dialogue with Trypho</u>,[41] and even deepened in the third and fourth centuries.[42] Around 200, when

36

the Mishnah was entering almost its final recension in the circles of R. Judah, the emphasis placed by a Greek-oriented proto-rabbi of pre-Hasmonean times upon selfless altruism would be a useful logion in the debate with Christianity. One must not underestimate the question in that polemic even if it does not come up specifically in that form. Matthew 6:1-4 implying that they act in the interest of glory would sting any believing Jew. Antigonus' logion, contra the pursuit of reward would be an antidote to this. Antigonus' maxim would be powerful as a pithy refutation of all of Mt. 6 which emphasizes reward for one's piety. Christian apologists interpreted the Old Testament spiritually rather than literally. Judaic apologists could turn that argument upon them and urge that all the this-worldly reward emphasized in the Old Testament is to be taken spiritually. Furthermore, this doctrine of selfless piety, stated at the beginning of the proto-rabbinic tradition becomes part of the program of rabbinic Judaism. For essentially M.Ab. 1:1-3 is programmatic of rabbinic Judaism, for its theology and ethics as well as methodology: a) deliberation in learned exchange; b) the establishment of networks of disciples; c) the interpretation of the written Torah through exegesis and by a definite hermeneutic that would preserve its essence;[43] d) the centrality of Torah, God, and Israel as the tripod of Judaism: study, the observance of worship forms, and benevolent relationships with one's fellow Jew; e) that all of this is to be in the service of God without thought of reward.

Thus rabbinic Judaism sees its essential nature encompassed in the fundamental maxims of M.Ab. 1:1-3. It is likely, therefore, that this was originally an independent pericope, and that it was ultimately joined to the rest of the chapter when the Mishnah was put into its present shape.[44]

C.   From the Earliest Proto-Rabbis to the Era of Jesus

1.   The Early "Fathers"

The "pairs" of proto-rabbinic scholars listed at M.Ab. 1:4-12 are traditionally referred to as Abot ha'Olam, "the fathers of the world," as are also Ishmael and Akiba, that is, founding fathers of rabbinic Judaism.[45] The list, including Gamaliel I, encompasses scholars who lived from the time of Yosi b. Yoezer ca.170 B.C. to Gamaliel I, who flourished in the first half of the first century A.D., a span of almost two-hundred and fifty years.[46] Despite the use of the term _Pharisaioi_ by Josephus and writers of the New Testament, this word is never found in the rabbinic tradition to refer to any of these scholars who are identified as "Pharisees" in virtually every book on the Judaism of antiquity. Of all these scholars named in Ab.1 only Gamaliel I is ever called a "pharisee," and that at Acts 5:34. The gospels name no scholars. Josephus refers only to a Simon b. Gamaliel[47] as of an illustrious family and of the "pharisees." He mentions Jesus ben Gamaliel, a priest, whom some take to be a proto-rabbi, but he names no other known proto-rabbis or rabbis as "pharisees." The Samaias and Pollion to whom Josephus refers[48] are certainly not to be identified as Shammai and Hillel,[49] for nothing that Josephus says points to those two gentlement being the famous "fathers of the world" Hillel and Shammai. When Abot de R.Nathan refers to _perushim_ as opposed to the Sadducees and Boethusians the reference is to separatist ascetic conduct (Ab. de R.N. A, 5, p.26). In much the same way the Sadducees and Boethusians are _perushim_, this is, they "separated" themselves from the circle of their teacher Antigonus (Ab. de R.N. B, 10, p.26). In short, neither the rabbinic tradition nor Josephus names any known proto-rabbis as "pharisees" except possibly Simon b. Gamaliel, if indeed it is he to whom Josephus refers. The New Testament refers to none except Gamaliel, father of this Simon. It would appear from this that father and son were indeed "pharisaic" proto-rabbis, _perushim_ in their life-style, and unusual, and hence so identified.

In addition to the sequence in M. Abot 1 we have scattered references to other pre-70 teachers. These are Yohanan the High Priest,[50] Honi the Circle-Maker,[51] Menahem,[52] and a number of others, more or less famous, with halakhic teaching transmitted in their names.[53] There should also be included such scholars as Yohanan b. Zakkai who is better known for his post-70 activity but who was a pre-70 proto-rabbi, and a contemporary of Jesus in Galilee.[54]

In these circles, in which rabbinic Judaism took root, the most productive groups were Bet Shammai and Bet Hillel. The Bet Shammai-Bet Hillel controversies produced much anonymous halakhah. During the years between the birth of Jesus and the outbreak of the war of 66-73 the two most famous proto-rabbis known by name after Hillel and Shammai were Gamaliel I and Yohanan b. Zakkai. It is difficult to ascertain why little halakhic tradition is ascribed to Gamaliel I. But the maxim given in his name at M. Ab. 1:16, to avoid doubt and to be careful to tithe with precision, sounds very "pharisaic," that is, <u>perushite</u>. It stamps Gamaliel as a "pharisee" type of proto-rabbi. He wrote letters,[55] and perhaps this became a model for one of his famous disciples, Saul of Tarsus. There is no direct historical evidence, however, that Yohanan was in Jerusalem as part of Gamaliel's circle. While Josephus refers to Simon ben Gamaliel as a Jerusalem leader he does not mention Yohanan b. Zakkai, nor does he ever refer to him or to Yabneh and the role he and the academy at Yabneh played in the emergence of rabbinic Judaism. We have the anomaly of Josephus writing his <u>Life</u> as late as 100 A.D. after both the <u>War</u> and <u>Antiquities</u> written in the 70's and 90's, and still never referring to Yohanan or to rabbinic Judaism.

For our present purposes, however, the Yohanan b. Zakkai of pre-66 interest us more. We are told that he, not Gamaliel I, "received" from Hillel and Shammai (M. Ab.2:9).[56] This supports the idea that Gamaliel I, a great pietist and communal leader, who was probably also a perceptive and diligent teacher (Ab. de R.N. A, 40, p. 127), may not have been a halakhic expert,[57] or if he was, his halakhah was suppressed because he was, at least on occasion, a Shammaite.[58] This brings into broad relief a contradiction between his being a Shammaite and being the grandson of Hillel. But the scope of this chapter does not permit a comprehensive discussion of the historical uncertainties of who Hillel really was, whether the historic line beginning with Gamaliel I and ending with the last Nasi, Gamaliel VI in the fifth century, was really the family of Hillel, and how ultimately Hillelite halakhah became predominant.[59] Most significant, as Neusner has pointed out,[60] is the fact that Gamaliel is nowhere related to Hillel nor to Bet Hillel. Neusner suggests that the Gamaliel family's Shammaite leanings, and with them, their halakhah, was suppressed, "a part of the price securing the support of the Hillelite faction, headed by Yohanan b. Zakkai."[61]

Whether this is true or not is beyond our ability to determine at the present time. It is clear, however, that the leading religious authority after the war of 66-73 was Yoḥanan ben Zakkai. Here was a man who was a disciple of both Hillel and Shammai, and a contemporary of Jesus. He was an anti-nationalist who withdrew from the siege of Jerusalem to join the sages engaged in religious learning at the coastal town of Yabneh.[62] When the smoke cleared, with the Gamaliel family in disrepute for being in rebellion, this independent scholar and friend of Rome was in a position to lead the restoration of Judaism and Judaic communal life. But in some mysterious manner, for which we have no definite information as to how and why, he was removed from leadership and replaced by Gamaliel II. It is my view, a view which is related to matters beyond the purview of this dissertation, that he was removed first of all because he experienced as much opposition in leading Jewish circles for his stance as the Christians who withdrew to Pella.[63] Secondly, perhaps his removal was instigated because the consensus around him felt he was "soft" on Christianity. And thirdly, he was probably superseded because the Romans felt it was time to return the helm to Rabban Gamaliel II, and restore the "pretender" to his "throne." The appointment of Gamaliel II opened the way for the expusion of the Christians from the synagogue, the alienation of Christianity, and its separation from Judaism.[64]

The foregoing discussion of the supplanting of Yoḥanan ben Zakkai requires a further word of explanation. Assuming what cannot be proven, but is taken for granted in modern scholarship, that the Simon ben Gamaliel mentioned by Josephus[65] is the son of Gamaliel I and father of Gamaliel II, it is clear that he was pro-war.[66] The precise fate of Simon b. Gamaliel I cannot be determined by our sources. [67] Eusebius tells us in the name of Hegesippus[68] that after the capture of Jerusalem Vespasian sought out descendants of David in order to bring the royal line to an end. This is not historically corroborated by other sources, but there is no reason to doubt the likelihood that the Romans would be antagonistic to Davidic descendants and would hardly see any difference between Davidides who were Christian and Davidides who were not. It is therefore a real probability that, first of all Simon b. Gamaliel I died during the siege in Jerusalem, since he is not again heard from, and that Gamaliel II could not serve as his successor because of the family's pro-war stance, and because its claims of maternal descent[69] from the House of David left it suspect in Roman eyes. There is a historical clue to this in a beraita (B.Taan.29a) which informs us that Gamaliel II was the leader in the academy at the time of the destruction of Jerusalem, and was warned that he was being sought by the Romans whereupon he was able to escape.

Thus we have Gamaliel II continuing the proto-rabbinic leadership in Jerusalem among the pro-war factions while Yohanan b. Zakkai was establishing himself at Yabneh as head of a rival center. That Yohanan b. Zakkai is reported to have asked Vespasian for the "chain" of Gamaliel (B.Git.56b) does not mean that he asked the Romans to spare him and his family,[70] but for the sign of his authority. At this point we may agree with Alon's account which is otherwise in error in matters of detail,[71] that Gamaliel patiently awaited an opportunity to supplant Yohanan b. Zakkai. How this occurred is not a matter of record. But we find Yohanan at Beror Hayil at the end of his life, there conducting a center of learning (B. San. 32 b, Sif. Deut. 144, T. Maas. 2:1) while Gamaliel II is the Nasi at Yabneh. It is likely that a coalition of Yohanan's opponents unseated him. These would consist of his own former associates and disciples, who opposed his anti-war posture,[72] the party of those loyal to Gamaliel II, the priests[73] who resented his anti-priestly position and persistent effort to "layicize" Judaism and grant equal authority to centers other than Jerusalem,[74] and finally the Sadducees.[75] It probably happened sometime early in the reign of Domitian (81-96) and before his volatile behavior after 88. Alon is correct the Büchler's reason[76] for priestly recalcitrance, their zeal for the war, cannot be correct, for priests, as we can see as far back as the time of Jesus, were not disposed to upsetting Roman power. Nevertheless it is quite possible that some priests were quite zealously in favor of the war, as one source hints rather strongly regarding Hanina Segan hakohanim.[77] But the main reason for priestly opposition was Yohanan's program of reducing their power. Furthermore, they would oppose him on the same grounds as Gamaliel II, that Yohanan was in the position of a usurper, ironically, being neither a priest nor a Davidide. For decades there must have been rivalry between priests and

41

rabbis. As late as the end of the century when Gamaliel II was deposed, R. Eliezer b. Azariah became Nasi, on the strength of his descent from Ezra (B. Ber 28a; P. Ber 7d).[78] Finally Yohanan's introduction of Ordination (P. San 19a) was a direct challenge to the priestly aristocracy, creating a wholly new formal and authoritative democratic body, a meritocracy, through which community leaders would be appointed by virtue of their attainment of a degree of competence in halakhah. This was to replace the hereditary aristocracy through which one attained power and authority by virtue of one's birth.

2. An Historical Resume

The foregoing has touched upon the scholars to whom I refer as proto-rabbis, who either preceded, or were contemporaries of Jesus. Their halakhic activity will help us understand that of Jesus. We have already seen that the term scribe in the New Testament, does not necessarily refer to proto-rabbis.[79] The New Testament does not define Pharisaioi. It only attaches that term to a group of people.

When we examine the sayings and concerns of the proto-rabbis from Simon the Righteous through Yohanan ben Zakkai, there is only slight coherence between these and what Josephus describes as "pharisaic" concerns.[80] Josephus has almost no information on proto-rabbinic ritual halakhah, Sabbath or Festival practices or halakhah of domestic relations. When he does comment on divorce halakhah, saying a divorced woman requires her former husband's consent to remarry, he is not citing proto-rabbinic halakhah (Ant. xv.7.10 (259)). He never mentions that important figure, Simon b. Shetah, of the reign of Alexander Janneus in which so much significant "Pharisaic" activity is related. His Pharisaioi are exceptionally fastidious about ritualism as they are in the New Testament. When Jesus is represented as demanding greater piety than that of the "Pharisees," (Mt. 5:20), it is because he regards them as hypocrites, not because their halakhah is not stringent.[81] In contrast to Josephus, on the other hand, the New Testament raises the halakhic issues that are found in proto-rabbinic Judaism.[82] But this does not mean that the "Pharisees" of the New Testament are indeed the proto-rabbis. It only means that these questions were of common halakhic concern among Jews of all groups, and that the writers made no effort to distinguish groups. That Josephus omits such details in his description of "Pharisees" is only due to his seeking to present them as a philosophical party, in a way familiar to a hellenistic audience. That he does not speak of the known rabbinnic figures who predominated at Yabneh after 70 A.D. may only reflect the fact that they were not yet considered the national authorities they became later. He does not even mention Yoḥanan b. Zakkai, who, like himself, had a pro-Roman disposition. It appears, therefore, that "rabbis" were not yet of such significance, and the direction Judaism was to take was not yet clear. This clarity probably emerged only after the Romans appointed Gamaliel II as Patriarch.[83]

This appointment was crucial. In matters of religion an effort was now made to establish a "normative" Judaism with the kind of muscle Nehemiah once possessed. The traditions of both Bet Hillel and Bet Shammai had to be fused, and were. Gamaliel II replaced Yoḥanan b. Zakkai who was not an "Establishment" man before 70 A.D., and was not acceptable for this reason among others, as well as for his anti-war position.[84] The appointment of Gamaliel II, nevertheless, would not have been fruitful had Gamaliel not incorporated Yoḥanan's innovations along with his disciples into the new Yabnean circles. This appointment of Gamaliel was also crucial to Christianity because Gamaliel II, unlike his famous grandfather, had no patience with the Christians.

Neusner[85] cannot be correct that the proto-rabbinic circles from Hillel on are "new" Pharisees, a religious sect born out of the chrysallis of a political party. Such a transformation would have been reflected either in Josephus or the New Testament or both. Neusner[86] is correct that the rabbinic record shows a group extending from Hillel to Gamaliel II which is very different from Josephus' Pharisees of the second and first centuries B.C. prior to the reign of Herod and the emergence of Hillel. But this is also true of the proto-rabbis from Simon the Just to Hillel. They simply do not represent what Josephus describes. And in the halakhah they taught they do not represent what the New Testament describes.

In the light of the foregoing I proceed on the

premise that the Pharisaioi of the New Testament are not the proto-rabbis of the Hillel and Shammai circles or of the school of Yoḥanan b. Zakkai. As a matter of fact, assuming the basic historicity of the Matthean account with which we are dealing, and assuming the date of the crucifixion to be 30,[87] Yoḥanan b. Zakkai possibly heard Jesus preach in Galilee and may even have had halakhic discourses with him. Considering, as we will see, the great diversity of the various "pharisaic" groups, and the proto-rabbinic freedom of approach to halakhah, it is highly unlikely that there was no room for Jesus to take an independent route. The controversialists who beset him are people who want him to be a parush, who press for a more pietistic halakhah and more stringency than the early proto-rabbis advocated. These early proto-rabbis, from Yosi b. Yoezer through Simon b. Shetah are innovators and advocates of leniency.[88]

As far as the written texts which we have are concerned, I proceed on the premise that much of this is pre-Hillel tradition which was transmitted not only orally, but also in notebooks, teaching pamphlets and the like. Neusner's caveat[89] that "the allegation that the present material about the pre-70 Pharisees consists of the written texts of traditions originally orally formulated and orally transmitted is groundless" is without any documentable warranty. The point is that when we erect a straw man, exclusive "oral transmission," we arrive at erroneous conclusions. Oral transmission was always a means of teaching. But there was also always written transmission preserved in the archives of the academies and extracts recorded in students' notebooks and teachers' materials.[90] The rabbinic literature, therefore, must be judged on its merits, with careful analysis given to each halakhah, not on the basis of form-criticism alone, but on the basis of how the halakhah matches the historical context, whose name it is attached to, and whether it appears plausible as a saying by that person at that time within that historical context. The sweeping generalization about certain "forms" such as "testimony-form," "ordinances," "chains and lists" being characteristic of a certain place (Yabneh) and certain circles,[91] is not in accord with historical probability for in history we experience overlapping, imitativeness, and simply conservative preservation of techniques used in previous generations. What can be identified as coming from Yabneh (70 - 130) or Usha (from 140) may

without much doubt be regarded as earlier tradition.
It is simply not reasonable to assume otherwise.

Summary

There is no source at all that tells us when,
where or how the so-called "Pharisees" emerged, or who
they really were. Josephus and the New Testament
speak of them in disparate manner. Rabbinic
literature refers to them only in negative terms, and
one of the most respected scholars of the entire
rabbinic literature, Hillel, taught that one must not
be parush from the community.[92] The Sadducees could
be haberim (B. Nid. 33b), so the latter term does not
necessarily designate "Pharisee." Yoḥanan b. Zakkai
reveals himself to be anti-perushim when he responds
to an attack on perushim with the line: "Is this the
only thing we have against perushim?" (M.Yad. 4:6).
Even in later sources only the anti-pharisee character
in the narration refers to "Pharisees" (perushim), in
naming his opponents in a famous story involving
John Hyrcanus or Alexander Jannaeus (B. Kid. 66a).
The rabbinic narrator calls the same persons hakmei
Yisrael (sages of Israel). So, too, Josephus
sometimes eschews the term Pharisaioi and refers to
sophistai.[93] This may suggest that those who opposed
the proto-rabbis tarred them with the anti-perushim
brush, seeking to identify them with a segment of the
community for which may had much disdain. This may
help explain the use of the term Pharisaioi in the New
Testament, as a general pejorative term to describe
separpatist-pietists, and if possible occasionally to
ensnare a proto-rabbi in the net. Nevertheless,
Josephus and the New Testament do not use the term the
same way, although scholars have equated their usage.
The halakhah of the Pharisaioi in the pericopae which
we will analyze, is not that of proto-rabbis, but
similar to that of Jubilees and Qumran.

The term perushim probably encompasses a variety
of extremists including Essenes, Qumranites, Zealots,
among others. Some proto-rabbis, in some matters such
as table-fellowship, purity regulations and tithing,
may have had a degree of sympathy and empathy with the
mass of perushim, but they opposed stringent halakhah,
separation from society, pietistic extremism and undue
asceticism. The affinities, however, explain why some
may interpret Josephus and the New Testament as
referring to proto-rabbis in the broad category of
Pharisaioi. The rabbis, however, clearly excluded

themselves from the category of _perushim_ because of their basic antipathy to extremism and social withdrawal. The _Sitz_ _Im_ _Leben_ of Jesus, 25-30, was a community in which proto-rabbis were not yet predominant and were themselves divided into a variety of "schools": those taking their names from Hillel and Shammai, and those which were probably independent of both, such as the one of Yoḥanan b. Zakkai. None of these were opposed to Jesus, and for this reason no anti-Christian or Jesus material survives in rabbinic literature from that period. Whatever there may have been that indicated a relationship was probably suppressed.

While it appears certain to me that _Pharisaioi_ in Matthew represent _perushim_ in general, and not the pre-70 proto-rabbis with whom we are acquainted, Matthew might at times have used that word against the latter as at Mt. 23. The effect of this would be to charge them as dissenters, as staying aloof from the true Israel, possibly in response to their using against him and Christians in general the _logion_ of Hillel against separatism.[94]

It remains now to describe as accurately as possible the development undertaken by these proto-rabbis from Simon the Righteous to Yoḥanan b. Zakkai. This will enable us to compare their halakhah with the positions Jesus is represented as taking in The Gospel of Matthew.

III. PROTO-RABBINIC HALAKHIC ACTIVITY

A. Factors in Reinterpretation and Innovation of Halakhah

1. Proto-Rabbinic Authority

All halakhic authority in Judaism traces itself to the Sinaitic revelation. This is clear from the Mishnah (Ab. 1:1). The legitimacy of any practice or custom that arose between Sinai and the hegemony of rabbinism was derived by exegesis or scriptural support from that same Sinaitic revelation, which was believed to be embodied in the Torah. The rabbis of the first and second centuries A.D. attributed much of the change in post-exilic Judaism to the Men of the Great Assembly.[1] The rabbis believed that a whole series of takanot (positive enactments) and gezerot (restrictive or prohibitory enactments) were instituted by Ezra and others.[2]

It is infinitely difficult to date with precision any given innovation. For example, one is hard put to determine when the innovative exegesis of Deut. 23:4 arose. Scripture says, "An Ammonite and a Moabite shall not come into the assembly of the Lord, even unto the tenth generation..." Rabbinic exegesis refers the prohibition only to males.[3] The right of females to enter the covenant community was considered a halakhic innovation of the pre-monarchal age, adopted in order to rationalize the legitimacy of Ruth the Moabite (Ruth 1:4) as an ancestor of King David. Nevertheless, it would be an unnecessarily harsh judgment on the integrity of the rabbis for modern scholarship to argue that this innovation was made by tannaites and that they deliberately falsely dated it to a pre-tannaitic period. It is my contention that when the first-second century literature specifically attributes an innovation or a reinterpretation of halakhah to a pre-tannaitic period it is because its authors were perfectly aware of not having been responsible for it themselves, and by natural inference realized it was pre-first-century.

Another point to be considered is that the literature has innovations specifically attributed to scholars who lived well before the first century. A primary example of this is the halakhah of Yosi b. Yoezer.[4] Yosi can serve as a paradigm of the sage who innovates halakhah contrary to the Torah. Jacob Z.

Lauterbach has persuasively argued that the midrash style seen in the tinnaitic halakhic midrashim[5] is to be traced to the Maccabean period, around 165 B.C.[6] This was a revolutionary age, and as in all crisis periods drastic solutions to new problems were introduced. Alexander the Great's introduction of Hellenism brought vast new changes to the Middle East in technology, politics, economics, culture and religion.[7] This cultural transmogrification of the hellenistic Middle East gave rise to conditions for which there was no precedent in halakhah. Authority in Judaism, previously centered in the High Priest, broke down when the high priesthood became discredited upon its usurpation by hellenistic non-Zadokite priests, and later by the ineligible Hasmonean family. Yosi b. Yoezer was a <u>hakham</u> of the pre-Hasmonean period, one of those who were engaged in the slow but steady process of taking spiritual authority out of the hands of the priesthood into their own hands, and this, despite the fact that he was himself a priest (M. Ḥag. 2:7). He sponsored the democratization of the academic community, urging "let your house be a gathering-place for sages" (M. Ab. 1:4). Yosi b. Yoezer is reported to have declared permissible three items that had been previously prohibited (M. Ed. 8:4).[8] The Mishnah (ibid.) reports that for his labors, and in all probability for many other innovations unknown to us, Yosi was called "<u>Sharyá</u>," "the permitter," by his colleagues. But his contemporaries did not overrule his opinions, nor did his successors into the talmudic era abrogate his innovations. His statements registered a point of view contrary to tradition. Most of all, his view that liquids of the slaughtering place at the altar were to be considered pure and not as imparting impurity was a wholly novel and lenient approach in a sphere (purities and impurities) often regarded as punctiliously maintained in a restrictive manner by so-called "pharisees" in whose earliest ranks one normally includes Yosi b. Yoezer.

Yosi was responsible for other innovations, and it would be naive to think that we have a full record of his activity. It is evident from how fragmentary is our knowledge of the third century B.C. and the first quarter of the second century that what we know of Yosi is only the tip of a massive iceberg. I have previously made reference to the technological revolution of the hellenistic period. The increased manufacture and use of glassware in Palestine is a

48

case in point.[9] This new product had in some way to be related to the halakhah governing purity and impurity of vessels, implements and containers. There was also the question of importation of glassware manufactured outside of Palestine, in consideration of the extent of economic impact such importation would have upon the local glassware and metalware industries. Under the impact of economic determinism as a leading method of interpretation of history in the nineteenth and early twentieth centuries many scholars have seen economics at the root of Yosi's approach to glassware.[10] He and his colleague Yosi b. Yoḥanan of Jerusalem decreed that glassware could become impure like other vessels although it is not mentioned in the Torah, and could therefore have been exempted from the Torah's regulations (beraitā, B. Shab. 14b; cf. A. Z. 8b).[11]

Involved in this delicate matter is the fact that prior to the growth of the glassware industry in Tiberius, Canaanite craftsmen in Tyre and Sidon were the major source of imported wares in Judea. These products were not subject to biblical restrictions and provisions that governed earthenware, wooden vessels and metalware, and so they became highly competitive to the disadvantage of Judean manufacturers of earthen and metal vessels. Later the local glass industry would constitute similar unfair competition. The protective decree by the two Yosis deprived glassware manufacturers of this advantage. Yet, the sages recognized that since glassware was made of sand it had the characteristic of earthenware for which there is no possibility of purification once it becomes impure (Lev. 11:32f). Nevertheless they permitted its purification, unlike earthenware, recognizing that new technology allows for freedom of interpretation, despite what appears to be an inclusive prohibition in the Torah which implies that any new type of vessel could not be given special status (Num. 19:15).[12] It does not matter here whether there was an econmic motive behind this decision, or whether it was based purely on the need to decide the status of a new product for ritual and doctrinal reasons.[13] What is of significance is that these men took upon themselves the right, and claimed the authority to introduce new halakhah that was sometimes merely innovative and sometimes in actual contradiction of the Torah. That the written rabbinic traditions concerning these matters are later than the first century [14] should not deter us from seeing the method and its product as pre-Christian. For it is clear from such examples as Yosi b. Yoezer that this process was in progress for centuries before the simultaneous rise of Christianity and Yabnean Judaism.

Returning to the pericope at M. Ed. 8:4, a word must perforce be added here concerning recent research touching upon the traditions of Yosi b. Yoezer.[15] Neusner[16] argues that the testimony-form used in that pericope derives from Yabneh (post-70 A.D.) and declines to suggest whether it is earlier, but concedes that both the content and language attributed to Yosi may possibly be earlier. Neusner,[17] however, misses a significant point in the third halakhah recorded in the name of Yosi, that "one who touches a corpse is made impure." Neusner wonders why Yosi restates Num. 19:11 and 16, that one who touches a corpse becomes impure, and suggests that "Temple priests...held the contrary." The "contrary" suggests they would hold such a one to be pure. How could Temple priests hold the contrary of their own levitical halakhah of the Pentateuch? And why, as Neusner curiously recognizes, would then Yosi be called "a permitter"? It would be the priests who are permitters! On this point of the corpse, however, Neusner's discussion does not reach a conclusion although he recognizes that on the other two items, that the áyil-locust and the liquids of the Temple slaughterhouse are pure, the Temple priests were more restrictive than Yosi. Neusner,[18] who argues that the sayings were a unit on the basis of form, concedes that the form is not clearly a mnemonic pattern, but I believe it to be unnecessary to approach this pericope from the standpoint of form. The editor of the Mishnah is simply recording old halakhah in the name of Yosi to explain why the sages support the current halakhah, although it is contrary to older priestly-traditions. On the question of the corpse, if Yosi was "a permitter," one must take it to mean that he somehow liberalized the previous norm. The solution must be found in his revising the overall effect of Num. 19:16, where we read that if one touched a smitten person or a corpse, a bone or a grave, one is impure for seven days. Yosi limits the impurity to the direct contact with a corpse, nullifying the more inconvenient effect of Num. 19:16 in favor of the simpler Num. 19:11. Thus this too, contrary to Neusner,[19] is a lenient decision by Yosi.

The foregoing discussion serves to illustrate the

proposition that proto-rabbis acted, out of considerations to be examined soon, to innovate halakhah which at times might abrogate the Torah's prior provision or violate the Torah's admonition to neither add nor subtract from it (Deut. 4:2).[20] The example of Yosi clearly shows a proto-rabbi assuming sufficient authority to assert his point of view even in the face of being reprobated with a pejorative epithet by his more conservative colleagues. It also evidences a proto-rabbi asserting halakhah contrary to the established and official religious authorities, the Temple priests. Yosi's actions were based upon a premise that become familiar to us in later texts. The proto-rabbis used one scriptural verse to reinterpret or annul another.[21] Even more forcefully we read in a <u>beraita</u> that contemporary authority takes precedence in the light of Deut. 17:8-11 (T.R.H. 1:17).[22] Enough has now been remarked to indicate the assumption of authority by proto-rabbis even in the face of the Torah. We must now examine cursorily the "profile of the halakhah" to perceive some of the factors that helped determine the proto-rabbinic halakhah. In the light of this we can gain some perspective into the teachings of Jesus. First, however, it is necessary to say a further word on the dating of texts.

2.   On Dating Rabbinic Texts

The problem of determining which elements of the "profile of halakhah" are pre-Christian is a complex one. Nevertheless there are certain elements which can readily be identifiable as such. The fact that our present literature is second century or later in composition and edition should not deter us from acknowledging that some of it can be pre-first century.[23]

Several illustrations from both ăgadah and halakhah will suffice. The first is a story related at B. Git. 57b concerning the killing of Zekhariah. The narrator is R. Ḥiyyah b. Abin of the third century. He attributes the information to R. Joshua b. Korḥa of the second century, and he in turn had related it in the name of a very old man of Jerusalem. The context signifies it was a tradition given by a man who lived in Jerusalem before 70 A.D. But from whom did the old man hear it? Quite possibly the story was a first century B.C. story, if not even older, and is also reflected in the New Testament.[24] Thus, the textual version before us may be a third century one, and perhaps even later, but the content is far older.

The second illustration involves a halakhic controversy at P. Shab. 3d between R. Zeira b. Abuna and R. Yonah over who had decreed impurity upon heathen lands and upon glassware (B. Shab. 14b). One the basis of the names in this passage Neusner[25] adjudges the beraitâ of B. Shab. 14b concerning the glassware to be mid-fourth century. He writes, "It is clear that until then there was no well-established tradition on who was responsible for the decree." By this reasoning there was still no well-established tradition, for they were still disagreeing whether it was Yosi b. Yoezer and Yosi b. Yohanan or Judah b. Tabbai. What is here overlooked is that it was a gezerah, a prohibitory enactment, and a gezerah was sometimes not accepted by everyone, or it fell into neglect and had to be reissued (B. Hul. 6a). In the case of glassware being subject to impurity, the controversy over who enacted it taking place in the fourth century is merely one for clarification. There were two traditions which were not contradictory. They were supplementary. The explanation is the the Yosis and Judah b. Tabbai, who lived about a century apart, had been authors of a similar decree. Judah found it necessary to reissue the decree once enacted by the Yosis. Perhaps it was no longer honored, or perhaps it had expired, its purpose for some time not applicable. The tradition embodied in the beraitâ that the Yosis enacted the decree and cited in a fourth century text, is therefore undoubtedly an authentic early one.

Furthermore, there are occasions when a sage only cites what he requires. This does not mean the rest of a text given along with this citation elsewhere is necessarily later than the other. For example, at Sifra 55a, of the three permissive rules of Yosi b. Yoezer we discussed earlier, only the one pertaining to the liquids of the slaughterhouse is give by R. Eliezer. Neusner[26] therefore dates this later than the M. Ed. 8:4 which contains all three. Actually R. Eliezer, as can be seen in the Sifra context, only needed the one to make his point. He therefore only cites that particular leniency. That does not mean the Mishnah is older. It only means that these three halakhic statements by Yosi b. Yoezer, among others, circulated in the schools, and the editor of Sifra used the one of them which he needed. When the editor of the Mishnah gathered his material, in order to be more thorough he gathered the three revolutionary logia for which Yosi had been reprimanded as a sharya[2], "a permitter." But the tradition itself was older than both Sifra and Mishnah.

The foregoing is designed to caution us on the question of dating. It is important to consider who is cited as having said what is significant in the context and for which it is primarily being cited. Thus it is the old man at Jerusalem who determines the date of the tradition in the first instance, and the fact that it relates to a first century text in the New Testament reinforces its antiquity. In the second instance it is the fact that Yosi b. Yoezer's logia are cited that counts, not whether part of all of them are cited. It should be noted in any case that even if the Yosi tradition is unhistorical, and the decree was really one by Judah b. Tabbai, it is still a pre-Christian item.[27]

A third illustration is a mixture of halakhah and agadah dealing with the recognition of a true prophet. Sifre Deut. 175 comments upon Deut. 18:15 "A prophet from your midst, from among your brethren, like myself, will the Lord your God set up for you; him must you obey." Sifre takes mekirbekha, "from your midst," to signify from within the land of Israel. Finkelstein[28] interestingly indicates that this points to a time when no prophet had yet arisen outside of Palestine, which must date the passage to a time before 597 B.C., before the time of Ezekiel who arose in Babylonia, and before Jeremiah preached in Egypt (Jer. 43:8ff). Sifre also comments on "from among your brethren" as signifying only from Israel, and "for you," meaning only for Israel. Finkelstein argues that these comments originated before Jeremiah 46:1, Is. 13-21, Ez. 25-32, 35, before Jonah is specifically told to preach to Nineveh (Jon. 1:2; 3:2), and before Obadiah and Nahum. As for Amos 1-2, Finkelstein argues that the prophecies concerning the gentiles here are merely part of, and related to his denunciation of Israel (2:6). The Sifre passage itself raises the question of a possible contradiction occasioned by Jer. 1:15, "I have made you a prophet to the nations," but interprets that verse to mean, "to those [Judeans] who conduct themselves according to the customs of the gentiles." This passage, therefore, may embody a very old exegesis despite the lateness of the composition of Sifre.

The closing part of this same passage reads,

> 'him must you obey,' even if he
> tells you to violate one of the
> mizvot stated in the Torah, as
> Elijah did at Carmel, in accordance
> with the need of the hour, obey him.

This passage thus retrieves for us a very early effort to justify needed revisions and served later rabbis in their need to rationalize revision of halakhah. We have already seen that we can trace such post-biblical revision to the early second century B.C., at least as far back as the time of the Yosis. A later editor could have added the last sentence in order to round out the exegesis of the entire verse but he could just as well have been citing a unit, all of which was old. The point is that this entire Sifre passage can be considerably older than the time of the editing of tannaitic literature.

A fourth illustration is from targum. The tradition preserved in what may be accounted as later literature, that Cain killed Abel by striking him with a stone upon his forehead,[29] is already found in pre-Christian literature (Jub. 4:31). Other examples may readily be brought forward.[30] In conformity with the above, the halakhic premises that I will demonstrate below will be only such as can reasonably be regarded to reflect pre-first-century data known from elsewhere.

B. A Profile of Proto-Rabbinic Halakhic Premises

1. Religio-Humanitarian Concerns in Halakhah

In this section I will attempt to demonstrate that the proto-rabbis acted halakhically in the spirit of the love command.[31] That is to say, they arrived at halakhic decisions in such a spirit as would take into primary consideration the welfare and needs of the human beings to whom they ministered. It was precisely in tune with this basic approach that Jesus taught halakhah. This, in turn, will imply that his antagonists were not proto-rabbis but perushim, pietist-separatists who did not necessarily make halakhic decisions on these grounds. It further indicates that in the chain of halakhic development between Ezra and Mishnah Jesus occupied a position of a first century proto-rabbi who transcended the halakhah of Jubilees and Qumran and stood in an antecedent position to that which emerges in the Mishnah.

The halakhic premises were not antithetical to prophetic Judaism but rather expressive of its objectives. Thus for Jesus it was both <u>ho nomos kai hoi prophētai</u> (the Torah and the Prophets)[32] that he was concerned with: halakhic obedience within the parameters of the prophetic interpretation. This interpretation is summed up by Hos. 6:6, "It is love I favor, not sacrifice, the love[33] of God rather than whole burnt offerings." Sand[34] correctly sees this in his presentation of the material.[35] Jesus (Mt. 5:17) argues that in what follows, that which is traditionally called "the Sermon on the Mount," he will adumbrate revisions in halakhah in order to better fulfill <u>nomos</u> in the spirit of the prophets. Indeed, even when he appears to make demands that will be more taxing than the current <u>nomos</u> (5:20), he is not abolishing the spirit of the prophets any more than he is abolishing the <u>nomos</u> itself. Only an exhaustive study of each item in the Sermon would bear this out. But Jesus emphasizes this with his climactic summation of the love command as the primary premise of all halakhah (Mt. 7:12; 22:40).

In his sermonette concerning John the Baptist (Mt. 11:7-15), Jesus is reported to have said that "all the prophets and the <u>nomos</u> prophesied until John."[36] Here the phrase does not have a relationship to the halakhic question. The very divergence of phrasing bears this out. The pericope is not a halakhic one. It is an àgadic sermonette on the theme of Elijah. "All of the prophets," and perhaps as an afterthought, Jesus is reported to have said, "and the <u>nomos</u>, prophesied until John," who is Elijah. Where do we have Elijah in "all of the prophets"? He is only mentioned at Mal. 3:23. Indeed it is correct to note as Meier[37] does that nowhere in the Greek Bible or New Testament does <u>propheteuō</u> govern <u>nomos</u>. But this is precisely the point. For àgadic purposes words and phrases are often given new meanings in order to clinch an argument. Thus Jesus is said to reverse the order of the phrase and use an unusual verb with <u>nomos</u> in order to stress that the eschatological convictions of the prophets, (hence, "all the prophets"), formulated in the last verses of the last canonical prophet, Malakhi, is also

pre-figured in the <u>nomos</u>. And here <u>nomos</u> really means
Torah, the Pentateuch. Where is Elijah or the
eschatological prophet prophesied in the Torah? We
may see here a midrashic allusion by Jesus to the
tradition of Phineas <u>redivivus</u>.[38] Elijah is Phineas.
John is Elijah. The midrashic link for the preacher
is Mal. 3:1 cited by Jesus (Mt. 11:10) which is
reflected at Mt. 11:14. In the Hebrew or Aramaic
there would be a real verbal allusion not evident in
the Greek <u>mellon</u> <u>erchesthai</u> (about to come). This is
the verbal form <u>heshib</u> (Mal. 3:24), that Elijah will
reconciliate the generations with the same zeal as
Phineas <u>heshib</u>, turned (appeased, conciliated) God's
wrath (Num. 25:11). In the Aramaic or Hebrew <u>Yashub</u>,
"will return" at Mt. 11:14 would trigger allusions
that we fail to note in the Greek.

With this understanding we can turn to the
principles current in the first century, through which
Jesus taught his own halakhic tenets. The oldest of
the midrashic collections, Genesis Rabbah, reflects a
fundamental philosophy of halakhah in its statement
that "the mizvot were only designed to refine humans"
(Gen. R. 44:1). The saying is given in the name of
Rab (Abba Arekha).[39] Rab is a second-third century
scholar who nevertheless could have heard what was
undoubtedly a pre-Christian saying in the latter part
of the second century as a student in Palestine. That
it did not originate with him or so late is clear from
the fact that it is a view already current in Philo.[40]
Philo saw the Torah as Moses' legacy that taught
"consideration and gentleness as fundamental to the
relations of men to their fellows" (<u>On the Virtues</u>,
81). Philo stresses the factor of "humanitarianism"
in relation to a number of specific tenets, or in his
own term <u>philanthrōpia</u>, "the love of man" (Ibid. 97,
99, 140, etc.). Philo continues to emphasize that the
injunctions are to teach one not to take pleasure in
another's adversities (ibid. 116), the measures are
conceived in a spirit of kindness and humanity (121),
moderation and gentleness (125, 134). It is of some
interest that the saying in Genesis Rabbah is related
specifically to food practices as are a number of
Philo's examples.

Bearing in mind then the idea that the mizvot
were designed for humanitarian purposes, we can
understand that just as the moral and ethical took
precedence in prophetic teaching, proto-rabbinic
halakhah, like that of Jesus, was to be expounded

within the paramenters of the love command. A mizvah
performed as a product of an illegal or unethical act
was considered sin, not mizvah.[41] It is true that the
rabbis did not write treatises like Philo expatiating
on these motives and objectives. They did not leave
tracts which trace how they philosophized upon and
classified these notions. But their appeal to such
motives speaks for itself.[42]

Humanitarian considerations served a wide variety
of purposes, from protecting the underprivileged to
elevating the status of women, from respect for the
dignity of the living to extending dignity to the
dead.[43] Above all, humanitarianism was recognized as
a premise of the halakhah in the formulation, "one
must not issue a decree which the majority of the
community is not able to abide" (T. Sot. 15:11). This
is given in the name of R. Ishmael.[44] But it is also
given in the names of two earlier sages, Simon b.
Gamaliel[45] and Eleazar b. Zadok,[46] (B. A. Z. 36a).[47]
One context in which both R. Joshua[48] and R. Ishmael
state the principle (B. B. B. 60b) is one in which
perushim promote the notion of prohibiting meat and
wine as a remembrance of the holocaust of the Temple.
This argument concerning decrees is put forward to
counter such extreme pietism, and it places rabbis in
juxtaposition to perushim, and reveals their halakhah
to be in opposition. It can be detected readily in
the text that neither Joshua nor Ishmael was inventing
a new principle. They were stating one that was
well-known in order to support the opposition to such
a pietistic program.

A whole array of halakhot was modified by
proto-rabbinic and early rabbinic Judaism out of
consideration of the poor. These modifications
affected various categories of ritual observances from
the size of the sukah[49] to the right to open places of
business on a festival day to allow the poor to
acquire their festival meal on credit.[50] The formula
which explained some of the halakhic revisions was
mipnei kevodan shel aneeyim, "out of respect for the
poor." A series of revisions of burial practices was
justified by this formula (B. M. K. 27a-b).[51] Several
beraitot record the changes some of which are linked
to Gamaliel I.[52] Special consideration for the poor
is given in a wide variety of halakhot, all of which
reflect a pre-70 context.[53] The custom promoted by
Gamaliel to be buried in simple shrouds is reflected
in other pre-rabbinic literature.[54]

Not even prayer escaped the sages' scalpel. first century tradition given in the name of R. Simo b. Nathanel (M. Ab. 2:18) reports opposition t perfunctory and vacuous worship; and tedium an boredom was to be avoided.[55] It is reasonable to se this tradition, that worship may be tailored in orde to meet the needs of greater spirituality and satisf the concentration-span of the worshipper, as one tha may be dated prior to the first century to th teachers of Yoḥanan b. Zakkai. That it was a genera teaching current in the circles of Yoḥanan is eviden from the fact that it is cited with a slight variatio by a colleague of R. Simon, R. Eliezer b. Hyrcanu (M. Ber. 4:4).[56] It is also reflected in the praye guidance given by Jesus to his disciples (Mt. 6:7).[57]

In the utilization of humanitarian criteria non had greater importance than <u>pikuaḥ</u> <u>nefesh</u>, the savin of life. This superseded all considerations, eve observance of the Sabbath, than which, as a perpetua sign of the covenant (Ex. 31:12-17), there was no mor significant institution in Judaism. More will be sai of this principle when dealing with the pericope a Mt. 12:1-8 and 9-14. Human life was so inviolabl that suicide was banned and a person was not eve permitted to injure himself.[58] Martyrdom wa discouraged and severely limited to four conditions and even then narrowly circumvented.[59]

We will see in Chapter Five that scholars wh attribute to Jesus the criterion of the love comman as his major instrument for advocating or denying specific halakhah are correct. But what many hav failed to notice is that Jesus' notion of the lov command is quite within the parameters of the Judais of his time. He would see no contradiction betwee Sabbath leniency out of humanitarian concern and rigidity in other halakhah that made exceptionall difficult demands, as in the case of insulting person verbally (Mt. 5:22).

2. The Historical Factor

Halakhah could not remain unaffected b historical factors. The events of the real worl projected themselves into the concrete application o the Torah to life. For example, how was one to obe the law of the gentile king? It is clear that whil Jews received certain rights of religious autonomy, they were not wholly free to violate the law of the king with impunity. In the purported document of King Artaxeres to Ezra (Ezra 7:11-26) we read,

> Whoever does not perform the law of your God and the law of the king, retribution will be promptly exacted of him, whether death or banishment, whether a monetary punishment or imprisonment (7:26).

It is the law of both God and the king that Ezra brings to Jerusalem. The Torah in a sense becomes the law of the king. And the king has the right to impose his own law alongside that of God (7:24).

It is not our concern here to settle the historical enigmas related to Ezra and Nehemiah.[60] The only matter of interest here is that the biblical evidence suggests that the law of the king and the law of God were parallel. Jeremiah[61] had long before encouraged adaptation to the environment. It is not surprising that out of the encouragement of Jeremiah there arose a coterie of Jewish functionaries who participated in government, an example of which we find in Nehemiah. There is insufficient material from which we can determine the stages and the process by which there developed the concept of dinâ demalkhutâ dinâ, "the law of the sovereign (or of the state) is binding," but it is gratuitous to argue that it is a concept that first arose with its earliest known reporter, the third century rabbi, Samuel.[62] Samuel studied under Judah the Nasi in Palestine during the second century and might just as well have learned that formulation there. Certainly, if not since Ezra, then since Pompey, there was need to accomodate the state law and the Roman Emperor's expectations.[63]

It is only in the light of this principle, that the sovereign's law is binding, that we are to understand the "render unto Caesar" pericope at Mt. 22:15-22. The "surprise" with which his interlocutors looked upon him was due to Jesus' apparent obedience to the sovereign law. The perushim who approached him did not favor the principle of dinâ demalkhutâ. For them this was valid only in the diaspora. Being extremist pietists and separatists they agreed with the Zealotic view that civil disobedience is a requirement. On the other hand the Herodians would be able to charge him with instigating civil disobedience if he rejected the validity of Roman taxation. The _perushim_ would be pleased to see him punished by Herodian standards because of his deviation from their norms. In other words, there was an unholy alliance of the _Pharisaioi_ and _Hērōdianoi_ (Mt. 22:16). The _Pharisaioi_ sent their disciples (Mt. 22:16; Mk. 12:13), or agents (Lk. 20:20) in order to confound him, but from opposing standpoints that would serve the same objective: to place him in an untenable position. Jesus surprised them both by accepting the principle of Roman taxation on the basis of the principle "render unto Caesar what is Caesar's" that the law of Caesar must be obeyed (Mt. 22:21).[64] He affirmed _dinā demalkhutā_!

Derrett[65] correctly sees that this pericope and its parallels (Mk 12:13-17; Lk. 20:20-26) is not intended to define the relations between church and state. But he is not correct in his ensuing analysis in which he rejects the notion that "Pharisees" or their students or Herodians may have something negative to say on the question of Roman taxes. This is not the place to enter into a critique of his entire discussion. Suffice it to say that I find his lengthy exposition off-target. The special problem raised with the phrase _ou gar blepeis eis prosōpon anthrōpos_ "you do not look to the face of men," is not as serious as Derrett imagines. It might simply be taken in its Old Testament sense, as signifying "you do not regard the person," that is, you are not partial.[66] This means, they expect him to respond candidly even when it involves Caesar and the law of the state. We see here, then, that as a proto-rabbi of his time Jesus taught the principle of _dinā demalkhutā_, and this would affect his halakhic teaching. It was in this case alone a major pronouncement. This was the reason he had to be "framed" before Pilate, and charged with opposing payment of taxes, when the opposite was true, as is clear when we read Mt. 27:13 and Mk. 15:3 in the light of Lk. 23:2. Rebellion against Rome, whether actual or potential, was what he had to be crucified for, not theology or halakhah.

3. Hermeneutics and Exegesis

The key to all proto-rabbinic halakhah given the fundamental premises upon which the motivating factors of exegesis rested, was hermeneutics. The application of generally known hellenistic hermeneutical principles[67] as well as those indigenous to Judaism[68] to scriptural texts, led to halakhic expansion that updated and revised the requirements of scripture. The hermeneutics used during the first century were quite traditional, having been employed, in some cases, for several centuries. Those Jews who became Christians would naturally apply the well-known tools of their matrix to their new faith. Thus, K. Stendahl[69] sees the basic explanation of Matthew's approach to be that it derived from a Qumran-type school. Robert H. Gundry[70] believes Qumran and rabbinic exegesis to have been atomistic, while the hermeneutic evident in Matthew has a special coherence, originated with Jesus and is wholly Christocentric.[71] Gundry, dealing primarily with Reflexionscitate, formula-quotations, and allusive quotation, does not deal with halakhah and can make no contribution to the question of the hermeneutic used by Jesus and then by his disciples and the early church toward the adjustment of halakhah. Gundry, however, is productively suggestive in his view that behind Matthew and the whole synoptic tradition stands a body of loose notes. This is also true of the rabbinic tradition, as noted earlier, and for this reason excessive skepticism about earlier dating of the received traditions is hardly warranted.

It is often simplistically generalized that one of the first century modes of exegesis was a literalist interpretation of scripture, along with the more intricate Qumran-type pesher and allegory.[72] In the realm of the halakhah, naturally, it is thought that literalism was the usual approach. But it must be emphasized that even "literalism" was open to the processes of midrash. The inevitable result was to decide what the "literal" meaning of scripture was in order to derive a new halakhah. Thus Deut. 23:4 enjoins that "an Ammonite and Moabite shall not enter the assembly of Yhwh." An initial reading of the text leads one to believe that it means precisely what it says: that marriage between Ammonites and Moabites with Israelites is prohibited. It might also signify that an Ammonite or Moabite cannot enter as a proselyte. In any event, the literal meaning of the text bars an Ammonite or Moabite from the assembly of Yhwh. But appearances are deceptive and the text was not understood so literally. The halakhah very early allowed the entry of female Ammonites and Moabites on the basis of a midrashic exegesis that inferred from the fact that the Hebrew terms for Ammonite and

Moabite were in the masculine, that females are excluded from the prohibition.[73] Longenecker is correct, however, to see rabbinic literalism in other instances.[74] In one of the instances he cites as an example, literalism itself is the product of midrashic limitations placed upon the provision at Deut. 21:18-21. The verses provide for parental power to condemn a perverse and rebellious son to death. There is no qualification whatever in the verses. The rabbinic exegesis, however, emphasizes the literal meaning of each word so as to limit the provision to a "son" and exclude a daughter, to require that the parents be able to "grasp" the son, to "lead him out" and to speak to the elders, thus being not maimed in hand, foot or tongue (M. San. 8:1-4). But Longenecker[75] fails to perceive that this exegesis is not only literalism. The Pentateuch does not have an age limitation. The Mishnah provides that the period during which a son may so be charged is drastically limited to the short time between the first appearance of his pubic hair to when his genitals have acquired the full "lower beard" (M. San. 8:1). This is exegeted as a derived halakhah from the notion that nobody is obligated to the miẓvot until he grows pubic hair (ibid.). On the other hand the word "son" is taken to be a "boy" and not a "man" stressing the literalism of a <u>ben</u> excluding an <u>ish</u> (ibid.).

The point is that rabbinic exegesis is a mixture of literalism and midrash; taking words literally virtually results in midrash. The same Torahitic provision is dealt with in both ways simultaneously. Thus the question arises: What is a perverse and rebellious son? The implication of the Mishnah's halakhah (M. San. 8:2) is that it is not a "perverse and rebellious son" after all that the rabbis see condemned at Deut. 21:18-21, but only a glutton and a drunkard (Deut. 21:20). In other words, the qualification added almost as an afterthought at v.20 limits the whole impact of the pericope. And then one must define "a glutton and a drunkard," leading to a whole series of other limitations (M. San. 8:2-3). But how did the teachers of the Mishnah arrive at the limitation of glutton and drunkard? This was the result of the hermeneutical principle of <u>gezerah</u> <u>shavah</u>, the analogy of words (Sifre Deut. 21:8). The <u>gezerah</u> <u>shavah</u> defines the perverse and rebellious son "who will not obey" (Deut. 21:18) by the glutton and drunkard "who will not obey" (v.20).

Longenecker[76] did not quite perceive this halakhic development. Therefore he over-simplified what he called the "woodenly literal" interpretation of the rabbis. The fact is that we have here a rabbinic exegesis based upon the hermeneutical principle of gezerah shavah, one of the oldest of the seven hermeneutical principles which have been ascribed to Hillel (Ab. de R. N. A,37).[77] some of which antedate him by over a century and more. The gezerah shavah is actually the key to the entire mishnaic halakhah at San. 8:1-4. It is on this basis that the "perverse and rebellious" son is limited to a glutton and drunkard, and all the limitations thereafter are rooted in this key hermeneutical rule. The perpetrator may only be charged, for instance, with imbibing wine and eating meat, the result of another gezerah shavah between Deut. 21:20 and Prov. 23:20.[78] This exegesis is already foreshadowed by the targum to Prov. 23:20 which reverses Proverb's textual order from sovēi and zolel to match Deuteronomy's zolel vesovēi. The conclusion to be drawn here is that even when rabbinic exegesis appears to be literal, it is not. The literal meanings of words give way to "interpretations," and these in turn are rooted in the hermeneutical canons by which the Graeco-Roman world read its literature, Jewish and pagan. Hermeneutics is the key to midrash in its original sense (Ezra 7:10). All forms of interpretation, whether pesher, allegory, parable or typology, are all midrash. Targum is translation, but targum also serves the purpose of midrash, as the example Prov. 23:20 indicates. There is hardly at all what one might call "literalism," and what is almost literalism is really a form of "strict construc-tionism," in which the interpreter strives to be as precise as possible in accord with the original wording. This is often taken to be a Sadducee trait, but it is also a proto-rabbinic characteristic, as we can see at Sifre to Deut. 21:18, reflected in the Mishnah (San. 8:1). The midrash approach, disciplined by hermeneutical principles, used throughout Graeco-Roman society, was characteristic of Philo, the Dead Sea Scrolls and the New Testament.[79] As J. Z. Lauterback has pointed out, the tannaitic sages believed that their midrash, being the true interpretation, is the real peshat, the actual and literal sense of scripture.[80]

Jesus, as presented in the Gospel of Matthew, will be seen to utilize midrash in reference to both

the Sabbath and divorce halakhah.[81] This element in
Jesus' sayings has been noted by others. Sometimes,
however, as in the case of Doeve, the emphasis is on
central christological questions or on ágadic
material.[82] Finkel provided only a few ágadic
examples.[83] The other writers whom I have cited
earlier frequently argue that Jesus "transcends" those
narrow "legalistic" arguments based upon hermeneutics.
Longenecker[84] provides halakhic examples and sees
clearly that Jesus is even what Longenecker calls
"atomistic." This, in fact, is the basis of Jesus'
halakhah as it was that of the proto-rabbis. But
Longenecker[85] does not quite comprehend the thrust of
Jesus' argument at Mt. 12:1-8. Longenecker asserts
that Jesus drew a kal vehomer (using a Latin term, a
minore and majorem), and he says that if "the Law
sanctions work for the priests on the Sabbath" how
much more "his presence among them was greater than
the cultic regulations." This is not the kal vehomer.
It is not Jesus' presence which can be compared to the
cult. Jesus is saying "here is something greater than
the Temple"--the love command is greater than the cult.
If one may waive the Sabbath for the cult, how much
more so for feeding a human being. Bornkamm and Held
both understand the role of the love command in
relation to the Sabbath but fail to grasp the kal
vehomer or the difference between the perushim and the
proto-rabbis.[86] Their views highlight clearly one of
the problems that stand in the way of correctly
perceiving the halakhah of Jesus: the tendency to see
everything Christologically, rather than in its own
Sitz im Leben. This same kal vehomer is also not
precisely understood by Doeve.[87] Doeve thinks it is
the food which is unlawful in both cases, and since it
becomes permitted to David, it is permitted to Jesus,
by gezerah Shavah; and then by kal vehomer if the
Temple service sets aside the Sabbath so does Jesus
who is greater. Again, Doeve misses the essential
point, that it is the love command which sets aside
the Sabbath as kal vehomer from the fact that the cult
does. Hence Jesus cites Hos. 6:6, love is greater
than the cult.

In general, in order to ascertain the state of
exegesis at the time of Jesus we must limit ourselves
to whatever evidence we have that is plainly pre-70.
On the other hand, one can use the exegesis of an
Akiba as witness because his work was largely based
upon the pre-70 work of Nahum of Gimzo. Nahum
followed the word-science techniques of his

Graeco-Roman environment which had rules for superfluous letters, redundant phrases, prefixes and suffixes. He therefore interpreted every particle, either to expand or contract the import or application of a verse.[88] This method and that of the Hillelite hermeneutical canons were prevalent in different schools during the era of Jesus.

Undoubtedly other canons of interpretation or similar ones going by other names were also in use. Thus Hillel himself is described as invoking a form of analogy, hekish. This was a very early hermeneutical rule, although it is later not found among the seven rules attributed to Hillel (P. Pes. 33a). It was a procedure used during the second century B.C. and referred to by Polybius as parathesis or syncresis, denoting a comparison or juxtaposition of two items.[89] Hillel permits slaughtering of a paschal lamb on the Sabbath by analogy to an ōlah, the daily tamid whole burnt offering. He argues that the tamid is an offering and waives the Sabbath (Num. 28:9) so by analogy the paschal lamb which is an offering, may waive the Sabbath; that is, the two serve the same function and by analogy enjoy the same rights. Hillel also adds the kal vehomer, that since omission of the tamid does not occasion the serious penalty of karet, being cut off from the assembly of Israel, and yet waives the Sabbath, how much more so the paschal lamb whose ommission is a cause for karet. Hillel then adds a third hermeneutical rule, the gazerah shavah, a verbal analogy, that both the tamid and the paschal lamb, is each to be offered bemoādo, "in its season" (Num. 9:3; 23:2).

Another hermeneutical rule identified as in use during this early proto-rabbinic period is kalal uperat, the general and particular.[90] At Sifra[91] to Lev. 5:2 it is used to arrive at a halakhah concerning impurity not communicated by a primary source which is precisely the conclusion of Yosi b. Yoezer before 160 B.C. (M. Ed. 8:4). Sifra refers to the halakhah as the opinion of "early sages." The very anonymity of these sages, the absence of such technical terms as hakhamim or sofrim pointing to the fifth to the second century B.C., indicates a time of such great antiquity that they were no longer identifiable.

Part of the problem that prevents greater perceptivity into the antiquity of hermeneutical principles, their function and their impact, is the scholarly convention of seeing a major gap between the pre-exilic Religion of Israel and post-exilic Judaism, as if a curtain came down on an act in 587 B.C. and did not rise again until 450 B.C., revealing a wholly new product. The fact that we know more about this hermeneutical science after 450 B.C. does not validate the view that prior to 450 B.C. prophets and colleagues, priests and wisdom teachers, did not engage in the same process.[92]

The hermeneutical process prevailed also at Qumran. Thus Lev. 18:13 prohibiting marriage with the sister of one's mother, the maternal aunt, is expanded at Qumran (C D C 5:7-11). The non-Qumran Jews who follow Jerusalem and proto-rabbinic halakhah are denounced because men marry their nieces. At Qumran they interpreted the prohibitions of incest at Lev. 18 more restrictively, to apply equally to women. Consequently, if a man cannot marry his aunt, a woman cannot marry her uncle, which means, conversely, that a man may not marry his niece.[93] In reference to this passage, Rabin calls attention to an interesting point which reinforces the argument that the perushim are not identical with rabbinic circles, and that, in the light of their more restrictive approach to halakhah, they may be identified with the Pharisaioi of the gospels.[94] The document cites Lev. 18:13 in a manner entirely different from that of the Masoretic Text. The latter reads "The nakedness of your mother's sister you shall not uncover..." The Qumran document reads, "And Moses said, 'the sister of your mother you shall not approach'..." The document is thereby projecting a euphemistic text on the question of incest, a procedure denounced in the literature of the rabbinic successors to the proto-rabbis (M. Meg. 4:9), who were as much opponents of Qumran as the perushim were of Jesus.

But what was the hermeneutical principle by which the Qumran sages expanded the halakhah of Lev. 18:12-13? It was a case of hekish, the comparison or juxtaposition of two items. A man was prohibited from marrying an aunt. By extension, an aunt was prohibited from marrying a nephew. The aunt is a sibling of a parent, and the nephew is a child of the sibling of the forbidden person. Thus any sibling of a parent (an uncle) is forbidden to any child (a daughter) of the sibling. This hekish is not explicated in the Zadokite document any more than hermeneutical principles are explicated in the Torah.

66

They can only be inferred. But in this case the use of <u>hekish</u> seems certain and reinformces the probability that the diverse Judaic communities (Qumranites, followers of proto-rabbis, Alexandrians, etc.) all used an inherited instrument of their Graeco-Roman environment for the exegesis of scripture. A recent study[95] has reviewed the common Near Eastern hermeneutical background and strongly supports this point of view.

It is necessary to see this Judaic hermeneutic behind the New Testament. Its importance becomes more evident only when we relinquish the tendency to insist that there is a great difference between Jesus and the proto-rabbis. Doeve[96] has indicated this tendency to be the weakness, for example, in the views of K. H. Rengstorf.[97] Rengstorf emphasizes that the great distinction between Jesus and the proto-rabbis is that while both see God's will revealed in scripture, for Jesus what really counts is "the fact of his self-awareness as the Son."[98] He writes, "...the Rabbis were increasingly characterized by learning as the continually necessary presupposition of teaching, and not so much by exemplary action."[99] Rengstorf cites statements from Sifre Deut. 41 and B. Kid. 40b where, he alleges, the Rabbis give "higher rank" to study as over against the doing. But unhappily, Rengstorf misunderstands the texts, a misunderstanding born from the persistent compulsion to force distinctions between Jesus and the proto-rabbis. This in turn is a function of a Christology which is an anachronism when referring to the time Jesus of Nazareth taught Torah during his ministry.[100]

The texts referred to by Rengstorf inform us that a group of rabbis were in process of discussing the relative importance of study and action. The relevant passage reads:

> R. Tarfon, R. Ăkiba and R. Yosi of Galilee were in session at a grape arbor in Lydda when this question was posed to them: 'what is greater: study or action?' R. Tarfon said, 'action is greater.' R. Ăkiba said, 'study is greater.' All then rejoined and said, 'study is greater because study brings to action.' (Sif. Deut. 41).[101]

The point made here is precisely that exemplary action is the objective, and therefore study "is great" as a mizvah because one can arrive at right action only as a consequence of study. This parallels the saying of Simon b. Hillel, a contemporary of Jesus, "Not study, but action, is primary" (M. Ab. 1:17).102 To imagine, as Rengstorf asserts, that study could have any other purpose for the proto-rabbis is to misread rabbinic literature.103

In concluding this section on hermeneutics it might be useful to indicate that a Torah verse could be made inoperative by applying another Torah verse against it. The very rabbinic enterprise itself was made possible by applying Deut. 17:9-11 against Deut. 4:2.104 The importance of this awareness is in the fact that Jesus proceeded similarly. Deut. 15:2 prohibits a creditor from demanding debts owing to him after the opening of the shemitah year, "the year of release." Deut. 15:9 prohibits the Israelite to refrain from lending money to a person in need. Yet,when commerce and finance became more significant in Graeco-Roman society it became evident that bankers, or wealthy persons with more cash than necessary even at the growing level of conspicuous consumption, will refrain from lending it out if it is to be forfeit upon the arrival of shemitah. Consequently, as noted earlier, the prozbul was devised (Sif. Deut. 113). Whether this was devised by Hillel or by a much earlier personage and later attributed to Hillel hardly matters (M. Shebi. 10:3-7). The point is that Hillel or a predecessor applied Deut. 15:9 against 15:2 and in effect made the latter inoperative. So, too, Jesus is said to apply Gen. 1:27 and 2:24 to make Deut. 24:1 inoperative. Since God created humans as male and female, and meant them to dwell together as one person, sending one's wife away is abhorrent and sinful (Mt. 19:4-6). His contemporary Yohanan b. Zakkai applied Hos. 4:14, a compassionate verse, to make the institution of sotah, the unfaithful wife (Num. 5:11-31), inoperative M. Sot. 9:9; B. Sot. 47b), as Jesus is said to use Hos. 6:6 at Mt. 12:7 to assert the primacy of love over cult and through the kal vehomer waive the sabbath prohibition.

Drawing superfluous distinctions between "the rabbis" and Jesus in hermeneutical matters105 only retards the process of understanding. More to the point is the conclusion by Doeve:[106]

> ...the Jewish method of using and
> expounding Scripture seems to
> contain the key to the solution of
> more than one problem in the New
> Testament.

4. The Tendency Toward Leniency

By "leniency" in the context of this discussion I
have in mind the selection of a lenient or permissive
option between two alternatives in a halakhah. The
technical terms used in rabbinic literature are koolah
and humrah, "the light" and "the weighty," more
properly, "the permissive" and "the stringent." When
a sage is mekil, he is selecting a permissive option.
When he is mahmir he is selecting a more rigorous or
restrictive viewpoint, whether in the interest of
greater piety, or caution in a time of laxity, or for
some other reason. We might glance at the first
pericope of the Mishnah for a convenient example
(M. Ber. 1:1). The question raised is: what is the
time-span within which the Shemâ of the evening must
be recited in order to fulfill properly the mizvah of
reciting the evening Shemâ? The view of R. Eliezer is
that it must be read no later than the end of the
first watch of the night.[107] A second view by
anonymous "sages" permitted the recital until midnight.
A third view, stated by R. Gamaliel I favored
permission for the Shemâ's recital until dawn. In
this example, R. Eliezer is mahmir since his position
is the most rigorous, while R. Gamaliel is mekil since
his view allows the greatest latitude.

This turn to the legitimacy of leniency was long
in process. During the second century B.C. we see the
rise of a new halakhic approach accompanied by the
gradual ascendancy of lay scholars. Ezra and
Nehemiah, as noted earlier,[108] established the
authority of the Torah. To teach and interpret the
Torah, the sofrim conducted schools. Many sofrim were
priests, but many might no longer have been priests.
Some teachers were of the hakhamim, the "wisdom
teacher" class, and probably both types now taught in
the same schools and the terms increasingly became
interchangeable. Simon the Righteous, as High Priest,
presided over the gerousia, the council of elders,
when Antiochus III recognized the legitimate authority
of both Torah and tradition for Judah and

Jerusalem.109   Since interpretive tradition was of
equal validity with Torah, a natural conflict arose
over authority: whose tradition and which authority
is valid? Would it be only the conservative priestly
"orthodoxy" in development since Ezra's time or would
there be room for innovative tradition that emanated
from both radical priests and non-priestly scholars?
The answer came with Yosi b. Yoezer, a priest, who was
a major instrument in the subsequent ascendancy of
koolah over humrah, the ascendancy of leniency over
stringency, as well as the rise to predominance of a
willingness to chart new imaginative courses.

The post-Simon the Righteous hellenistic
priesthood brought into disrepute the very legitimacy
of the priesthood and resulted in the shift of
religious evolution to a new track, from that of the
priestly schools and Establiment to what became the
tannaitic-amoraic progression. The bridge was
Antigonus of Sokho.110 As even the sons of Simon the
Righteous were considered inappropriate for the
priesthood (B. Men. 109b), halakhic hegemony moved
from the priestly authorities to circles in which
Antigonus was predominant. Of Antigonus nothing is
known. He became the conduit in history who served
for a brief brilliant moment as a link in the chain of
tradition as it moved away from the conservative,
stringent humrah posture originated by Ezra and
Nehemiah and continued by the circles in which
Jubilees was written, as well as at Qumran. The focus
that determined tradition now shifted to a coalition
of liberal priest and lay scholar. Religious
discipline in the community, and the avoidance of
inordinate schism, was maintained by a tacit agreement
for the legitimacy of halakhic options. The public
was free to follow the stringent or the lenient view.
Authority was shared by at least two leading schools
of thought, a historic reality reflected in the unique
diumvirate, the zugot, from whose midst arose the
teachers called tannaim and the hegemony of the
liberal trend in the evolution of halakhah. This
emergence of the diumvirate begins with Yosi b. Yoezer
and Yosi b. Yohanan.111 The rise of hellenistic
Judaism, the dissent of hasidim, the organization of
Qumran, the proliferation of Essene communities, war
and civil war, all made for the possibility of total
disintegration. The accomodation between permissive
and stringent halakhic views made possible a broad
coalition and consensus within the remainder of the
community. In this consensus were the Sadducean

70

followers of the priesthood and the circles attached to the proto-rabbis, as well as the ammei-haárez.

The older Ezra-Nehemiah retrenchment conservatism, what one might even term classical post-pentateuchal halakhah is reflected in the Book of Jubilees and in the Zadokite Fragments. This halakhic approach was the pietistic reaction to the incursions of Hellenism. This restrictive pattern, as we will see, [112] can be traced in the Sabbath halakhah. But the proto-rabbinic sages moved into a more imaginative system of religious interpretation and decision-making. Perhaps the earliest example of this is the permission to bear arms on the Sabbath in self-defense (I Macc. 2:40-42), a decision which is contemporary with Yosi b. Yoezer.

Major innovations were possible because Yosi introduced the era of halakhic individualism. Prior to his time, the halakhah was anonymous, given in the name of sages without individual attribution. [113] In a giant step forward, as noted earlier, Yosi advocated three innovative permissive decisions and was labelled "the permitter" (M. Ed. 8:4). [114] To arrive at his positions Yosi used the hermeneutical rule of kelal uperat, ein bekelal élah mah shebeperat, "when scripture records a general term and a specific term, the general includes no more than is delineated by the particular." His colleagues were pleased with neither the hermeneutical rule nor his halakhah, and hurled at him a very opprobrious epithet, sharyá, "one who unbinds," thus virtually accusing him of destroying the scholastic discipline carefully nurtured since Ezra. [115]

Another pre-Christian illustration is found in the controversies of Bet Shammai and Bet Hillel which undoubtedly mirror even earlier views. As Solomon Zeitlin[116] has shown, the "Schools" may be named for disciples and not for the original masters. The controversies of the "Schools," therefore, may be much older than the texts in which they are embodied and represent teachings of masters who preceded Shammai and Hillel. An analysis of the Hillel-Shammai, Bet Hillel-Bet Shammai halakhah indicates that neither School may be labelled liberal (lenient) or conservative (stringent). The conclusion one must draw is that there is a tendency for the lenient halakhah to be preferred over the stringent without regard to whether it is Shammaite or Hillelite. [117]

One illustration can suffice for our purposes. Bet Hillel (M. Git. 4:5) states that if a person is half-slave and half-free, that is, someone owns half of him, he may serve his master one day and work for himself one day, in regular alternation. Bet Shammai disputes this on the grounds that the slave remains at a disadvantage doomed to bachelorhood and celibacy. He cannot marry a slave because he is half-free, and he cannot marry a free woman because he is half-slave (ibid.). Bet Shammai, therefore, maintains that a court must compel his master to emancipate him (ibid.). Here we have an example of Shammaite liberalism. This became the prevailing halakhah.

Another aspect of the tendency toward leniency is found in the pervasive principle that the <u>koah deheterá ádif</u>, "the power of the permissive argument is preferable."[118] This simply means that the explanation of the words of the permitter is more significant because the permissive view is given out of the strength of conviction. On the other hand, when one prohibits it may only be due to assuming a stringent view as the safer course in the absence of real conviction. One permits out of certainty. One may prohibit out of pietistic fear and anxiety lest one anger God. Whether this is indeed a psychological reality is not germane to us. But it was utilized in the halakhic armory.

Each of the instances cited in the talmudic texts[119] is a third century explanation of a first- or second-century tannaitic discussion. The third century scholar is explaining the reason for a view cited from a first- or second-century <u>beraitá</u>, or in one case cited from the Mishnah (Nid. 9:1f.). In other words, the later scholar attributes the form of the earlier citation to this rule that the pwoer of the permissive argument gives it priority. This rule is never questioned. It is evident that it is taken for granted as a well-known principle that motivated some of the sages in their halakhic decisions.

One curious example will suffice to illustrate this. The Mishnah (ibid.) teaches that if a woman passed water in a vessel and observed blood, R. Meir ruled she is impure and R. Yosi ruled her pure, because it cannot be certain that the blood is of a menstrual flow. The question is discussed in the Talmud (B. Nid. 59b). The halakhic transaction there has no interest for us. But the last line of this talmudic segment is significant. It states that "the power of a lenient view is preferred," and therefore the position of R. Yosi is given priority for discussion. While this example revolves around a dispute between R. Meir and R. Yosi, first- and second-century scholars, we also have illustrations that involve the views of Bet Shammai and Bet Hillel, early first-century schools which reflect even earlier traditions (B. Bez. 2b; Er. 72b).

In the light of this one may conjecture that this principle, the priority and superior validity of the permissive argument, was one of the prevailing canons of proto-rabbinic halakhah-making. It follows from this that Jesus would find it to be a natural instrument in his own ministry. Thus, where Matthew presents Jesus as differing with other halakhah which he cites, as in the case of the antitheses (Mt. 5:21-48), or where he presents Jesus as only alluding to uncited halakhah, offering halakhah which can be shown to be at variance from later rabbinic halakhah, for example, whether to wash one's hands before eating (Mt. 15:20 contra M. Ber. 8:2), we may assume that Matthew is presenting Jesus as applying, among other arguments, the view that <u>Koah deheterá ádif</u>. One might assume that whether or <u>not</u> unwashed hands will necessarily convey impurity is a case of double doubt: whether the hands are impure from contact with a source of impurity, and whether they will touch liquid which in turn will convey impurity. But as with R. Yosi, the Matthean Jesus may argue that even a single doubt alone suffices to bring into question the need to wash hands. The argument then takes an allegorical turn. What is the purpose of washing hands? It is to erase impurity. But the real impurity a person must erase is evil thought and evil deeds (Mt. 15:19). Here, according to Matthew, Jesus supports the proto-rabbinic argument with a touch of Alexandrian-type allegory. But it should be noted, in any case, that the controversy is with <u>perushim</u>[120] who conveyed to Jesus' disciples their displeasure (15:12) over what Jesus taught (15:10-11) and not over an incident they witnessed. We have only the halakhah stated at Mt. 15:20, based on the midrash of vv. 11, 17-19. Had Jesus been included in a talmudic discussion, his disputant's halakhah would have been given, but Jesus' view would have been more fully aired because <u>koah deheterá ádif</u>.

The above might appear to be an invalid argument

73

in the light of the ultimate stabilization of the
halakhah in favor of washing the hands before meals.
But the ultimate evolution of the halakhah as
presented in the Mishnah is the product of much
agonizing during an era in which, as in the days of
Ezra and Nehemiah, power went to those who deemed it
exceedingly important to consolidate and retrench in
ritual observance if the religion were to survive.
The ultimate halakhah as presented in the Mishnah,
furthermore, incorporates the product of
generations-long polemic against Christianity. We
have no way of knowing how it would have looked if
Jesus' arguments had been admitted into the literature.
On the contrary, the emphasis of the perushim upon
washings prevailed as a function of the rabbinic
strategy to bring under the umbrella of rabbinism the
various surviving tendencies within Judaism after
70 A.D. This explains the presence of a tractate
known as Mishnat Hasidim, "the Mishnah of the
Pietists" (P. Ter. 46b), in the literature, a guide
which undoubtedly strongly influenced the received
text of our Mishnah.

5.   The Principle of Lifnim Meshurat Hadin

The phrase lifnat meshurat hadin refers to a
halakhic decision which goes beyond the boundaries of
the law. It signifies that, although the established
norm or precept requires a given response, the spirit
of the norm or precept (or law) requires that people
respond in a nobler way. Put another way, it means
that the requirement of scripture, or the right
allowed by scripture, is one thing, but the sages
instituted a practice which either demands more or
recommends ignoring the warrant of scripture.

An example of virtually setting scripture aside
is found in the case of vows. The Torah teaches
(Deut. 23:22) that if one makes a pledge to God one
must not delay its fulfillment. On the other hand, if
one refrains from pledging, it will not be a sin
(23:23). But whatever one speaks one must perform
willingly (v. 24). We see an ambiguity reflected in
this passage. It is evident that vows are permitted.
But three statements indicate they are not encouraged.
The first is that fulfillment must not be tardy, for
tardiness is sinful. The second is even stronger,
that in contrast to the sin of tardiness, not to vow
at all is not a sin. The third discouraging statement
is the further caution that fulfillment is required,

74

further reinforcing v. 22. The author of Ecclesiastes picked up on Deut. 23:23 and declared it preferable not to vow at all (Ecc. 5:3-4).

We have here as case as early as pre-exilic times in which the Torah and later writings reflect the changing mores of an evolving society. Vows, as a medium of religious devotion, are accepted. But they are discouraged. It is required to fulfill a vow. But it is even better not to vow. Not to vow at all, therefore, become lifnim meshurat hadin, a virtue that goes beyond the boundary of the halakic permission to vow. Jesus also took up on Deut. 23:22-24 (Mt. 5:33-37) and sharpened it ambiguity as the author of Ecclesiastes did. The earlier view, that refraining from vowing is not a sin, is transformed in Ecclesiastes into the higher notion that it is better not to vow at all. And in the sayings of the Matthean Jesus the attitude to vows is radicalized to the extent that vows are pronounced evil (5:37). Thus not to vow indicates a loftier religious spirit, proceeding from lifnim meshurat hadin, for the din permits vows.

The failure to see this relationship between the principle of lifnim meshurat hadin and the question of vows has misled scholars on this particular antithesis. Thus Meier sees this as one of the antitheses that "revokes" an "important O.T. institution."[121] Does Matthew really represent Jesus as revoking every halakhah related to vows and oaths, such as the necessary oath one would be required to take before a court in a judicial proceeding (Ex. 22:10) as Meier claims?[122] Furthermore, is it correct, as Meier argues, that a chapter dealing with personal vows and oaths (Num. 30:17), "These are the statutes which the Lord commanded Moses, to obtain between a man and his wife, and a father an his daughter..." transfers its status to the judicial oath at Ex. 22:10?[123] Meier does not evince any awareness of the vast distinction between Num. 30 and Ex. 22:10. The former deals with acts of piety and the latter with a question of civil suit. Mt. 5:34 refers to the type of oath or vow referred to at Num. 30. The rest of the pericope attributes to Jesus the use of the hermeneutical principle of kelal uperat,[124] the general and the particular. "Swear not at all" is followed by specific formulae of oaths. The redactor is therefore indicating that Jesus opposed certain types of hastily-made oaths in the process of daily life in society. It has no relationship whatever to the judicial process. Mt. 5:37 simply shifts the type of oath-taking from the pious type of abstention or devotion to the ordinary daily transactions among members of society.[125]

Oaths taken "by heaven" (M. Sheb. 4:13), "by earth" (ibid.), "by Jerusalem" (M. Ned. 1:3), "by the head" (M. San. 3:2), as enumerated at Mt. 5:34-36 are also recorded as typical in tannaitic literature. As Lieberman[126] has shown, there was a great propensity for oath-taking which was interchangeable with vows in Graeco-Roman society, and many forms of the oath or vow were not recognized as binding by the proto-rabbis and the later rabbis. Nevertheless the populace did accept these formulae in inter-personal transactions. Jesus is thus cited as opposing the making of hasty oaths and vows in the manner other proto-rabbis opposed it. At Mt. 23:16-22 where Jesus is represented as making the halakhah of oaths appear absurd[127] the attack is really upon the popular approach.

We can now return to our original point. As Lieberman shows, the authorities were opposed to the vow-oath syndrome but were compelled to accept it and to regulate it. For an individual to give up all oath-vow making would be lifnim meshurat hadin, going beyond what is the accepted precept. This is what Jesus desired in his attitude toward vows and oaths. He wanted his disciples to surpass the virtue of other pietists (Mt. 5:20), and reach out for perfection (v.48).

In the light of this radical demand that Jesus is represented as making, Finkel[128] is not correct in attributing Hillel's "leniency" to Jesus. For one thing, as noted previously, Hillel is not always lenient. For another, Jesus is not represented simply as an expounder of leniency. To demand lifnim meshurat hadin is not to be "lenient." What Jesus is cited as saying at Mt. 11:28-30 is not meant to lead his follower to believe it will be easy to attain the aim of 5:48. It is a logion that states the other side of the coin of Jesus' halakhah. On one side there is the radical demand of lifnim; on the other side there is the lenient interpretation when the burden becomes heavy. For in the final analysis, to act lifnim is the voluntary response of the disciple. What is mandatory, however, must be made lenient.

76

This brings us to a consideration of the halakhic role of lifnim meshurat hadin.[129] The term shurat hadin occurs at M. Git. 4:4. There it denotes the "strict law" as over against a flexibility that takes into account human welfare, and is called "equity" in legal systems.[130] It is incorrect, however, to assume as Finkel does, that this "equity" principle of lifnim applies only to lex talionis which he equates with "the strict letter of the law."[131] Finkel cites civil cases as his only examples of lifnim. The fact is that there are also cases that occur in ritualistic contexts. (T. Ter. 2:1-3; Pes. 3:7), where the shurat hadin is that one is not to be believed when he testifies that he has committed a ritual sin, while an alternate view is that shurat hadin be set aside. And this is so despite the halakhah that one witness be adequate in cases of ritual (B. Git. 2b, 3a; Ḥul. 10b). The shurat hadin is one thing, but there exist possibilities of going lifnim, beyond, or outside of the shurat hadin. Thus the concept is applied theologically at B. Ber. 7a where the first-century sage, Ismael b. Elisha prays that God will show His mercy by entering into a lifnim meshurat hadin relationship with his people. Again, in reference to God's judgment, the phrase is used to express the hope that God will act lifnim (B.A.Z. 4b).

Saul Berman[132] discusses the Mekhilta's exegesis of Ex. 18:20.[133] Scripture reads "...And you shall make them aware of the way in which they should walk, and the deed they are to perform." The midrash records an Akiban-type exegesis based upon the utilization of every word. The word "the deed" is taken to refer to the shurat hadin, the precise requirement, and "they are to perform" signifies lifnim meshurat hadin, going beyond that requirement. In some instances it can mean accepting a loss the law does not require in order to benefit others. In other cases it can mean extending oneself to do more than the halakhah requires. Thus the Palestinian Targum to Ex. 18:20 indicates one is to act in justice, shurat dina and to go beyond the norms of justice for the guilty, milgav leshurata lerashiayin. While these standards evidently are addressed to judges (v.19) rabbinic exegesis applied them to all the people. The targum here undoubtedly reflects a very early tradition which requires that, most especially toward the guilty, one must show special compassion (B.B.K. 99b: B.M. 30b). The talmudic exegesis of the

Summary

In the foregoing there have been adumbrated a
number of areas of importance to the understanding of
the halakhic process. This in turn aids us in
comprehending the halakhic posture of the New
Testament in general, and of the Matthean Jesus in
particular. From the moment the Pentateuch was edited
and made into the official scripture of Jerusalem's
temple, the synagogues and the schools, scholars were
confronted with new socio-economic and technological
realities. The sacred word of scripture had to be
interpreted to meet the challenges of historic change.
The process of midrash, already detected in the Bible,
became the method whereby Pentateuchal norms and
precepts could be applied centuries later to new
conditions.

The authorities we know as priests, prophets,
hakhamim, sofrim, and finally proto-rabbis, do not
only form a sequence. They are often contemporaries,
each new era overlapping with the old, with old titles
continuing in use. Thus the sofrim acquire
significance during the post-Ezraic era while priests
still hold hegemony. This is so possibly until the
time shortly after Ben Sira. But then the authority
seems to shift to persons referred to as hakhamim who
emerge as the proto-rabbis of the early first century,
while the function of those called sofrim begins to
change. These hakhamim occupy a variant "profession"
from that of the hakhamim of the Old Testament, and
are the persons we can identify as the proto-rabbis,
the predecessors of those who assume the title "rabbi"
after 70 A.D. Yet the priests of Jerusalem remain the
religious Establishment and hold formal authority.[135]
Despite this, however, an ancillary or parallel
tradition of exegesis is growing among the hakhamim,
and ultimately this tradition is incorporated into
rabbinism, and the old priestly or Sadducean tradition
of exegesis and halakhah is suppressed.[136]

The proto-rabbinic tradition is characterized by
a number of features. The exegesis and halakhic
conclusions can be shown to have had humanitarian
underpinnings. The basic criterion for a decision
would frequently be the concern for the poor, the
individual, or the welfare of society as a whole. In
addition to the hermeneutical rules which served as
their scientific method of exegeting texts, the sages
tended to favor the lenient option in deciding

78

questions of halakhah. Nevertheless, they were men of piety, and were challenged even more vigorously by separatist-pietists who dissented from both the Jerusalem Establishment and the proto-rabbinic alternative. Consequently, proto-rabbis sometimes encouraged going beyond the strict requirement of law or the literal reading of a text. In this way they inspired some to sacrificee their monetary or property right under law in order to extend equity to others. This is how we are to understand Mt. 5:40. Similarly, the proto-rabbis persuaded people to accept provisions in ritual that were not necessarily demanded by a strict reading of the Torah.

A major characteristic of this proto-rabbinic development, however, was the assumption of religious authority by individuals. These individuals, by force of personality and learning, were capable of changing previous halakhah, unsettling tradition and inaugurating new trends. Not everyone accepted their gezerot or halakhic decision, and so diversity was the rule. For centuries Shammaite views were maintained long after the hegemony gained by Hillelites at Yaḥneh, just as Ishmaelite views were preserved into Gaonic times despite the "official" academy decisions in favor of Akiba. It is this diversity which in great measure is the key to our understanding of the Matthean Jesus. The Mishnah, though a much later document, is a collection containing old traditions. We can see from it how contemporaries differed, and frequently we note no effort on the part of the editor to indicate by which view an adherent of Judaism must live. Tractate Eduyot is an excellent case study.[137] Here we find that a majority of proto-rabbis sometimes overrule individual opinions, but what is of greater significance is that individual opinions sometimes are accepted to become majority views.[138] We find here examples of the many differences between R. Akiba and R. Ishmael, the views of both remaining legitimate (T. Ed. 1:8-15; M. Ed. 2:4-10).

We also have here an interesting report concerning a contemporary of Jesus, Akabya ben Mahalalel (M. Ed. 5:6).[139] Akabya affirmed four opinions, and his colleagues asked him to retract, offering him the office of second in command of the Bet Din.[140] But he scornfully rejected the offer and maintained his views. His four halakhot are then listed. We are informed that his colleagues cited Shemáyah and Abtalyon against him on a halakhah in

79

which Akabya refused ritual equality to proselytes.141 Akabya in turn rejected those venerable scholars with the remark that they acted in the interests of people like themselves. This was an oblique reference to the tradition that Shemᵃyah and Abtalyon were proselytes.142 In consequence of making this remark, a clause in the pericope informs us that Akabya was placed under excommunication, that he died under excommunication, and that his coffin was stoned. R. Judah then denied the parenthetical anecdote of the excommunication and said the report was confused with the excommunication of another person.

What we derive from this extended text at Ed. 5:6 is firstly that, even if Akabya was excommunicated, it was not for his halakhic viewpoint but for insulting the memory of two venerable sages by casting aspersion upon them as proselytes. Secondly, even if the alternate version is correct, that not Akabyah, but a certain Elazar ben Ḥanokh was excommunicated for persisting in disagreeing with the majority of his colleagues over a question of purity-halakhah, the punishment meted out was only excommunication and not crucifixion. It must be stressed that Elazar's view was the stringent one.

These facts, along with the other points derived from this pericope and other passages in Eduyot dealing with the question of how first-century sages related to colleagues who sharply diverged from the consensus, help us in thinking through the relationship of Jesus to the proto-rabbis. This also aids in ascertaining what the possible consequence would be for Jesus when teaching the halakhah represented to be that of Jesus by the author of the first gospel. In the light of this, the statement at Mt. 12:14 where _Pharisaioi_ deliberate on how "to destroy" Jesus must be interpreted cautiously. Its parallel, Mk. 3:6, where _Pharisaioi_ deliberate with Herodians how "to destroy" Jesus, should be seen as a careful, albeit mistaken, correction of Mt. 12:14 where _Pharisaioi_ act without Herodians.143 The proto-rabbis in no event would seek to do more than excommunicate a defiant or frustrating colleague, and even this is doubtful. But the author of Mark did not quite understand what lay behind Mt. 12:14. The _Pharisaioi_ are not proto-rabbis, but even the extremist variety of separatist _perushim_ would not seek to destroy Jesus for his halakhah. At most they would ostracize him, for example, because they resent

80

his attitude toward what is regarded as essential in their circles, purity-halakhah. At M. Ed. 5:6 the substitute victim of excommunication suffers his sentence for stringency in purity-halakhah indicating some distance between proto-rabbis and perushim, in regard to the degree of severity mandated in purity matters. The Herodians are concerned that some people follow Jesus as a Davidic national liberator-messiah. We can assume that Mark reflects the view that the Herodians fear any messianic talk and would enter into collusion to destroy anyone who might appear to threaten the stability of the entrenched regime.[144]

The author of Matthew is in struggle with rabbis, and undoubtedly prefers to leave the term Pharisaioi in his sources as a pejorative designation of contemporary rabbinic opponents. He is, therefore, also ambiguous as to whether the perushim were seeking to place Jesus under excommunication or to destroy him literally. The Aramaic behind the Greek, "to destroy," might very well have been a form of haram, which in biblical Hebrew denoted "to destroy utterly" or "to devote, consecrate," but came to denote in rabbinic Aramaic "to excommunicate."[145] The Greek translator took it to have the stronger sense. But the author of Mark was not able to leave it in a questionable form, for if it did signify "to destroy" he knew neither the perushim nor the proto-rabbis killed a defiant colleague. He therefore added "the Herodians" to clarify the objective to kill Jesus. When Luke wrote his version of the episode (6:11) he made no reference to Herodians and knowing the tradition that a defiant sage would not be put to death for halakhic dissent, he omitted the notion altogether.

One further comment may be of value at this juncture. The form with which Jesus presents his strongest halakhic remarks, "I say unto you," (Mt. 5:20, 22, 25, 32, 34, 39, 44) should not be regarded as evidence of anything more than proto-rabbinic insistence upon one's own view even when it contradicts and abolishes earlier teaching. It is found used by the first-second century sage, R. Simon b. Yoḥai, at T. Sot. 6:6-11 along with the amplifying remark "my opinion is preferable" (ibid. 6:6,11), and in a later source at B. Kid. 60b, pointing to its naturalness in the asseveration of a view contrary to a strong position.[146] No purpose can be served here by enumerating the many instances in

which the proto-rabbis and rabbis utilized the phrase
"I say" and similar phrases to contradict earlier
teaching. It is self-evident that people "marvelled"
at Menahem b. Sungai (T. Ed. 3:1) as they did at Jesus
(Mt. 7;28). Even if these sources are later, and
Jesus' uses are the earliest on record, he was active
in a period when halakhic teaching had become
individualized, and there is reason to think some such
phrase as "I think," or even "I insist" (when the
usual "I say" is prefaced by amen) would become
acceptable. At Jer. 28:6 when one removes the
editorial "And Jeremiah the prophet said," one is left
with a sentence opening with "amen": "Indeed may God
so act." Jesus is represented as opening sentences
with amen at 5:18, 26; 6:2, 5. This manner of opening
sentences is paralleled in older Greek usage. For
example the idiom ē mēn is found in Plato. Mēn is a
particle which reinforces affirmation, meaning "in
truth." The phrase ē mēn was used to open an oath.[147]
In rabbinic literature "amen" used in response was
taken to imply an oath, an obligation or an
affirmation (B. Sheb. 29b, 36a). There is therefore
no warrant at all for the statement of Ethelbert
Stauffer that Jesus' use of this formula "schliesst
eine Epoche ab."[148] Another tannaitic way of
expressing the same certainty or determination was to
use beēmet (M. B. M. 4:11) to open a halakhic
logion.[149] It is conceivable, if undocumentable at
this time, that Matthew originally used beēmet and his
translator used amen because it was a more familiar
term.

The foregoing places Jesus into the Sitz im Leben
of an early first-century proto-rabbi, albeit an
unusually charismatic one. All of these details
should serve to create the background for our
examination of the relationship between Jesus and the
halakhah of the proto-rabbis. These particulars
should also aid in our quest for the halakhic Jesus
and the methodology by which he arrived at his
halakhic teaching. In this effort we will limit
ourselves to the halakhah of divorce and the Sabbath.

IV. THE MATTHEAN JESUS AND THE HALAKHAH OF DIVORCE

A. A General Overview

The halakhah of divorce (Mt. 5:31-32) constitutes the third of the six antitheses of the Sermon on the Mount. Views have varied from one end of the spectrum to the other regarding whether these antitheses are traditional or redactional, and which among them abrogate the Torah.[1] Rudolf Bultmann[2] regards the third antithesis as redactional and as overthrowing Deut. 24:1. J. Jeremias[3] considers the third antithesis as revoking the Torah, but he sees it as traditional. J. Suggs[4] considers the divorce pericope both as redactional and as abrogating the Torah's provision on divorce. Where he differs with Bultmann is in his regarding all the antitheses as redactional while Bultmann sees the first, second and fourth as traditional. R. Guelich[5] considers the divorce pericope as redactional and as abrogating Deut. 24:1ff. Examples of varying positions on this question may be multiplied. These positions and critiques of a number of viewpoints are briefly surveyed by J. P. Meier.[6] It appears that regardless of the conclusions of redaction and form criticism on whether the pericope in the Sermon is original with Matthew or found by him in the tradition, there is a consensus that it abrogates or revokes Deut. 24:1ff. Exceptions to this consensus are, however, in evidence. While Banks[7] also regards the pericope as redactional and as harmoniously integrated with Jesus' absolute prohibition of divorce, he hedges on whether it is "strictly" an abrogation, although that "appears to be involved." A. Finkel[8] does not regard this pericope as an abrogation but rather as the selection of one of two possible options for interpreting Deut. 24:1ff. Finkel avers that the author of Mt. 5:31-32 allows divorce, but limits Deut. 24:1ff. to a case of fornication. He thus takes himself out of the consensus referred to above.

It will be useful to present the complete divorce texts at this juncture. Concerning these two texts, (Mt. 5:31-32; 19:1-9) a note of explanation is also relevant: in this dissertation, as noted earlier, there is not effort to separate tradition from redaction.

1. **Mt. 5:31-32; The Greek Text:**

> 31. Ερρεθη δε Ος αν απολυση την
> γυναικα αυτου, δοτω αυτη
> αποστασιον;[9]
>
> 32. Εγω δε λεγω υμιν οτι πας ο
> απολυων την γυναικα αυτου
> παρεκτος λογυν πορνειας ποιει
> αυτην μοιχευθηναι, και ος εαν
> απολελυμενην γαμηση μοιχαται.

Textual Comment

The reading rendered here is the preferred reading of the Aland Greek New Testament text used for this dissertation.[10] The minor differences in some of the reading, such as gamēsei for gamēsē,[11] or the omission of the last clause of v.32, kai hos...moikhatai,[12] do not change the halakhic meaning of the pericope insofar as divorce halakhah is concerned.[13]

Mt. 5:31-32, the Translation:

> 31. It has been said: the one who divorces his wife must give her a bill of divorce.
>
> 32. But I say to you, that anyone who divorces his wife, except for the reason of porneia[14] makes her an adulteress, and whoever marries the divorced woman commits adultery.

2. **Mt. 19:3-9; the Greek Text:**

> 3. Και προσηλθον αυτω θαρισαιοι
> πειραζοντες αυτον και λεγοντες,
> Ει εξεστιν ανθρωπω απολυσαι την
> γυναικα αυτου κατα πασαν αιτιαν;
>
> 4. Ο δε αποκριθεις ειπεν, Ουκ
> ανεγνωτε οτι ο κτισας απ αρχης
> απσεν και θελυ εποιησεν αυτους;
>
> 5. Και ειπεν, Ενεκα τουτου καταλειψει
> ανθρωπος τον πατερα και την μητερα
> και κολληθησεται τη γυναικι αυτου,
> και εσονται οι δυο εις σαρκαμιαν.

6. Ωστε ουκετι εισιν δυο αλλα σαρξ
μια. Ο ουν ο θεος συνεζευζεν
ανθρωπος μη χωριςετω.

7. Λεγυνσιν αυτω τι ουν Μωυσης
ενετειλατο δουναι βιβλιον
αποστασιον και απολυσαι
[α υτην];[15]

8. Λεγει αυτοις οτι Μωυσης, προς την
σκληροκαρδιαν υμων επετρεψεν υμιν
απολυσαι τας γυναικας υμων, απ
αρχης δεον γεγονεγ ουτως.

9. Λεγω δε υμιν οτι ος αν απολυση
την γυναικα αυτου μη επι πορνεια[16]
και γαμηση αλλην μοιχαται.[17]

Textual Comment

The rendering of this pericope again follows the
Aland Greek New Testament. There are minor variant
readings. The most significant differences are found
for v. 9. But Metzger retains the text I have here,
and in any case the variants do not alter the halakhic
meaning of our passage.

Mt. 19:3-9; the Translation:

3. Pharisees approached him,
testing him, saying: "Is it
allowed for a man to divorce his
wife for any reason?"

4. He answered, saying: "Do you
not know that the Creator, at
the beginning made them male and
female?"

5. And He said, 'Therefore a man
leaves his father and his mother
and clings to his wife, and
these two become one flesh;'

6. So that they are no longer two
but one body. Now, that which
God joined together let man not
separate."

7. They said to him, "Why then did
Moses command to give a bill of
divorce and to send her away?"

8. He said to them "Moses, because
of your hard-heartedness,
permitted you to send away your
wives, but at the beginning it

was not this way.

9.   I say to you that the one who
     sends away his wife, but not for
     the reason of <u>porneia</u>, and
     marries another, commits
     adultery."

Provisionally it may be noted that the halakhah presented in both of these texts by Matthew consists of the following: a) a person should not divorce his wife (19:6); b) any person who divorces his wife except where the charge of <u>porneia</u> against her is made is an agent of her becoming an adulteress (5:32); c) any person who marries the divorced woman commits adultery (5:32); d) 19:6 is in effect where there has been no adultery; and e) if one divorces his wife and remarries, he commits adultery unless the divorce was on grounds of <u>porneia</u> (19:9).   In order, however, to place this halakhah in perspective we will now examine precisely what Deut. 24 provides.

<u>Deut. 24:1-4</u>

1. כי יקח איש אשה ובעלה והיה אם לא
   חמצא חן בעיניו כי מצא בה ערות דבר
   וכתב לה ספר כריתות ונתן בידה
   ושלחה מביתו--

2. ויצאה מביתו והלכה והיתה לאיש אחר--

3. ושנאה האיש האחרון וכתב לה ספר
   כריתות ונתן בידה ושלחה מביתו או כי
   ימות האיש האחרון אשר לקחה לו
   לאשה--

4. לא יוכל בעלה הראשון אשר שלחה לשוב
   לקחתה להיות לו לאשה אחרי אשר הטמאה
   כי תועבה היא לפני ה' ולא תחטיא את
   הארץ אשר ה' אלהיך נתן לך נחלה.

<u>Textual Comment</u>

The rendering is in accord with the received Masoretic text.   There are no emendations recommended.18   I have placed dashes at the end of the verses to signify that they have a continuous thread of thought.   The text is composed of protases at vv. 1-3 and the apodosis at v. 4.19   It is apparent from this construction that these verses do not constitute a halakhah of divorce.   The institution of divorce is assumed in the Pentateuch (Lev. 21:7, 14; 22:13; Num. 30:10) and forfeited under certain conditions (Deut. 22:19, 29).   But there is no halakhah indicating on what grounds a person may

86

divorce his or her spouse, or how the divorce is to be effected. Deut. 24:1 leads us to believe that a written document was normal practice.

Deut. 24:1-4; the Translation:

1. When (or if) a man takes a woman as wife, but she finds no favor in his eyes because he detects an &rvat dabar[20] concerning her, and he writes her a bill of divorce and places it in her hand and send her from his home--

2. And she departs from his home and becomes the wife of another--

3. And her second husband despises her and writes for her a bill of divorce, gives it to her and sends her from his home, or, the second man to whom she was married, dies--

4. Then[21] the first husband who divorced her cannot take her again to be his wife, because she has been defiled (for that is an abomination before the Lord) in order that you do not cause guilt to be upon the land which the Lord your God gives you as an inheritance.

The halakhah presented or reflected in this unit consists of the following particulars: a) a man has the right to divorce his wife for an &rvat dabar (24:1) although this right is nowhere explicitly stated; b) the act of divorce involved the transfer or delivery of a document of divorce to the wife (24:1); c) the divorced woman may contract a legal marriage, (24:2) but the marriage, though legal, constitutes a morally abominable act (v. 4).[22] We cannot determine what the author of Deuteronomy meant by &rvat dabar. This term came in for much exegesis later on, and we will have occasion to discuss it more fully in a subsequent section of this chapter. At this juncture it need only be said that the targum Onkelos and the Palestinian Targum interpreted it to mean any sinful matter (&berat pitgam). We will see that this is neither the precise view of the Hillelites nor that of the Shammaites for grounds for divorce (M. Git. 9:10; Sif. Deut. 269), although it may serve both. Furthermore, it is relevant here to note that M. Ket. 7:6 provides a listing of sundry grounds for divorce when it describes such cases as where a divorced woman is not entitled to her <u>ketubah</u>, her marriage settlement.

When synchronizing Mt. 5:31-32; 19:3-9 with Deut. 24:1-4 we find certain correspondences and certain divergences. Although we have yet to consider the meanings of <u>ἔrvat dabar</u> and <u>porneia</u>, we may posit that Deut. 24:1 and Mat. 5:32, 19:9 are in harmony. Both do no more than allow a husband to divorce his wife on grounds of <u>ἔrvat dabar</u>--<u>porneia</u>. The question to be more carefully examined is whether these terms represent the same grounds for divorce or whether the latter exegetes the former. From the Greek Old Testament (Deut. 24:3), we learn that the term <u>ἔrvat dabar</u> meant, at least to some segments of Judaism, <u>askhēmon pragma</u>. This Greek term can mean a variety of things just as <u>ἔrvat dabar</u> may mean a variety of things. But what is clear from all of the lexical attempts to define it is that <u>askhēmon</u> signifies "indecorous" and "indecent" and may extend so far as to include sexual indecency but need not.[23] In other words, the term used is a mild euphemism which may describe sexual immorality as it assuredly does at Lev. 18. This is indeed the meaning of the term many times in the Old Testament outside of Deut. 24:1. At Lev. 18, this Greek is used for the Hebrew <u>ἔrvah</u> throughout. Nevertheless, where precisely the same Hebrew term as of Deut. 24:1, <u>ἔrvat dabar</u>, is used at Deut. 23:15 (LXX 23:14), the Greek offers exactly the same translation (with allowance for varying grammatical forms). The obvious problem here is that 23:15 has no sexual connotation at all. It is therefore quite plausible to conclude that both the Hebrew and Greek idioms <u>ἔrvat dabar</u> and <u>askhēmon pragma</u> did not necessarily convey a sexual misdeed although it could have done so. This is certainly clear in the targums which render <u>ἔrvat dabar</u> as "some sinful deed."

The outcome of what has been said is that divorce was possible from the earliest times in Israel neither in precise accordance with the Shammaite view nor with that of the Hillelite view, and most certainly not in accordance with the post-Hillel reform by the Hillelite Akiba who allowed divorce for any reason whatever, including a roving eye to prettier women (M. Git. 9:10). Apparently, the Bet Shammai sought to limit divorce to reasons of sexual indecency, exegeting ĕrvat dabar of Deut. 24:1 as any dabar which can be defined as ĕrvah, sexual indecency, although not necessarily adultery. The Hillelites agreed with the targumists that divorce may be executed for lesser reasons than sexual indecency but disagreed that the reasons could only be such as may be defined as ăberah, "sin." The Greek translator understood Deut. 24:1 to convey a rather serious matter, at least equal to that of 23:15, and therefore used the same idiom. Probably the original Deuteronomic writer and the Greek translator were in closer harmony with the thought of the targumists. But Bet Shammai felt that all of these efforts to interpret Deut. 24:1 departed too far from the indigenous opposition to divorce found in the Old Testament. We will have occasion to examine this view a little later. To anticipate our conclusions then, the Matthean Jesus engaged in an effort to recapture the spirit of Malakhi (2:14-16), a prophet with a high degree of significance in early Christianity. Nevertheless, he cannot do more than exegete Deut. 24:1, and so he exegetes it in the strictest possible way: for porneia alone may a person terminate his marriage. It is true that God hates divorce altogether (Mal. 2:16), but God also prefers that people who are in a state of porneia be separated from future sexual relations with their spouses. We will see a little further on, however, that Jesus' view presented by Matthew, that divorce on the grounds of porneia may be countenanced, is not the same as the view of Bet Shammai.

Banks[24] fails to come to grips with the real halakhah here because he approaches the subject with three faulty presuppositions. First, he believes Jesus has to be above the halakhic disputes of his time. And secondly he thinks the Pharisaioi who approach Jesus are "rabbis" who have in mind "the discussions current" then. Thirdly, Banks propounds the notion that God and Moses are here represented as teaching divergent halakhah. That is, Banks believes God is opposed to divorce (19:4,6) but Moses allows it to them (19:8), an impossibility in the light of how scripture was looked upon as the word of God in the first century. Obviously first-century Jews would believe that whatever is in the Torah of Moses was divinely revealed. The same prophet Malakhi who is of importance in early Christianity, closes his message with the admonition, "remember the Torah of Moses my servant which I (God) commanded him" (3:22). It is clear from the following eschatological verses concerning Elijah _redivivus,_ that the prophet seeks to connect the Torah of Moses with the messianic herald. What Moses "permitted" (Deut. 24:1), is what God revealed to him to permit in first-century thinking. Nevertheless, when that is all said, the proto-rabbis allowed for much space for reinterpretation of the word of God given through Moses. And this is essentially what Jesus is engaged in doing. The question is: on what grounds did God allow Moses to permit divorce? The Greek translator, the targums, Bet Shammai, Bet Hillel, Qumran, and the Matthean Jesus, among others, all had their independent views.

In Matthew's version the _Pharisaioi-perushim_ approached Jesus, "testing him." Matthew often presents them dogging Jesus' footsteps. They were disappointed that John did not remain one of them. Perhaps they had experienced Jesus' presence among them. Josephus had been an Essene and gave it up.[25] He passed Essene requirements and after that decided on an even more rigorous life.[26] Undoubtedly, many people tried the pietist ascetic life and either lost the fervor, or like Jesus, decided on a different course. We have about 20 years of Jesus' life to account for. We hear of him at twelve years of age (Lk. 2:41), and then do not know of his whereabouts until he appears before John at the age of approximately 30-33.[27] The _perushim_ have never given up on him. They have a love-hate relationship with him, and this explains their constant presence in his entourage.

We have no way of knowing what the relevance of the _perushim's_ question was at that moment. Two hypotheses are preferable. The first is that when he arrived at Peraea (Mt. 19:1),[28] he may have entered a village where a divorce dispute was in progress or where a divorce had already taken place and the man or woman had remarried, an act opposed by _perushim_ as we will see later. They sought the halakhic views of Jesus. They were "testing" him only insofar as the questioners hoped he will back them up. A second hypothesis is that it was the week when the lection of Sabbath morning or of Monday or Thursday[29] included Deut. 24:1-4. It would be natural at that time to engage a visiting proto-rabbi in interpretive discourse. Assuming either hypothesis, the _perushim_

90

ask him how he interprets Deut. 24:1, whether "any reason" is sufficient for divorcing one's wife. Their question is aimed against the background of the views of Greek translation, the targumists and the "schools." As far as the rigorist thinking of perushim is concerned, even the Shammaite definition of 24:1 as an "indecent" matter was inaccurate. Jesus' response was a typical midrashic exercise. He did not respond directly to the question, whether yes or no, nor did he provide grounds for divorce. He presented other texts (Gen. 1:27; 2:24), and echoed a term known to us from the Palestinian Targum (Deut. 34:6) dezaveg, that God united Adam and Eve as a couple. This is to be understood as standing behind Jesus' statement, "What God has joined together man is not to sunder" (Mt. 19:6).[30] He has not said so in so many words, but it appears that it was in the light of targumic evidence of first-century belief that God unites males and females before they are born, that he opposes divorce on any grounds. His interlocutors then challenge his opposition to divorce (Mt. 19:7), on the grounds that Moses commanded it (Deut. 24:1), in certain instances. Jesus corrects them (Mt. 19:8), pointing out that Moses did not command it, but merely allowed it because of hard-heartedness, and insisting that at creation God intended marriage to be indissoluble and Himself even engages in coupling. It should be noted the ap arkhēs of vv. 4,8 must mean the same thing: at creation, God's design expressed at Gen. 1:27 and 2:24 predates the sin of Adam, the corruption of the human race in the time of Noah and so forth. When Moses permitted divorce--under the impact of revelation--it was because God's design for the human race had gone awry. True, what God prefers is the unity of male and female as a pre-figuring of the cosmic unity. Jesus opposes divorce, as did Malakhi. Therefore, the Matthean Jesus adds, because this is so, anyone who divorces his wife and marries another, commits adultery (Mt. 19:9). Nevertheless, he has Deut. 24:1 to contend with, which implies the tacit permission of the Torah to divorce one's wife. And this, Jesus says, can only be for porneia.

In effect, then, Jesus does not abrogate Deut. 24:1. He exegetes ervat dabar to mean porneia. But with this he abrogates the ḥalakhah of polygamy, denying a man's right to have more than one wife. That Jesus abrogated polygamy is a logical deduction. He would not call a divorced man's remarriage adultery, even if the divorce is not legitimate and he continues in the marital relationship to the first woman, if he was permitted a second wife. Thus in recapitulating the provisional statement of the halakhah which was reviewed earlier, we find explicitly that: a) Deut. 24:1 is to be understood as meaning a person should not divorce his wife unless a charge of _porneia_ can be sustained; b) in instances where there has been no _porneia_ the divorce is not legitimate, the first husband and wife remain married, and consequently she and the second man who marries her commit adultery, and if the first husband remarries he commits adultery; and implicitly: c) the husband who divorces his wife unhalakhically is unable to invoke his right to polygamy to remarry. Nevertheless with this we have not yet exhausted the possibilities and ramifications of these divorce pericopae.

For one thing, there has to be a reason for Jesus' correcting the _perushim_ from understanding Deut. 24:1 as implying a "command" to indicating "permission." The _perushim_, it will be recalled, are strict constructionists. As they read other protases and apodoses in scripture, generally the _kee_ (protasis) is followed by a "must," a structural apodosis. They would assume that to be the case here too. Nevertheless, as in all cases the "must" can be set aside in order to practice _lifnit meshurat hadin_. Here too Jesus is saying, one "may" divorce, but one need not. And in any case the right to divorce is restricted to _porneia_.[31]

When we understand Jesus' halakhah in this way we can perceive that those who find him merely Shammaitic and those who see him as "_ein pharisäischer Scriftgelehrter_" are missing a significant point.[32] Jesus is a charismatic blend of prophet and proto-rabbi and therefore he stands with neither Hillel nor Shammai nor with the other proto-rabbis whom Merkel means when he refers to the _pharisäischer schriftgelehrter_."[33] For that matter, the _perushim_ would not be interested in either the Hillelite or Shammaite schools since they were opposed to both. Thus Isaksson[34] is entirely off the track when he asserts that both schools were engaged in an effort to make Jesus unacceptable. The questioners were not members of either the Bet Shammai or the Bet Hillel. In any case, Jesus stands with Malakhi (2:14-16). Malakhi too refers to the event of creation (2:10) and roots his attack on both mixed marriage and divorce in

92

the original design of God. At 2:15 Malakhi refers to the "single being" that God created, an allusion to Gen. 1:27 and 2:24, and reaches a climax with the line "For I hate divorce" (2:16). Jesus uses the same verses. The perushim are silent, because, as we will see, their confreres at Qumran used the verses in a similar context. Jesus stands with Malakhi, and in line with Malakhi's admonition to "remember the Torah of Moses." Jesus exegetes Deut. 24:1 in the light of Malakhi. While the Shammaites would allow remarriage even when the divorce was not in accord with their halakhah (M. E. 4:7-10), Jesus rejects it. At Mt. 19:9 Jesus underscores his belief that the concession Moses made at Deut. 24:1 was for porneia alone, and he is therefore unwilling to accept remarriage as legitimate in any other divorce context. Contrary to Catchpole,[35] however, Jesus is not thereby annulling Deut. 24:1. He is only exegeting it. Surprisingly, the scholars who have written on this pericope, including Merkel and Catchpole, among others, do not notice that what Jesus is radicalizing or annulling is polygamy. And again, there is no evidence whatsoever that Bet Shammai ever rejected polygamy. Others, Isaksson among them,[36] have denied that Mal. 2:14-16 speaks of divorce. Nevertheless their arguments are not persuasive. These verses were taken as referring to divorce in the Talmud (B. Git. 90b), and it is not what modern scholars ingeniously determine the original meaning of verses to have been that counts in this connection, but how this meaning was understood in ancient Judaism.

To sum up, then, the Matthean Jesus preached that a person may divorce his wife only if a charge of porneia can be sustained against her. In the light of this, Jesus is insisting that if a person chooses any of the options offered by other interpretations of érvat dabar one becomes ensnared in the sin of adultery. Furthermore, this is so despite the right of a man to marry more than one woman, for Jesus is rescinding that right. It need occasion no surprise that he does not specify what he is doing. Proto-rabbis often spoke elliptically. The halakhah of polygamy is a clear inference from the charge of adultery. If a person were allowed to marry another woman after he divorced his wife he would not be an adulterer, and the strict construction of the divorce halakhah would be defeated. By clear implication Jesus introduces one other new halakhah. It is self-evident that a divorced man who remarries,

marries a single woman. Yet Jesus calls this adultery. Adultery is usually only defined as a sexual act with a married woman (Deut. 22:22; Lev. 18:20). Thus Jesus is elevating the status of women in sexual matters and forbids men their wonted power to abuse them. He is expanding adultery to include sexual relations of any married man with a woman not his wife, whether or not she is anyone else's wife. This, too, is a halakhah with which Bet Shammai would not concur. And finally, contrary to T. Sot. 5:9, Jesus would not allow a man to divorce his wife simply because she is flirtatious or participates in public bathing, again elevating her public status as an individual.

With this background we can turn to an examination of the use of the term _porneia_ in order to confirm the limited grounds upon which Jesus permits divorce.

B. Mt. 5:32 and 19:9 and the Use of the Term _Porneia_

Fleming[37] is among those who define _porneia_ as adultery. He refers to Jer. 3:9 (8) where the term _porneia_ defines the Hebrew naăf, adultery (Ex. 20:14). For the adultery of Israel God divorced her, giving her a writ of divorce, an event expressed very much in the language of Deut. 24:1 both in the Hebrew and the Greek (and cf. Jer. 3:1). It is clear from this verse, despite any other meaning Fleming and others would attribute to it, that God favors divorce for adultery, despite Gen. 1:27 and 2:24. Thus the Matthean Jesus' view[38] that _porneia_ is to be excluded from the prohibition on divorce is very much in tune with the action described of God at Jer. 3:8f. Fleming,[39] therefore, who sees Jesus' statement as "stricter" than the view of Shammai overlooks the fact that the more you curtail the husband's power of divorce, the more "liberal" you are in the matter of the status of women. This is also the case with Deut. 22:19,29. In any event what we have now is a clue that _porneia_ refers to adultery, and that Jesus allows divorce to a man only if his wife has been guilty of adultery.

This is how we may read Mt. 5:32 and 19:9: when a person divorces his wife for a reason other than adultery, he causes her and the one who marries her, to commit adultery, and when he (the first husband in question) marries another woman he commits adultery. It is inevitable to ask: what is the status of these

94

people when a man divorces his wife for adultery? May
he remarry? May anyone else marry her? There is
nothing to be gained by turning to Mk. 10:1-12 to
infer that Jesus prohibited all divorce and remarriage.
It remains the onus of others to prove that the author
of Mark did not represent another interpretation of
the words of Jesus long after Matthew wrote his
version. I Cor. 7:11 may be a general statement in
which Paul omitted to qualify his remarks with the
adultery exception. Paul's problem at hand was mixed
marriage, and he was interested in having the
Christian partner save the pagan. He therefore
discountenanced divorce. Furthermore, he may have
taken it for granted that the _porneia_ exception was
well known.

There are those, however, who hold that Jesus
taught that when a person divorces his wife, even
before he remarries, he already is guilty of
adultery.[40] Fitzmyer[41] argues that Jesus prohibited
all divorce because all disciples are priests, and a
priest cannot marry a divorcee (Lev. 21:7; Ez. 44:22).
This argument has much merit. But just as in the
light of Mt. 19:9 Fitzmyer's equation of divorce and
adultery is open to question, so Fitzmyer's analogy
here is not iron-clad. Lev. 21:7 and Ez. 44:22 do
prohibit a priest from marrying a divorcee, but that
does not prohibit a priest from divorcing an
unsatisfactory wife. The problem that leads to so
many theories is the presupposition which insists
Jesus was doing something unique, and that what he
did, or what Matthew represented him as doing, was in
some way connected with the Christology. The simple
way to read the text is that Jesus was opposed to
divorce, as was Malakhi, and that he regarded divorce
for _porneia_ as punitive, as did Moses and Jeremiah.
Moses sought to circumscribe divorce by limiting it to
èrvat dabar, but the meaning of that term soon came
under question. Jesus' definition of it was _porneia_.
He viewed divorce for any other reason as hateful and
maintained that in such cases there ought to be no
remarriage. In order to safeguard the design of
creation, he opposed any further licit polygamy.
Such, briefly, was the interpretive Torah of Jesus on
the subject of divorce. But he conceded that where
there was _porneia_ his strictures are to be waived.
Where divorce was for _porneia_ the husband may also
remarry, for why should he be penalized for his wife's
misbehavior? It is now essential to consider the term
porneia.[42]

95

Michael Goulder[43] speaks for a whole school of thought when he denies a connection between _porneia_ and _ervah_ of Lev. 18. He equates _porneia_ with _moikhea_.[44] The woman in the case contemplated in Matthew commits _porneia_, adultery, and the man who remarries in the event of divorce is guilty of _moikhea_ (Mt. 19:9). Similarly, T. L. Thompson[45] has argued that to insist upon a distinction between _porneia_ and _moikhea_ is "groundless and implies a very mechanical idea of language." That both of these words can be used for adultery is, in fact, clear in the LXX at Jer. 3:8-9. To present the text of v.8 in English with Greek and Hebrew inserts will suffice for our purpose.

> _v.8_: And she[46] saw that entirely on account of wayward Israel committing adultery [_niafah_, _emoikhato_] I sent her away, and I gave her a writ of divorce; but her sister treacherous Judah, was not afraid, and she went and also committed adultery, [_vatizen_, _eporneuse_].

We see here that both the Hebrew and the Greek use synonyms for adultery. The same effect, incidentally, is not afforded by English translations seeking variety by using whoring,[47] fornication[48] or harlot[49] to stand in for the Hebrew _niáfah_ or _vatizen_. When Jesus permits divorce for _porneia_ he is permitting divorce for adultery alone, in turn with Jer. 3:8f. Israel's sin of idolatry is always adultery for Israel is "married" to God. Fornication, harlotry, and other forms of illicit sex such as incest, for example, when committed by unmarried women, are not adultery according to biblical norms. In his initial statement of the halakhah, the Matthean Jesus limits divorce to a case where the wife has committed adultery. By using _porneia_ and _moikhea_ together Matthew makes that limitation precise and specific.

Fitzmyer[50] correctly refers to all attempts to read the exceptive clauses as anything other than excepting as "tortuous" and as "subterfuges to avoid the obvious." The major problem is to determine what the Matthean Jesus was "excepting" when he excepted _porneia_. Fitzmyer[51] concludes that _porneia_ in Matthew refers to the illicit marital unions of Lev. 18:6-8. But as I have indicated earlier _porneia_ is not the

96

term that would be familiar to the tongue of a
first-century Jew who read Lev. 18 in the Septuagint.
It is unlikely that he would introduce a term into so
technical a subject that was not the familiar
technical term. It is true that at Mt. 15:19
moikheiai and porneia are listed together and
therefore may be used in a manner distinct from one
another. On the other hand, in the context of
divorce, because at both Mt. 5:32 and 19:9 the author
has to use the word "adultery" twice, once for the
only reason one may divorce his wife, her adultery,
and a second time to describe the consequence of
inappropriate divorce, he chooses synonyms. The first
term applies to the action of the woman; the second to
that of the man. In effect, Jesus is represented as
saying "anyone who divorces his wife for a reason
other than her adultery and remarries, himself commits
adultery." Though aware that porneia need not mean
adultery, in that particular context it appeared
better to the author to use synonyms than to be
redundant by using moikheia twice.

It is clear from M. Sot. 5:1 that an adulteress
becomes sexually forbidden to her husband.[52] Thus the
climate of the first century was such that in a case
of adultery there was no possibility of maintaining
the relationship of Gen. 1:27; 2:24 in any case. And
so, in such cases, Jesus is said to permit divorce.
There is also to consider what Jesus might have said
in the Hebrew or Aramaic. In the style of
M. Git. 9:10 he might have said "A person must not
divorce his wife except for zenut [or neuf]." This
would obviously be a fourth halakhic alternative to
the three listed in that pericope.[53] The emphasis
upon adultery in Jesus' reputed words is also seen in
one understanding of Mt. 5:32. Lenski[54] has drawn
attention to the passive character of the term
moikheuthenai and argues that it carries the sense of
stigmatization. By Lenski's reasoning, it can be said
that the very act of divorce stigmatizes the divorced
wife as having preceded the divorce with an act of
infidelity for which her husband takes advantage of
the implications at M. Sot. 5:1. Banks[55] rejects
this, but his view is open to question. Banks argues
that the emphasis of Matthew's statement is on
remarriage at 19:9, and in tandem with Mk. 10:11 and
Lk. 16:18 Banks believes this to be primary. On the
other hand it can be argued that by the divergent
phrasing concerning remarriage found at 5:32 and 19:9
the author has provided a two-sided halakhah: a) the

prohibition against stigmatizing his wife (Mt. 5:32) which would be in the spirit of Deut. 22:13f.; b) the prohibition of remarriage. The two divorce pericopae, therefore, should be read as two separate halakhic statements arising in different situations, there being no evident compulsion to harmonize them in every particular.

Earlier it was stated that the _Sitz im Leben_ of Mt. 19:1-9 might have been an actual case of divorce in which Jesus' opinion was solicited, or a discourse he was solicited to participate in on a day the lection included Deut. 24:1-4. The _Sitz im Leben_ of Mt. 5:31-32 is self-evidently of a similar nature. Assuming the Sermon on the Mount to be a collection of sermons,[56] vv. 31-32 might represent the summation of a discourse on Deut. 24:1-4. The view of Jesus, as represented by Matthew, is then said to have been that what Moses really meant to do at Deut. 24:1 was only to permit divorce in cases of adultery. According to Matthew, Jesus teaches that Moses is misinterpreted by all those, including the Shammaites, who approach the verse on the basis of any looser construction. The "hard-heartedness" of 19:8 refers to the fact that they have not transcended the sin of adultery. Jesus offers his interpretation of Deut. 24:1, and while this exegesis obviously is a stricter construction than any current in his day, therefore "new" as Banks[57] would have it for other reasons, it is not radically new. Banks[58] argues that "No rabbi (sic!) would have regarded the remarriage of a divorced wife as adultery..." That is not correct. Many, if not all proto-rabbis, would argue that where a _get_, the bill of divorce, is not valid, remarriage of the wife is adultery. Therefore, when Jesus argues that only when it is written for reason of adultery is the _get_ valid, remarriage in any other instance would constitute adultery.

In this interpretation of the pericopae the halakhah of Jesus concerning divorce as presented in Matthew, neither abrogates nor transcends the Torah's divorce halakhah. It brings it into focus. Jesus is utilizing the third of the hermeneutical rules, _binyan ab_, by which a major principle is derived from one or two texts. In this instance Jesus derives the major principle, man and wife are to be united for life, from the two Genesis texts, and this principle takes precedence over a secondary verse like Deut. 24:1. Deut. 24:1 establishes no principle nor does it record

98

a basic halakhah. It merely provides information concerning an operative practice and provides limiting halakhah in regard top it. While Jesus' reported exegesis and halakhic conclusions are certainly original in the matter at hand, they are not unique in terms of the matrix from which he arises, first-century proto-rabbinic Judaism. Banks[59] adjudges Jesus' teaching as condemning "those who refuse to accept the new state of affairs which has now come into existence." This Christological allusion may be a valid homiletical exercise but has no relationship to the text of Matthew. Jesus lays before his questioners the principle that the natural state of humanity, ap arkhēs, as described by Gen. 1:27 and 2:24 was to brook no marital severance. But conditions have changed since the sin of Adam. Within the paramenters of the real world, adultery is a fact of life. But because adultery is in itself a severance of the unity of flesh envisioned at Gen. 2:24, divorce was allowed in order to give the innocent party a new opportunity at a sacred marriage. That other instances were well-known where changing conditions called forth even the abrogation of the Torah's provisions is evident from M. Sot. 9:9-10, which also include pre-Christian abrogations.[60]

Egō de legō at Mt. 5:32 must introduce a statement that contrasts with what came before. It either rejects or contradicts the previous statement. What does it reject or contradict in this case? One may misread Josephus[61] where it appears upon first glance that the prevailing view on divorce was the Hillelite position during the first century. There is no way to tell whether Josephus errs in presenting an "orthodoxy," or whether he reflects only the post-70 halakhah or a halakhah that had long been in ascendancy. But no matter, for we are perfectly aware that Bet Shammai and Bet Hillel never agreed on the halakhah of domestic relations, and that both positions were openly practiced in the community (M. Ed. 4:7-10). Nevertheless, we are informed that although one declares ineligible for marriage a person considered eligible by the other, they continued to allow intermarriage among followers of the two schools (ibid. 4:8). What Josephus reflects, therefore, is easy divorce which is in keeping with the climate of his Roman society. What the Matthean Jesus is saying is that if one, indeed, does follow either the Hillelite or the Shammaite position, he is guilty of adultery. The Matthean Jesus argues that neither one

of them is close enough to what Moses intended. At
Mt. 5:31 we find either an amputated statement from
Deuteronomy or an alternative reading, which is in
accord with neither the Masoretic text nor the Greek
Bible.[62] If we are thinking of a discourse _Sitz_ im
Leben, we may reconstruct the pericope this way: "It
has been said, whoever divorces his wife must give her
a bill of divorce. . ." But that is not all Jesus
would have said in a discourse. He would have
reviewed how the passage is interpreted by others, and
then he would add, "But I say unto you. . . only for
adultery."

Aside from a few similar Greek words, Mt. 5:31
has no real connection with the text of LXX Deut. 24:3.
Matthew is not here necessarily attributing a
quotation to Jesus. Although Gundry[63] includes this
among the formal quotations peculiar to Mt. it appears
to me to belong even more accurately among the
allusive quotations peculiar to Matthew. Therefore,
egō de legō signifies a total rejection of the divorce
halakhah of any school of thought current around the
year 30. Jesus teaches that a divorce is valid only
if it is on the grounds of adultery. Egō de legō does
not reject Deut. 24:1. It rejects the loose
interpretation placed upon it which amounts to the
statement paraphrased at Mt. 5:31, that whoever
divorces his wife [without proper limitation of valid
cause] gives her a get, a writ of severance. In
effect Jesus is saying: "You think. . . but I tell
you. . . ," for errethē does not have to refer to the
Torah. The formulae opening the antitheses differ,
but antitheses one and four have the same formula
similar to one another, as do antitheses two, five and
six. Only antithesis three stands out alone with a
truncated opening formula, "It has been said." Jesus
is here not reported to be quoting, but to be saying:
"It has been said Deut. 24:1 means easy divorce. . . I
say, not so at all, it really means divorce must be
limited to porneia."

One final word is in order considering porneia.
Many scholars insist that it denotes prostitution or
harlotry. There are those who see in it only the
illicit marital unions of Lev. 8:6-18 and argue that
it is used in this way at Acts 15:20,29,[64] a view
wholly and correctly rejected by Sand.[65] Fitzmyer,
Schmid, and other who see porneia as the ĕrvah of
Lev. 18, fail to note that in all of those cases, if
marriage were entered into, by proto-rabbinic norms

100

the marriage would be retroactively null and void and would not require a get. Where there is no marriage there is no need for a divorce. The principle involved is kiddushin éinan tofsin, a valid betrothal is not transacted.[66] There was a difference of opinion as to when there can be no kiddushin, but it is clear that there was a consensus that no person could legally betroth any of the women listed at Lev. 18:6-18 (M. Kid. 3:12). This means that when one had violated the ̇ervah precepts of that chapter a court would enforce a separation without a divorce. Jesus, therefore, could not have been allowing divorce in a case of the ̇ervah violations of Lev. 18. The earliest person to whom this principle is attributed is R. Akiba, who included the case of one who remarries the woman he divorced among those in which the kiddushin is not valid (M. Yeb. 4:12). By strictest canons, one might legitimately suggest that the halakhah had not yet been operative in the time of Jesus. Logic, however, would tend to refute this. If a sinful union were transacted, the court could with ease declare it terminated. Furthermore, it is rather gratuitous to discuss the relative "priority" of Akiba's halakhah to that of Jesus. If Jesus stated his halakhah before this principle was enunciated, that hardly matters. It is inconceivable that Jesus would have regarded a marriage that violated Lev. 18 as valid. And since Jesus' thrust, in all the synoptics, is represented as being to eliminate divorce, he certainly would not be reported by Matthew as instituting it to sever an invalid marriage. The evangelist can be speaking only of a valid marriage, a marriage which has been broken in spirit by adultery, and therefore now has to be severed halakhically. In this way he presents Jesus in the prophetic tradition as reflected in Malakhi and Jeremiah. This tradition is antipathetic to divorce. For this reason Jesus argues that Deut. 24:1 is limited to adultery. Hence Matthew introduced the specificity of parektos logou porneias and mē epi porneia. This is all in perfectly appropriate harmony with proto-rabbinic methodology. Catchpole's[67] view that Jesus' radicalism left him subject to the charge of   M. San. 43a, that he "led Israel astray," is without any warrant.

We may look at this question from another point of departure. We have no hard evidence for an indigenous divorce institution in the Pentateuch. For example, when a husband hates his wife, why would he not divorce her if he could instead of going to great lengths to besmirch her name (Deut. 22:13-19)? This pericope must imply that in early times he could not have applied an extant divorce norm. When the husband is proven to have levelled false charges against his wife, he is told he can never divorce her (v.19). But this does not imply that there existed an established and recommended system of divorce. It only implies that the Torah tolerated people taking advantage of general Near Eastern custom to shed their wives and in this case the court will prevent it on the moral grounds of the Torah's injunction. Divorce was deplored by Malakhi, and by the author of Deut. 24:4. The act of remarriage to the divorced spouse after the severance of a second marriage was regarded as toévah (Deut. 24:4), an "abomination," the same term as is used for homosexuality at Lev. 18:22, and sexual immorality in general at Lev. 18:26. In effect, the Torah did not initiate a divorce halakhah. It sought to curb Near Eastern custom. The description of the woman's defiled moral state, hutamaắh, is the same term as is used of the sotah, the unfaithful wife at Lev. 18:20 and Num. 5 (vv. 13, 20 etc.). The same is true at Deut. 22: 28-29. That passage issues an injunction to support the woman against anyone taking advantage of the customary system. Jesus acts within the spirit of this tradition. God despises divorce. God designed the harmony of male and female. Remarriage of a divorced person borders on adultery and therefore Ăkiba refused to recognize it as valid. And so the Matthean Jesus takes the halakhah to its logical conclusion: he prohibits all divorce except where the marriage has already been spiritually severed by adultery.[68]

C. Mt. 5:17-19 and the Divorce Pericopae

In his famous preface to the Sermon on the Mount, Jesus is reported as having assured his listerners that he has not come to abolish the nomos but plērōsai, "to fulfill it." He further guaranteed that in the spirit of Deut. 4:2 and 13:1 not a jot or tittle will pass from the nomos. How do these verses stand up to Mt. 5:32; 19:6,9?

When one clearly perceives the proto-rabbinic characteristics of Jesus, there is no problem in Matthew attributing both sets of verses to the same person. As has already been shown,[69] proto-rabbis used a variety of techniques and followed a given set of literary or exegetical rules to revise written

102

Torah and produce interpretive torah. The latter, part of it preserved in notes, school texts and collections of logia, but taught orally, was then seen to be as valid as the former, and to actually participate in the legitimacy of the former, so much so that it came to be "Torah." For both Hillel and Shammai, first century B.C., the interpretive teaching was subsumed under the rubric Torah (beraitá at B. Shab. 31a). Jesus would see no contradiction between his views of divorce and Deut. 4:2; 13:1; Mt. 5:17-19, any more than proto-rabbis would consider Ezekiel as contradicting Leviticus in matters of cult. Jesus can still be reported as upholding the Pentateuch in the normal proto-rabbinic fashion. One reads each portion of the Pentateuch in the light of the entire work. Various proto-rabbis invoked some verses to cancel the effect of others,[70] thereby still upholding the Pentateuch in a higher, or prophetic sense. Jesus, too, employed this technique, the interpretation of scripture by scripture. He invoked Gen. 1:27; 2:24, to interpret the sense of Deut. 24:1. Since there was no statement anywhere in the Pentateuch delineating the right or mandate to divorce, or grounds therefor, the task of all sages was to interpret the implications of Deut. 24:1. Jesus exegeted the verse to imply that for porneia alone may a man divorce his wife. This upheld the Pentateuch and the Prophets, for he stood upon Malakhi 2:14-16. There was no way then, and there is no way to this day, to reject the Matthean Jesus' interpretation of Deut. 24:1 as error. Although proto-rabbis abrogated or made inoperative a variety of Pentateuchal statements or norms, and Jesus could have done this with divorce, as it happens, he did not. The divorce antithesis does not revoke the Torah. Deut. 24:1 declares that for ẽrvat dabar a man may divorce his wife. Bet Shammai interpreted this to mean for indecency bordering on sexual unseemliness (but less than adultery)(M. Git. 9:10). Bet Hillel interpreted it to refer to any unsatisfactory behavior, even such as it is without sexual connotations (ibid.). The targumist at Deut. 24:1 represented a conservative view in opposition to the Hillelites, insisting that the behavior had to partake of a "sinful" nature. Jesus rejected all of these contemporary opinions including the Greek targumist's (LXX Deut. 24:3), who much earlier had anticipated the Shammaite position that Deut. 24:1 referred to a looseness in sexual conduct, short of adultery.

The Greek targumist had seen _ḗrvat dabar_ as _askhēmon pragma_. As indicated earlier, although _askhēmon pragma_ can relate to the _ḗrvah_ of Lev. 18 and therefore denote incestuous behavior, and illicit marriages, it does not in this halakhic context. In the case of illicit marriages or incest there is not _kidushin_, no valid marriage is contracted, and therefore no divorce is required.[71] Both Deut. 24:1 and Jesus' statements would in that event be superfluous. _Askhēmon pragma_, therefore, refers in our context only to indecent behavior which may or may not include sexual matters, such as flirtatiousness, and whatever else might be subsumed under that umbrella. This is how the Greek targumist conveyed the interpretation prevalent during the era between Ezra and Bet Shammai. Bet Shammai clearly picked up on that and comes closest to representing the older interpretation, contrary to G. F. Moore[72] who sees the Hillelite as older. The Aramaic targumist represented an alternative which sympathized with this view, but insisted that the behavior had to be classifiable as _āberah_, "sin," and then possibly unrelated to sexual unseemliness. Bet Hillel rejected these positions in favor of a far more contemporary approach, making for easier divorce, in the style of the Graeco-Roman environment. Jesus was aware of all these views. He was undoubtedly fully aware of other views that appear at Elephantine and Qumran, and perhaps of those of Philo. We have yet to look briefly at these sources. But regardless of how these other segments of the community looked upon the halakhah, Jesus preached in the mainstream of the community where the Bet Shammai--Bet Hillel halakhah was operative along with the halakhah of the Jerusalem Priesthood. And Jesus, according to Matthew, rejected all of these views in favor of the intent of creation, with but one exception, where the intent of creation has already been disrupted by the sinful act of adultery. With this we may turn to evaluate where Jesus stood in the sequence of the divorce halakhah between the Pentateuch and the Mishnah.

D. Divorce in Post-Pentateuchal Sources

1. Elephantine

The information from Elephantine is not abundant. But it does provide us with sufficient data for tentative conclusions.[73] It appears that divorce was practiced more fully at Elephantine, as it was throughout the Near East, and that on occasion a woman initiated and executed the divorce.[74] No document informs us of the causes for which a divorce may be issued. It is clear that, to the extent that the papyri reflect Judaic religious life in the Elephantine diaspora, the Jews there did not necessarily take a conservative attitude toward divorce. On the other hand, the Elephantine community preceded historically[75] all of the exegesis we have discussed, and undoubtedly did not yet know of Malakhi's teaching. They probably were not even aware of the actions of Ezra and Nehemiah regarding non-Jewish wives, nor would they have cared.

2. Ezra and Nehemiah

Ezra 10. The question of divorce arises in Ezra in the context of mixed marriages in the post-exilic community (Ezra 10: 2f.). The covenant the leaders suggest to Ezra which includes the dismissal of all the gentile wives states that this is to be done katorah (v.3), "according to the Torah" or "according to practice (custom)." It is difficult on linguistic basis alone to determine what meaning "Torah" has in this context. It might refer to the Torah's injunction against mixed marriages (Ex. 34:16; Deut. 7:3-4), but those verses do not provide for dismissal. The internal meaning in our verse appears to be that the wives are to be dismissed "according to torah," that is, the instruction to be issued by Ezra now. At 10:11 Ezra enjoins upon the guilty of the community to separate themselves from their gentile wives. We see here incidentally, insofar as Ezra's role of priest is singled out, that the Priestly Establishment represented by Ezra is still in charge of formal religious authority. There is no provision in the Torah for divorcing gentile wives. Superficially, it would appear that the Ezraic solution is merely separation. The text reads hibadlou, "be separated," as if the men are simply to separate themselves from their wives. There appears to be no need or call for a written document. The "separation" would then be a mental and physical determination. On the other hand, from the fact that the community persuaded Ezra that it would take too long to do this in the rainy weather which they were then experiencing, another conclusion is possible. Why would it take too long if it is to be a simply private act that each husband will effect? There must, therefore, have been something to do that would take time. Each husband would have to register his marriage and perhaps the date of separation. This is implied at 10:16f. in the light of the preservation of a list at 10:18-44 and the renewed statement "they agreed to dismiss their wives" (v.19). But then, from the term lehozi (v.19), to dismiss, the term regularly used in Mishnaic references to divorce,[76] it appears that more than "separation" was ultimately involved.

Nehemiah 13:23-29. This passage corroborates the post-exilic mixed marriage problem brought forward in the Book of Ezra.[77] Nehemiah seems to employ a degree of muscle (v.25) to end the marriages but teaches nothing new on divorce. It appears that Nehemiah did not even attempt to bring about mass divorce in the style of Ezra, rather employing his harsh measures only to prevent future mixed marriage.

On the whole neither the passage in Ezra nor that in Nehemiah expands our perceptions of the halakhah of divorce in the post-Pentateuchal era. We may infer no more than that Ezra introduced compulsory divorce for cases of mixed marriage, but the evidence is slender that his innovation succeeded. As with all of Ezra's authority, this too was only moral. As has been suggested, the brevity of the list of offenders at Ezra 10 may indicate that Ezra's policy was not a smashing hit.[78] Evidently mixed marriage was still a reality in Nehemiah's later governorship. But this in any case teaches us nothing new about grounds for divorce in ordinary marriage, and we remain with only the Pentateuch as guide. From this it would appear that, at about 400 B.C., the halakhah of divorce was in flux. There were no specific grounds that allowed it or called for it, except Ezra's attempt to make mixed marriage such a ground. That divorce was an ongoing convention is evident from the Pentateuch, but while Deut. 24:1 teaches us that ervat dabar was probably the basic grounds for divorce, there is no way to determine what that term meant to the community. Diaspora Jews in Egypt apparently followed their own arrangements. We have no knowledge for this period for the Jews of Babylonia or the eastern diaspora in general.

3. The Apocrypha and Pseudpigrapha

References to divorce in the intertestamental literature are sparse. Marcus[79] apparently saw no need to include the subject in his discussion of halakhah in the Apocrypha, or to include the Pseudepigrapha under his purview. Only three passages in Ben Sira possibly relate the termination of marriage. These are Ben Sira 23:22ff.; 25:26; and 42:9. Closer scrutiny indicates that 23:22ff. does not really refer to divorce. Verse 42:9 utilizes the same term, "to hate" which occurs at Elephantine and at Deut. 24:3, and which is taken as introductory to divorce. Ben Sira 25:26 appears to allow divorce for any reason, Hillelite-style.

Ben Sira 25:26 occurs in a passage on the evil of a wicked woman (vv. 16-26). The woman is apparently a wife (vv. 16, 18, 22ff.). The verse in question reads[80] "If she go not as thou wouldst have her,[81] cut her off from thy flesh." This is taken to be a suggestion for divorce. Other reading are provided by different versions, but there is no substantial difference in the way to understand the text. It appears that it allows severance of the marital relationship for reasons less than were later required by Bet Shammai. The only inference to be made is that throughout the post-exilic period there were at least two competitive attitudes toward divorce. The first was anti-divorce, expressed by Malakhi. The second was for easy divorce, reflective of male dominance and the willingness to use that power to abuse the female, expressed in such texts as Ben Sira and those of Elephantine, with the exception that at Elephantine the woman, too, could execute the divorce.

The Apocrypha adds nothing beyond that awareness of theological and halakhic diversity to our understanding of the divorce halakhah. The Book of Jubilees betrays no evidence of a divorce halakhah alternative to that of the Pentateuch, despite the various other divergences between the two works.[82] Perhaps that is the result of our not having the version of Deuteronomy the Jubilees circle produced.[83] Finally, it appears that both the Greek and the Aramaic targumists of the Pentateuch were more conservative than Ben Sira.[84] But without doubt Ben Sira represents a stage on the road to Hillelite halakhah, and this text is one of the many that reinforce what has been said earlier[85] concerning Ben Sira as an early proto-rabbi.

4. Philo

The halakhah of divorce in Philo cannot with

certainty necessarily be said to have played a role in the thought patterns of Jesus. It is essential, however, to include the halakhah by which Egyptian or Alexandrian Jews who were closest to Palestinian traditions, lived, if we are to paint a comprehensive picture of the halakhah of divorce in the time of Jesus. There is a degree of controversy over whether there is affinity between Philo's halakhah and that of proto-rabbinic Palestine.[86] I have enlarged on this matter elsewhere,[87] but here it will suffice for our purposes to state that I adopt the view of which Belkin[88] and Wolfson[89] are leading exponents. Briefly stated, this is that Philo's halakhah is frequently close to that of Palestine, that Philo had good knowledge of Hebrew, and that at times he utilized the Hebrew text rather than the Greek.[90]

On the subject of divorce there are at least two useful references in Philo.[91] In the first,[92] Philo has direct reference to the situation presupposed at Deut. 24:1-4. In this context Philo refers to the woman as having been divorced "for any cause whatever."[93] He does not object to divorce "for any cause," and in the context appears to take it for granted as a perfectly appropriate situation. The question that arises is: does Philo here reflect the lax Hillelite attitude toward grounds for divorce and an open-ended interpretation of Deut. 24:1? That this was not Philo's view appears from another passage in Philo where he did not think in terms of easy, Hillelite-style divorce. In reference to Deut. 22:13-19, Philo is adamant that the whole <u>gerousia</u> must assemble to adjudicate as at Deut. 22:15. If he had believed in the validity or desirability of easy divorce, Philo would have commented less bitingly on the type of man under question at Deut. 22:13.[95] Had grounds for divorce in Philo's circles in Alexandria been Hillelite, or had Philo wished to advocate such general grounds, he would have reflected so in this context. The man under question would not have been compelled to try to frame his wife in order to achieve a divorce on the grounds of unchastity.[96] Thus, when we read the former passage of Philo in the light of the latter we can conclude that Alexandrian halakhah as Philo taught it did not embody divorce "for any reason." How then does one explain Philo's statement concerning the woman divorced <u>kath hēn an tukhē prophasin</u>, "under any pretense whatever"[97]?

Belkin's approach[98] is to indicate that Bet

Shammai did not limit the right of divorce to adultery alone. But while this view is correct, Belkin's evidence for this (M. Ket. 5:6) is open to question.[99] That passage provides according to Bet Shammai, that a man must not vow sexual abstinence from his wife for more than two weeks. The verse upon which is based a husband's obligation to provide sexual life for his wife (Ex. 21:10), is seen in this mishnaic context to be interpreted as having a mandatory force which cannot be postponed indefinitely even by a vow. Bet Shammai teaches there can be no postponement of the obligation for more than two weeks. Should the husband violate this, the wife is free (Ex. 21:11). This can imply that he must divorce her (Mekh. to Ex. 21:11) but it need not. It may mean precisely what it states, that she goes free without a formal divorce. Does this mean that she must go free or that she may go free? There is no clue to this in the Bible. At Deut. 22:19 where a man is enjoined from divorcing a wife whom he has wronged by falsely accusing her of non-virginity, Philo[100] says the husband cannot divorce her, and if she desires to continue living with him she may. For her it may be an economic necessity to remain with her husband. She is permitted to make this choice, for it is the husband who is penalized, not the wife. Similarly, one might supply a kal vehomer in the instance at M. Ket. 5:6: if at Deut. 22:19 the wife may choose to remain with her husband where she has been horribly and falsely accused of infidelity, how much more so, at M. Ket. 5:6 where the issue is merely a vow of abstinence! We must assume the court will enjoin the husband from abstaining more than two weeks, and the wife may choose to remain with him despite his erratic sex interests. M. Ket. 5:6 is therefore no evidence for a Bet Shammai view of grounds of divorce for anything less than sexual unseemliness, albeit not only for adultery. Nevertheless, while Belkin may be open to criticism in detail, the insight is probably correct that Philo may be teaching Shammaite halakhah, and that "for any reason" would mean any acceptable reason. In reference to Deut. 22:13ff. he evidently assumes the husband cannot simply divorce her because "he hates her" (v.13).

Philo interest us for another reason. He says the wife may "stay or separate" as she wishes. This implies that the wife may freely choose to leave him. Would she then give him a divorce? This is a difficult question to answer. While biblically it might appear there were occasions when a divorce was not required (Ex. 21:11), this may be subject to careful consideration. For example, Deut. 21:14, with the use of the technical term shalah, "he shall send her to her freedom," is at the very best ambiguous. Even if it might be taken as not requiring a formal document, it might at least equally imply that the husband is to give her a writ of divorce which will then be evidence for her eligibility for remarriage. Certainly it was taken so in the traditions of the school of Ishmael and may, therefore, in the person of Ishmael, be considered a first-century tradition, possibly also derived from pre-Christian Bet Shammai. The evidence for this is not found in the Mekhilta of R. Ishmael where it is stated that Ex. 21:11 requires a get,[101] but is substantiated in a passage of Sifre Deut. 214 at Deut. 21:14. The get requirement is there given in the name of R. Yonatan, a leading disciple of R. Ishmael.[102] In the light of the likelihood that in accord with Near Eastern custom and the practical needs of settling marriage contracts such as we find at Elephantine, and the need to be assured of eligibility for remarriage, it is logical to conclude that the termination of marriage was generally accompanied by a writ of divorce. Conversely, if it is the woman who has the freedom of choice as Philo interprets Deut. 22:19 (and one might add Deut. 22:29), it would appear that she had a pre-rabbinic right to divorce her husband. We have seen this at Elephantine.[103] It was customary throughout the Graeco-Roman world. But by the time Josephus writes, with rabbinic halakhah in dominant position, he says this is contrary to halakhah.[104] It appears, as well, from references in the Palestinian Talmud that Philo's statement implying a woman may freely choose to divorce her husband, was the earlier halakhah.[105] Mk. 10:12 is testimony to this halakhic alternative. It need not be taken as a statement for a gentile audience or as one written by a person unfamiliar with halakhic options.

There are several conclusions to draw from our discussion of Philo. First, Philo refers to the wife of Deut. 24:2 as having "broken with the rules of the past" (Spec. Laws III, 5(30)). This may be an allusion to Gen. 1:27; 2:24. In that event Philo is defending one-time marriage, but accepting divorce as part of the general culture as well as an integral part of the halakhah of Judaism. As an Egyptian Jew he could not possibly bring divorce to an end. It

110

would be a gezerah the community could not abide.[106]
That Philo is unhappy with the case under
consideration (Deut. 24:1-4), is evident from his
strong language in reference to it. Secondly, it
becomes evident that, when possible, Philo stresses
the conservative approach to divorce. Belkin[107] is
therefore correct in interpreting Philo's "for
whatever reason" as meaning for whatever reason within
the parameters of allowable grounds. For Philo,
allowable grounds would not be Hillelite. They would
come closer to being Shammaite, for some form of
sexual indecency. Thirdly, Philo reflects Alexandrian
and earlier proto-rabbinic halakhah in which a woman
was able to divorce her husband. This would be the
result of applying halakhah of domestic relations to
men and women equally as at Qumran.[108] In sum,
therefore, Philo's halakhah of divorce exhibits that
element of diversity and independence which we have
come to associate with first-century Judaism. It has
continued the tradition of Elephantine which embodies
an older halakhah than the one we know as rabbinic.
It is therefore one more item of evidence that Jesus
did not function in a monolithic Judaism, and when he
taught his halakhah differently from others, his
teaching would not be condemned.

5. Qumran

The basic source for all discussions of the
halakhah of divorce at Qumran is the passage at
CDC 4:20-5:2:[109]

הם נ·חפשים בשחים ,בזנות: לקחח 4:20
שח· נשים בח··הם ·יסוד הבריאה: 4:21
זכר ונקבה ברא אותם[110]
ובא· התיבה: שנים שנ·ם באו אל 5:1
התבה [111]ועל הנש·א כחוב
לא ·רבה לו נש·ם. . [112] 5:2

4:20   They are trapped on two counts:
       a) in zenut[113] by taking
  21   two wives during their lifetimes,
       whereas the fundamental of creation
       is that "He created them male and
       female";
 5.1   And as for those who came into the
       Ark, "two by two they came into the
       Ark"; and for the prince it is
       written,
   2   "He shall not multiply wives for
       himself."

There are a number of problems in this text that have by no means been solved to the satisfaction of all.[114] It has been understood to condemn divorce,[115] or polygamy.[116] It has also been interpreted according to variations of these two general views.[117] The scope of this dissertation does not call for a careful analysis of the text or a comprehensive critique of all who have written on the subject. Suffice it to say that scholars like Dupont-Sommer,[118] who see this as condemning all polygamy including a second marriage after a divorce, are probably correct. But it must be conceded that the second part of that halakhah prohibiting a second marriage after divorce is only an inference.[119] In the event of divorce, a second marriage would be tantamount to polygamy only if the first marriage is not severable. This begs the question. Whether marriage was severable in the halakhah of Qumran is not ascertainable for lack of iron-clad evidence, and it is only possible to conjecture and to apply hermeneutical rules. We will return to this later. At this juncture it is necessary to point out that, if the scroll teaches that a second marriage during the lifetime of one's first spouse is zenut, adultery,[120] in effect the people at Qumran are ruling that any sexual relationship between a married man and a woman not his first wife is considered adultery. This is parallel to the teaching of the Matthean Jesus as we saw earlier. Thus both the Zadokite Document and Jesus prohibit polygamy and a second marriage after divorce, albeit Jesus would permit a second marriage after an appropriate divorce, in a case where there has been adultery. Rabin[121] has pointed out that the Palestinian Targum to Gen. 1:27 reads "male and his mate, He created them." Although Rabin draws no conclusions from this relevant to our subject, it may immediately be inferred that Qumran, like the Palestinian Targum to Deut. 34:6, based itself on a tradition that God created the first pair as mates, and it was typological for all future pairs: hence Gen. 1:27 forbids polygamy. The same midrashic tradition is reflected in Matthew.

Rabin[122] believes that Qumran permitted divorce at CDC 13:17. There is a basis, however, upon which to seriously question this view.[123] It is quite possible that Fitzmyer[124] correctly interprets the Temple Scroll 57:17-19, "she alone shall be with him all the days of her life"[125] as signifying a king must not divorce his wife. Hence Dupont-Sommer[126] may be correct in his translation at CDC 13:17, "whoever is expelled," with the term not signifying divorce, contra Rabin.[127] Jesus' response to the perushim at Mt. 19:3-9 appears to have satisfied them with his ban on polygamy. His extremely strict construction placed upon èrvat dabar at Deut. 24:1 would not, for they prohibited divorce, and while Jesus' permission of it was only on a very strict basis he did not issue an absolute prohibition as they did at Qumran. Jesus used Gen. 1:27 to make his point, as they did, and apparently interpreted that verse, in the spirit of the Palestinian Targum, to signify monogamy.[128] So too, probably the Karaite Kirkisani[129] reinforces the notion that Qumran forbade divorce, and the inference we are allowed to draw from their challenge to Jesus would imply that the perushim also opposed it.

It is difficult to ascertain the state of the halakhah of polygamy in the early first century in proto-rabbinic circles. We see that some perushim opposed it, specifically the Qumran people. Their pressure, as is the case normally with pietists, must have been challenging, if not persuasively influential. Later on we do find negative rabbinic attitudes toward polygamy (B. Yeb. 65a). Another aspect of this question is whether CDC 4:21 prohibits any second marriage at all either after widowhood or after divorce. It appears, as Fitzmyer[130] has pointed out, that if the "king" and the "congregation" are equated in the Zadokite Fragment,[131] remarriage after the death of the spouse is permitted. This is based upon the Temple Scroll 57:17-19 which permits a king to marry another woman after his wife dies.[132] On this score, then, both Qumran and the New Testament (Rom. 7:3f.), are in accord with rabbinic halakhah. Polygamy is to be defined as having more than one wife at the same time, but not prohibiting more than one wife in sequence. Where rabbinic halakhah and Paul part company is on remarriage after divorce. Here Paul would reject the implications of Deut. 24:2 as proposed by contemporary exegesis but he would be in accord with the implications proposed by the Temple Scroll 57:17-19. Both Paul and the Scroll permit remarriage after death of the spouse, but not after divorce.

We may now conclude on the basis of the Temple Scroll that Qumran did not allow divorce. Hence Fitzmyer[131] has a strong argument that CDC 4:20f. declares both polygamy and remarriage after divorce to be _zenut_, adultery, since the marriage cannot be severed. This brings us full circle back to Solomon Schechter who was among the first to conjecture that Qumran objected to divorce as well as polygamy. He took an educated guess which has been borne out by the Temple Scroll. Indeed, CDC 4:20f. says nothing about divorce. But the inference must be made that remarriage after divorce would be adultery since the divorce is not valid and polygamy is forbidden. If divorce were valid the remarriage would be permitted and it would be neither adultery nor polygamy.

The Qumran text (4:20) says their opponents are caught in _zenut_ on two counts. The first is that they practice polygamy. The second is not reached until 5:7ff., that they marry their nieces. For Qumran then, the _ĕrvah_ of Lev. 18:13-14 where an aunt is forbidden, is extended to the niece, and its violation is considered _zenut_. This implies that the term _zenut_ refers to illicit marriages as well as adultery. Hence Fitzmyer[134] interprets the exceptive clauses of Matthew to allow divorce where there has been an illicit or incestuous union. Fitzmyer here fails in his application of Judaic halakhah. First, the passage at Lev. 18:6-20 has no relationship to marriage. It does not presuppose a marital arrangement any more than Lev. 18:22-23. It refers to promiscuous, incestuous and adulterous sexual conduct. Secondly, as noted earlier, in these unions there would be no _kiddushin_, no valid sacrament of marriage, and the union would therefore require no formal severance. This leaves us once again with adultery alone as the exception made by the Matthean Jesus. And in the light of the absolute ban on divorce at Qumran, here as in all matters the Qumranites are more stringent than Jesus.

Summary

The foregoing review of the halakhah of divorce as presented in Matthew indicates that in some aspect of _hilkhot ishut_ (the halakhah pertaining to domestic relations) the halakhah of the Matthean Jesus was close to but less stringent than that of Qumran. All known interpreters of Deut. 24:1 accepted a variety of grounds for divorce, ranging from sexual promiscuity to male fickleness in taste for females. These interpreters included the Greek and Aramaic targumists, Bet Shammai, Bet Hillel, and Rabbi Ăkiba. All were working within a moral tradition which was

114

historically anti-divorce.[135] The other side of this
tradition, which tolerated the act of divorce
juridically, was inimical to the woman.[136] The Bet
Shammai halakhah limiting grounds for divorce was a
step forward in Palestine in protecting the rights of
women. Jesus' severely strict construction of Deut.
24:1 was even more important in advancing the status
of women. There is no evidence that the opinions of
Jesus had any direct influence upon the academies
after 70. But during the first century, women in
Palestine must have heard of some of the advantages
their sisters in Alexandria enjoyed under hellenistic
law.[137] This was bound to influence debate in
Palestine. There is no warrant to doubt that Jesus'
opinions might have become part of the content of
discussion. A careful scrutiny of the evolution of
the details of the halakhah of the execution and
delivery of a get reflected in the Mishnah, verifies a
steady improvement in the status of the woman and an
ongoing curtailment of absolute and inordinate power
of the husband.

Some Jews recognized the right of women to
initiate and execute the divorce, as at Elephantine.
The divorce procedure there was antecedent to the
tradition of easy divorce found in the Hillelite
circles. The post-exilic communities of Ezra and
Nehemiah must have accepted Deut. 24:1 at face value,
but we have no way of knowing whether they followed
the halakhah reflected in the Greek or Aramaic targums.
Their innovation of compulsory divorce in cases of
mixed marriage was ultimately superfluous. Divorce in
cases of mixed marriage became halakhically
unnecessary because there was no kiddushin, as in the
case of incestuous unions (M. Kid. 3:12).

The Apocrypha and Philo, along with the data
reviewed above all point to the diversity and
flexibility in the divorce halakhah in the first
century. The apocrypha provides no further
information of substance. Our overview of Philo
indicates that he may have followed a Shammaite view
in matters of divorce, being opposed to divorce on
ethical grounds, but accepting it as an integral
aspect of Judaic practice. He limited the husband's
freedom to divorce, but unlike the Shammaites, Philo
allowed the women the right to divorce their husbands.
On the whole his halakhah cannot be equated precisely
with the Shammaites or Hillelites, with Qumran or with
Jesus. He represents one more independent option or

tributary of the stream of first-century Judaism.

Qumran, as we saw, objected to divorce and to polygamy.[138] The Bet Shammai opposed this pietistic halakhah, while the Matthean Jesus sought to interpret scripture as close to the stricter Qumran construction as possible.[139] Bet Hillel was furthest removed (aside from R. Ákiba) from the Matthean halakhah. But Bet Shammai clearly did not go as far as Matthew. This is not only evident from the exegesis of ervat dabar but also from statements attributed to Bet Shammai elsewhere, indicating that certain sexually suggestive acts are enough to bring the wife to the hazard of divorce (P. Git. 50d; Sot. 16b). Furthermore, Bet Shammai never agued that a man is committing adultery in a sexual act with an unmarried woman, which is the clear implication of Mt. 19:9; Bet Shammai never prohibited polygamy, and there is no evidence that Bet Shammai allowed a woman to execute a divorce.

In sum, then, the halakhah of divorce practiced by the diverse communities of a many-faceted Judaism was in no way monolithic. There was no orthodoxy and no orthopraxy. The Matthean Jesus narrowed the grounds for divorce because, in line with prophetic tradition, he regarded divorce as contrary to God's will. He reduced the inordinate power of the male by abolishing the right to polygamy. He took a step toward equalizing the dignity of women with that of men by making the married male subject to charges of adultery even if he had relations with an unmarried female, just as the married woman who had sexual relations with an unmarried man was guilty of adultery.

The Matthean Jesus did not abolish the Torah's tacit acceptance of divorce, but he exegeted Deut. 24:1 in the prophetic manner. On a halakhah index he stands between Qumran and the Mishnah. Qumran prohibited polygamy (CDC 4:20-5:2); it probably abolished divorce (Temple Scroll 57:17-19) by applying the halakhah of the king to the whole congregation by equating "king" and "congregation" midrashically (CDC 7:16f.); and it established the equal obligation of men and women under Lev. 18 (CDC 5:9-10). Scholars who speak of the right of a person to marry a niece as "Pharisaic" (that is, "rabbinic") halakhah in opposition to "heretical" views,[140] are of course conventionally misreading the term "Pharisee." It was perushite halakhah ("Pharisee"), but not "heretical," that prohibited this form of marriage while proto-rabbinic and rabbinic halakhah permitted it.[141] The oldest halakhah, therefore, contrary to Ginzberg[142] was probably based upon a face-value reading of Lev. 18 with the hermeneutical reinforcement we find at Sifra 86a. This halakhah excluded the marriage of an uncle and niece from the prohibitions of Lev. 18. A difference of opinion arose over the exegesis, however, and based upon the hekish, the hermeneutical rule of juxtaposition, the aunt and nephew were juxtaposed with uncle and niece, the prohibition of marrying an aunt was applied to the niece, and in general all the regulations were declared to be applicable equally to males and females. The perushite halakhah on the marriage of a niece was therefore the later, dissenting view, or a contemporary alternative exegesis.

The Matthean Jesus, like Qumran, prohibited polygamy. He differed considerably from what ultimately became rabbinic halakhah, embodied in both the Tosefta and the Mishnah, which continued to recognize the validity of polygamy (M. Yeb. 1:1; Ket. 10:1ff.).[143] Unlike Qumran, the Matthean Jesus did not abolish divorce, but unlike his fellow proto-rabbis and the later rabbinic authorities, he severly limited it and allowed it only on the grounds of adultery. The Matthean Jesus applied domestic relations halakhah equally to male and female at least on the question of divorce, remarriage and adultery (Mt. 19:9). It is therefore likely that he would agree with Qumran on the degrees of marriage listed at Lev. 18. Nevertheless, we do not have an explicit statement attributed to Jesus on the question of a man marrying his niece, and so we can only conjecture.

The rabbinic tradition ultimately, and possibly as a result of anti-Christian polemic, accepted the easier Hillelite divorce halakhah, but labored at improving the rights of women. Marriage to a niece continued to be permitted despite the broad expansion of the Lev. 18 list in rabbinic literature (T. Yeb. 2:4; B. Yeb. 21a-22a; P. Yeb. 3d). This may have been due to the pejorative attitude taken in the Zadokite Document toward those who permit it. Polemics tend to drive the participating parties to opposite extremes. Christianity thus adopted a no-divorce halakhah while rabbinic Judaism adopted the Hillelite halakhah.

In sum, the foregoing leads to the conclusion that, in matters of divorce, or <u>hilkot ishut</u> broadly, the Matthean Jesus was an independent proto-rabbi who adhered to no particular school of halakhah.

V. THE MATTHEAN JESUS AND THE SABBATH HALAKHAH

A. A General Overview

There are a relatively large number of passages relating to the Sabbath in the Old Testament.[1] The basic pericope, as noted earlier,[2] is that of Ex. 31:12-17, a judgement based upon its historic inclusion in the liturgy of the synagogue. This includes all the elements of importance in the Sabbath theology: its status as an everlasting covenant, its symbolic value as a sign between God and Israel, its sanctifying function for Israel, its observance as an absolute obligation upon Israel at pain of death,[3] and its role as a sign of God's creation of the heavens and the earth. Bound up in this one pericope are two fundamental theological motifs of Judaism: the Covenant and the doctrine of Creation.[4] A special detail to be noted in this pericope is that "anyone who performs a melakhah on the Sabbath will be 'cut off' (v. 14). . . anyone who performs a melakhah on the Sabbath will assuredly be put to death" (v.15). It is important, however, to note that nowhere in the entire Old Testament is melakhah defined. Upon this fact hinges the wide disparity of Sabbath halakhah and the ultimate question of whether Jesus or his disciples violated the Sabbath. What we have in a variety of sources are certain specifications of forbidden activities,[5] but no broad definition of the nature of melakhah. Furthermore, as I will indicate later, at no time was the threat of death alluded to against Jesus for the violation of the Sabbath despite the practice being know even to Philo.[6]

The Sabbath remained an institution of utmost significance in the post-exilic period.[7] It was seen from both a humanitarian aspect (Ex. 23:12; Deut. 5:14) and a cultic one (Num. 28:9-10; I. Chron. 23:30-31). In addition to the references to the Sabbath in the intertestamental works,[8] the significance of the day is attested in the writings of Philo and Josephus.[9] A strong Sabbath statement is found in Jubilees, which makes it rather surprising that Ralph Marcus[10] asserts that there is no allusion to the Sabbath in the Apocrypha outside of Judith (8:6), and I and II Maccabees.[11] It is of special importance to relate the halakhah of Jubilees and Qumran to that of the proto-rabbis and the New Testament.

The available literature points to a diversity in the Sabbath halakhah. One example is the question of conducting defensive warfare on the Sabbath. While it is clear at I Macc. 2:40f. that the first generation of Hasmonean leaders permitted resistance on the Sabbath, II Macc. 5:25ff. raises some doubt whether they were yet wont to practice that, and II. Macc. 15:1-5 implies that the Jews would not have resisted if Nicanor had attacked on the Sabbath. More to the point, II Macc. 6:11 indicates that their conscience would still impel Jews not to defend themselves on the Sabbath. This reluctance would be reinforced by Jub. 50:12. What we detect here is that restrictive attitude toward the Sabbath that had become part of the framework of Judaism since the consolidation and retrenchment policies of Ezra and Nehemiah gained hegemony. Jubilees and the Zadokite Document will be seen to reflect this Sabbath stringency at its peak. As late as the middle of the first century some Jews still did not defend themselves on the Sabbath.[12] Proto-rabbinic halakhah and the teachings of Jesus were in opposition to this type of stringency. The Mishnah later reflects rabbinic attempts to modify the most restrictive features of the halakhah.

The question of waging war on the Sabbath is interesting for another reason. The halakhah of Jubilees (50:12) ordains that making war on the Sabbath is a capital offense (vv. 8,13). It is not feasible here to enter into a discussion of the dating of Jubilees, but if, as seems likely, Finkelstein[13] is correct in his recent early dating of the book, and even more so, should the dating of Vander Kam[14] prove correct,[15] the stringent rule of Jub. 50:12 fits well with Sabbath restrictiveness clearly evident in the Zadokite Document where there is no provision for waiving Sabbath observance in order to save life.[16] Finkelstein[17] correctly argues that the author of Jubilees seeks a return to the pre-Maccabean halakhah. This more stringent Ezraic-Nehemian attitude is reflected in the pietistic circles which produced Jubilees and the Zadokite Document. The effort by the first Hasmoneans to rescind this prohibition was not immediately successful. It probably did not become successful until the proto-rabbis introduced the principle that one may violate the Sabbath for the purpose of saving life.[18]

What becomes evident in the first instance,

however, is that the halakhah of the Old Testament was supplemented from the earliest times. The Sabbath halakhah of the Pentateuch is enlarged in Jeremiah and Nehemiah, further intensified in the Book of Jubilees and the Zadokite Document, and ultimately modified in the New Testament and in the proto-rabbinic tradition, all of which will be discussed further on in this chapter. It is not correct to assert, as Marcus[19] does, that "the ceremonial and civil laws of the Old Testament were interpreted and expanded in the oral law," unless we modify oral to mean "interpretive," frequently orally transmitted. But it is not possible to accept the other part of his statement,[20] that for this interpretation and expansion "instruction was given by a class of men, known as scribes, in large part drawn from the sect of the Pharisees..." In using this term in the context in which he includes it, Marcus here refers to proto-rabbis. But it is highly instructive that nowhere in these works is there found a term remotely related to "Pharisees." We know that <u>sofrim</u> and <u>hakhamim</u>[21] carried out this interpretive function, but the apocryphal sources we have referred to: Judith (no fasting on the Sabbath), II Maccabees (apparently resisting the permission to wage war on the Sabbath), Jubilees (with its stringent halakhah to be discussed separately below) do not produce a halakhah that meets with the proto-rabbinic standards[22] discussed earlier. Only I Maccabees 2:41 serves as an early herald of the proto-rabbinic attitude toward the Sabbath. Indeed, in a way not contemplated by Marcus, the halakhah embodied in these apocryphal writings are "pharisaic" in the sense of being <u>perushite</u> non-proto-rabbinnic, similar to the halakhah of the opponents of the proto-rabbis and the halakhah of the opponents of Jesus. A separate monograph is desirable to analyze this halakhah comprehensively in order to demonstrate that this may be one of the major reasons why the apocryphal books were not included in the rabbinic canon. As I have adumbrated in the previous chapters, I will again be stressing in this chapter that the complex of ideas that is conveniently summed up by Moore[23] as "normative Judaism" simply do not constitute such a "normative" tradition. Furthermore, the conventional notion summed up by Marcus[24] that this "normative Judaism"..."the religion of the Tannaim, is essentially the same as that which is reflected in the apocryphal books. . ." is not accurate. Much of the theology and halakhah is naturally similar, in much the same manner as the modern denominations within

Judaism share many affinities in belief and practice. But the teachers of the apocrypha's halakhah and the teachers who emerge as the founders of rabbinic Judaism belonged to different "denominations."

In the light of what has just been said, H. Loewe[25] misses the target when he suggests that those who would be opposed, for example, to Jesus' healing on the Sabbath, would be those who opposed the halakhah of the Pharisees, namely the Sadducees. On the contrary, it was the pharisees-perushim who opposed Jesus' healing. We have no way of knowing how the Sadducees felt about healing on the Sabbath. And we will see later on that the proto-rabbis have a more lenient position than the one attributed to so-called "Pharisees" at Mt. 12:9-14. For some strange reason Loewe backed away from an accurate guess when he momentarily suggested[26] that the "Pharisees" attacked by Jesus might have been sectarians who were "mistaken for Pharisees." They were perushim who represented a very stringent approach to the halakhah. They did not exegete Hos. 6:6 the way both Jesus and his contemporary fellow-proto-rabbi Yohanan b. Zakkai were wont to do.[27] The latter, a Galilean contemporary of Jesus', stressed that acts of love are primary for salvation, basing his claim upon the same verse as Jesus who argued that acts of love are valid for waiving the requirements of the Sabbath (Mt. 12:7).

This leads to a second thought. The proto-rabbininc usage of Hos. 6:6 in some quarters saw love as superior to the Temple cult. Manson[28] therefore has a case in point when he stresses that Mt. 10:9-10, where Jesus is said to admonish his disciples not to take any symbols of material goods on their mission, is parallel to the notion that such objects as a staff, sandals and a wallet are not to be carried into the Temple. The mission is the act of bringing the Kingdom and is parallel to the Temple, and even greater (Mt. 12:6). Therefore, in the service of the Kingdom (the Temple) the Sabbath is a secondary consideration. At this juncture it should be observed that Mt. 12:1, "At that time" reverts to the mission (Mt. 10-11). When Jesus defends his disciples he is alluding to more halakhah than is evident in the text, all of which is designed to argue for a Sabbath exemption.

Jesus defended his disciples at Mt. 12:1-8. If he was opposed to the very premise of the perushim he

122

could simply reject their argument as invalid in much the same manner as he does at Mt. 15:1-20. It is therefore evident he had no intention of rejecting the Sabbath as he rejected <u>perushite</u> purity taboos. The view of G. Barth[29] that the decision at Mt. 12:14 to kill Jesus is a consequence of his attitude toward the Sabbath may be questioned.[30] Is it at all possible to kill a proto-rabbi for his halakhic divergencies related to the Sabbath? So, too, Severino Pancaro[31] seriously misses the mark when he asserts that the charges made by the Pharisees against Jesus related to the Sabbath is one of the four major charges that constituted the "case" that "orthodox Judaism" made against Jesus. First of all, that there was no "orthodox Judaism" has been demonstrated in the earlier discussion of the wide diversity prevalent in the first century. Secondly, had there been an "orthodoxy" it would have been the priestly Establishment in Jerusalem which continued to wield religious authority.[32] Thirdly, when that religious Establishment did contribute to Jesus' death its action had no relationship to the Sabbath.

Banks[33] assesses Mt. 12:1-8 as a proper sequence to Mt. 11:28-30. The latter saying expresses the idea that Jesus' yoke is easy and his burden is light. Banks sees this as a natural prelude to a controversy with Pharisees whose burdens are presumably heavy. There are others who see the approach of the Pharisees at Mt. 12:2, as designed to warn Jesus of his culpability in accordance with the judicial requirement that, before the death penalty can be exacted, the offender must be warned that he is culpable for the action he is about to perform.[34] That only begs the question: could a teacher like Jesus be put to death judicially in the first century for having an independent view of a given halakhah? Everything we know about first-century Judaism refutes that. It is logical, however, with Banks to think that the Pharisees accosted Jesus on the basis of their heavier burdens. Where Banks fails is first in missing the basic point that the Pharisees are pietistic separatists who represent a Sabbath halakhah that was not yet the prevalent form. And secondly, Banks errs concerning the action in the Sabbath pericope because of his interpretation of the halakhic controversies as being related to the Christology.[35]

On the other hand, both Barth[36] and Hummel[37] are correct in seeing Jesus' attitude in both Sabbath pericopae as a function of the love command,[38] or, as I indicated earlier, the application of the humanitarian motive in proto-rabbinic halakhah. At no time, contrary to Banks,[39] does Jesus' healing actions on the Sabbath run counter to the so-called "Mosaic Law." David Flusser[40] discusses the Sabbath passages briefly and seeks to associate Jesus with a customary Galilean practice as far as "rubbing" grain is concerned (Lk. 6:1). He argues that some of the Pharisees found fault with his disciples accepting Galilean tradition.[41] He attributes the addition of "plucking" (at Lk 6:1 and parallels), to the unfamiliarity of the Greek translator with Galilean custom, coupled with his desire "to make the scene more vivid." Flusser thus sees the plucking of corn as "the one and only act of transgression of the law recorded in the synoptic tradition."[42] This is not the place to offer a critique of Flusser's general approach to the halakhah. I will come back to the question of "plucking" and "rubbing" later. Here it will suffice to point out that Bet Shammai was Galilean, and if Flusser sees "Pharisees" in the conventional light, one could hardly expect such a violent reaction by Pharisees against Galilean custom. Furthermore, the argument can be turned around. Flusser calls this the "one and only" transgression in the synoptic tradition, and yet it is not after this one, but after the healing (Lk. 6:11; Mk. 3:6; Mt. 12:14), an act Flusser sees as "permissible,"[43] that the Pharisees allegedly decide to destroy Jesus.

In the foregoing I have adumbrated the difficulty of defining the nature of Sabbath prohibitions, and of ascertaining the precise violations with which Jesus or his disciples may be charged. A cursory scan of the material in the four gospels will reveal that there are a number of Sabbath halakhot involved that are related to Jesus' actions or to those of his disciples. These include: a) picking grain (Mt. 12:1 and parallels); b) rubbing grain (Lk 6:1); c) healing (Mt. 12:13, and parallels); d) carrying (Jn. 5:8); e) mixing a healing potion (Jn. 9:6). In addition four other halakhot are alluded to: a) lifting an animal up out of a pit (Mt. 12:11); b) flight from danger (Mt. 24:20);c) circumcision (Jn. 7:22-23); d) Temple worship(Mt. 12:5). Evidently there is a sizable body of halakhah, and each item has its own ramifications and complications.

There are several halakhic principles that come

under scrutiny. Among these are the two most prominent: a) temple worhip or abodah os exempt from Sabbath prohibition;[44] b) the need to save life supersedes the Sabbath.[45] The alleged violations must be measured against the general principles of Sabbath halakhah. Furthermore, when Jesus or his disciples are accused of a violation, the question must be asked: according to whose halakhah? One must never lose sight of the fact that halakhah has alwasy been in flux, and the first century was no different from the twentieth century. Except where a central secular government exercises it civil power to enforce a system of practice, the writ of authority of each rabbi runs as far as those who accept his view.[46]

It is not anachronistic to adjudge the Jesus incidents in this light. Like many other proto-rabbis and their successors, the rabbis, Jesus expressed his own halakhic viewpoint based upon his own interpretation and application of the traditional hermeneutics and principles. Jesus did not innovate new hermeneutics or frame new underlying philosophical principles by which to enunciate halakhah. But he must have taken a hard look at the prevalent Sabbath halakhah of his time and rejected the stringencies of Jubilees and of the perushim who followed a halakhah similar to what we now know was the Qumran halakhah. Perhaps he anticipated rabbinic halakhah in some particulars. This can be determined only by a careful and comprehensive examination of his Sabbath halakhah. It would be too formidable a task to undertake here an evaluation of each of the items listed above. For our purposes, therefore, and in the interests of limiting ourselves to Matthew, I am here examining only the two pericopae at Mt. 12:1-8; 9-14. A careful analysis of these icidents and the attendant halakhah will provide us with a picture of where Jesus stood in his Sabbath halakhah between the Pentateuch and the Mishnah. Most importantly, however, we must not confuse the halakhah of the Pharisees in the New Testament with that of the later rabbis, and we must liberate ourselves from what have become classic errors in all studies of New Testament halakhah, that the halakhah of the Pharisees became "normative" Judaism,[47] and that the Pharisees are identical with the rabbis who gained hegemony after 70 A.D.[48]

Certainly in relation to the Sabbath above all, but also in general, one must ask why halakhah plays so great a role in the ministry of Jesus. If Jesus was not a charismatic proto-rabhbi among proto-rabbis, why has the Matthean tradition such concern for the halakhah, not only at 5:17-20, but throughout the Gospel? Nowhere is Jesus made to reject halakhah as a system. He reinterprets or he rescinds an individual halakhah. He differs over particulars, but never brings the system into question. At 23:3 he attacks hypocrisy, not halakhah. Throughout that vehement chapter Jesus is made to question particulars, or integrity, but never the responsibility to the halakhah as a method of concretizing God's covenant with Israel. Scholars such as Guelich[49] engage in tortuous exegesis to separate Jesus and his halakhah from the first-century environment by arguing that Hos. 6:6 is being used to rebuke the Pharisees for not understanding and recognizing the function of Jesus, thereby missing the opportunity to exhibit hesed. Neither this notion nor Strecker's proposal[50] that its use by Jesus indicates the superior importance of the moral over the ceremonial law, correctly explains Jesus' use of Hos. 6:6. This is a matter to which I will return when exegeting the pericope.

After establishing the Sabbath halakhah of the Matthean Jesus at least insofar as the pericopae of Mt. 12:1-8, 9-14 are concerned, I will review the extra-Pentateuchal Sabbath halakhah found in the Prophets, Ezra-Nehemiah, Jubilees, Philo and The Dead Sea Scrolls, in order to indicate where the halakhah of Jesus falls in this sequence leading to the Toseftá and the Mishnah. Zekhariah Frankel[51] indicates his conviction that halakhot found in the Toseftá are earlier than some of those found in the Mishnah. This may help at times to clarify why Philo's more stringent halakhah has greater affinity with that of the Toseftá and the perushim. It may also explain why there are times when the stringent perushite halakhah is reflected in the Mishnah. This would indicate it was absorbed into rabbinic Judaism after 70 A.D. in the effort of Jamnia to create a halakhic consensus. On the other hand when the perushite and Toseftá halakhah is apparently more stringent than that of the Mishnah, it is probably because the latter is the product of later rabbinic efforts to create a more lenient halakhah.

One more word is in order here. There is a view in the Mishnah (Shab. 16:8) that prohibits a Jew from using a gangway, even if it is made by a gentile, to disembark from a ship on the Sabbath, if this gangway

126

was made on the Sabbath and was made specifically for the Jew. The Mishnah continues with an episode in which it reports that Gamaliel and other sages used a gangway made on the Sabbath by a gentile. Since the Mishnah had already stated a unanimous view (ibid.) that when a gentile made a gangway in order to disembark, a Jew may follow him, the Gamaliel episode is redundant if it is taken to relate to that clause. Rather, it must relate to the next clause which prohibited the use of the gangway if the gentile made it on the Sabbath expressly for the Jew. In other words one must infer that the Gamaliel episode is reported in order to refute this prohibition of the Mishnah. A glance at the passage, Clauses C and D of the pericope, will help to understand this inference:

> C) (1) If a non-Jew made a gangway by which to disembark, a Jew may disembark after him; (2) but if he made it expressly for the Jew, it is prohibited.

> D) There was an incident when Gamaliel and elders who arrived in a ship when a gentile made a gangway for disembarking, and R. Gamaliel and the elders disembarked.

Clause D is superfluous if it illustrates C (1), but has importance if it is designed to refute C (2). There is no need to cite a corroborative episode to C (1) since there was no dispute on the question. The dispute therefore consists of whether a Jew may use a gangway when it is made expressly for him. The Mishnah indicates that certain proto-rabbis allowed this, thus implying a leniency as compared to C (2). There are other examples where a story does not corroborate an undisputed halakhah, but rather disputes a point expressed in the Mishnah (Suk. 2:4-5).

The foregoing is important for two reasons unrelated to the actual halakhic questions involved. First of all, the example from M. Shab. 16:8 provides clear evidence of some proto-rabbis rejecting the stated halakhah of other proto-rabbis on a Sabbath question, reinforcing our understanding of the Matthean pericopae under discussion. Secondly, the example from M. Suk. 2:4-5 cautions us against hastily labelling any individual. One of the persons involved there is Yoḥanan b. Zakkai who, though frequently an innovator (M. Suk. 3:12; R.H. 4:1, 3f.), decides more stringently in this case, as he also does in certain Sabbath halakhot in which there was a degree of doubt (M. Shab. 16:7; 22:3). Similarly, when Jesus differs from stated Sabbath halakhah, it need occasion no surprise, and need not lead to crucifixion. Secondly, one should not seek consistency in leniency or stringency from the same sage. Although Jesus' demands are for extreme righteousness, and he often requires lifnim meshurat hadin, as noted earlier, it should occasion no surprise that he also follows a more lenient approach at other times, as here in the case of the Sabbath.

B. Plucking, Picking and/or Rubbing Grain on the Sabbath (Mt. 12:1-8)

Mt. 12:1-8 provides us with a Sabbath story in which the disciples of Jesus are said to be violating the Sabbath. Jesus offers two rationales (vv. 3-6), to declare their behavior legitimate. Contrary to what the perushim have asserted (v.2), that the disciples have done what is not allowed on the Sabbath, Jesus simply delivers a brief halakhic discourse in which, as we will see, he makes it clear that what the disciples did is permissible. To this he adds an ágadic exhortative lesson, as an addendum to his halakhic words (vv. 7-8).[53]

Scholars[54] correctly emphasize that Jesus here uses the hermeneutical rule kal vehomer. But he does much more. At vv. 3-5, Jesus offers two other halakhic principles. Confronted by the assumption asserted by the Pharisees that what the disciples did was forbidden on the Sabbath, Jesus neither rejected the Sabbath nor consented to the assumption of violation. He referred to the incident at I. Sam. 21:2-7 as a parallel for the action of his disciples (3-4). He then also referred to the activity of the priests in the Temple as a parallel for the action of his disciples (v.5). He follows up these two arguments with a kal vehomer (v.6), and with another major halakhic principle (v.7), finally closing his argument with a theological or ágadic teaching which can be used as an underlying concept by which to measure Sabbath halakhah.

It will be most convenient to present a more
formal interpretation of this pericope and an
exposition of the halakhic particulars and principles
involved by examining each verse in sequence.

12:1 Εν εκεινω τω καιρω επορευϑη ο
Ιησους τοις σαββυσιν δια των
σποριμων. Οι δε μαϑηται αυτου
εττεινασαν και κρζαυτο τιλλειν
σταχυας και εσϑιειν.[55]

Jesus is here described as passing through a field of
grain on his journey. It must be assumed from 1b that
his disciples were proceeding through the field with
him. While he was able to exercise greater
abstemiousness (once before, Mt. 4:2, he had fasted
for forty days before becoming hungry), his disciples
stripped ears of grain, pulling off the ripe grains
from the ears to eat.[56]

12:2. What, in fact, had the disciples done to
bring forth the Pharisaic assertion that they were
doing something forbidden on the Sabbath? There are
many halakhot to select from. Some may compare the
action to trimming or weeding, all depending upon
precisely what they did and how the beholder
interpreted the action. One who weeds or trims either
dry twigs or young shoots is culpable for the
violation of the Sabbath (M. Shab. 12:2). On the
other hand the action of tolesh, "plucking,"
separating a twig or a fruit from a plant that is
still rooted in the soil, or removing the plant itself
by such an action, is not unanimously prohibited
(M. Shab. 10:6). Furthermore, such removal, the
action of tolesh, is not one of the thirty-nine
categories of prohibitied primary forms of work (M.
Shab. 7:2).[57] Again, at M. Shab. 12:2 we are told
that, if one gathers vegatative growth in order
letaken, to improve upon the land, he is culpable for
violating the Sabbath. Other examples of activities
similar to the action of the disciples may be
multiplied many times over. But a careful scrutiny of
the sources will indicate they involve either land
improvement or general agricultural tasks. The
tannaitic sources contain no real parallel of a hungry
person returning from a journey,[58] especially from a
sacred journey, or still engaged in such a journey,
having had no time to prepare his food on Friday,
receiving no succor from villagers,[59] simply pulling
off some seeds from ears of grain in order to reduce
hunger pangs. There is, however, precedent for

waiving the Sabbath prohibition on carrying from one domain to another (M. Shab. 1:1) in order to save food from a fire on the Sabbath in order to enjoy three Sabbath meals (M. Shab. 16:2ff.). There can be no doubt that Jesus did not prevent his disciples from consummating their action because he did not regard the action under the circumstances as forbidden. He offers several arguments to sustain his view once he is challenged, but a priori he would simply reflect on the commonly used exegesis of Lev. 18:5, "and you shall live by them" (B. Yom. 85a-b), or upon a common view that in cases of serious doubt one does not enforce a halakhah.60

It was an old tradition among those circles that produced Jubilees and Judith not to fast on the Sabbath (Jub. 50:11; Jud. 8:6). This tradition was probably widespread and appears as a favorable practice in rabbinic literature (M. Ned. 9:6), although it is not found as an explicit prohibition in early rabbinic sources. The Qumran people opposed voluntary "hungering," or fasting on the Sabbath (CDC 11:4-5).61 Later rabbinic literature both disapproves62 and allows it.63 Considering the reluctance of the disciples to fast at any time (Mt. 9:14-17), one can be certain they would not wish to fast on the Sabbath. In the light of the discussion above, it is unlikely that they would identify any extant halakhah about not picking grains off the plant as superseding the prevalent sentiment against fasting.

At Num. 15:32-36 where a man who is gathering sticks on the Sabbath is stoned for violating the Sabbath, Sifre 113 raises the question: what was his sin? One view was that he was guilty of tolesh, separating an object rooted in the ground. At B. Shab. 96b three views are given, and a beraita there, probably identical with the passage in Sifre, also declares the sin to be tolesh. At B. Shab. 103a another beraita is cited which indicates that, if one is guilty of tolesh, even for food consumption, he is culpable. But we must see this passage in perspective. First of all, tolesh is not one of the thirty-nine primary prohibited works (M. Shab. 7:2), and therefore the beraita of B. Shab. 103a and Sifre Num. 113 are in conflict with the catalogue of primary forbidden activities at M. Shab. 7:2. Only this catalogue was regarded as transmitted by Moses at Sinai.64 The activity of the disciples, therefore, falls into at

least two permissable spheres. First, not all would
see this activity as tolesh. Hence halakhically there
is a double doubt: whether the act can be defined in
a particular way, and whether the act is necessarily
strictly forbidden.[65] Secondly, and perhaps most
importantly, in the disciples' thinking, which is not
reflected in the pericope, there would be an implicit
awareness that the dictum of Is. 58:13 "to call the
Sabbath a delight" allows them the freedom to select
their halakhic option to strip some grains and eat
them.

12:3-4. In the light of this we fully understand
Jesus' response. Jesus asks the Pharisees whether
they do not recall the action of David (I Sam. 21:2-7)
when he and his followers were hungry, and they ate
the artuous tēs protheseōs.[66] Mt. 12:4 refers to
these as loaves meant only for priests. The priest in
the David episode does not indicate priests may eat
the bread that he gives to David. He merely pleads
that the only bread available is "holy bread" (v.5).
Actually this holy bread was to be offered upon the
altar (Lev. 6:16). At I Sam. 21:7 the author informs
us that the priest gave to David this holy bread, for
otherwise the only bread there was the lehem hapanim
which is changed weekly, but which cannot be removed
until that time. If the episode occurred on the
Sabbath, the priest could bake new griddle-cakes to
offer upon the alter (M. Men. 11:3), but he could not
bake new lehem hepanim. If the episode did not occur
on the Sabbath, the lehem hapanim was not even
scheduled for change. In either case he could not
give the lehem hapanim to David. But in either case
he was able to give him the holy food which the priest
was to burn on the altar, and bake substitute cakes.[67]

Despite Schlatter,[68] the thrust of Jesus'
argument is not merely that moral factors take
precedence over the ceremonial. It is that David ate
holy bread meant only to be offered on the altar. He
violated the sanctity of the altar itself. Jesus is
thus offering a hekish, the hermeneutical rule of
juxtaposition of two persons and situations.[69] David
infringed what is kodesh, holy, the priests' breads
which constitute the daily meal-offering, and the
disciples are infringing upon what is kodesh, the
Sabbath. As a matter of fact, the case of David is
more serious, for there it is clearly holy bread
destined to be a holocaust, which he infringes. In
the case of the disciples, it is not at all clear that

131

their activity is forbidden. Thus   vv. 3-4
constitute a combined hekish and an implied kal
vehomer. After the hekish one must understand Jesus
as arguing that, if David could do so in a case of
definite infringement, the disciples may certainly do
so in a case of doubtful infringement.

   12.5. The evangelist then has Jesus present a
second illustration. He asks the Pharisees whether
they are not aware of the halakhah that priests may
perform acts that are customarily considered
violations of the Sabbath but are held guiltless when
these are performed in the Temple.[70] Here Jesus
clearly has reference to the principle that abodah
doheh et hashabat, the cult supersedes the Sabbath,[71]
the natural inference from the biblical provisions for
Sabbath offerings on the altar, and the evidence that
this was indeed Temple practice.[72] There is no need
here for a kal vehomer, nor any other hermeneutical
rule. But Jesus is said to supply it (v.6), because
he wishes to reinforce both the hekish of v.4 and the
principle of v.5. In effect he is offering two
arguments in each illustration: in the matter of
David, a hekish and a kal vehomer; in the matter of
priests, a halakhic principle and a kal vehomer.

   12:6-8. Verses 6 and 8 are unnecessarily seen
Christologically.[73] As for v.6, what is here "greater
than the Temple" is not Jesus. The two are not a
natural analogy. What is "greater" is the call to
provide for human life, the required response to the
love command. The analogy is between two obligations,
love of humans and the cult. Jesus is said to tell
the Pharisees that, if they recognized that it is
hesed which God requires (v.7), they would not have
held the disciples guilty . The beauty in Jesus'
response is that, while it is quite possible the
disciples have acted perfectly in accord with one view
of what is allowed on the Sabbath, and require no
halakhic defense at all, Jesus tackles the perushim
(Pharisees) on the basis of their own stringent
pietistic halakhah. He offers them several iron-clad
halakhic arguments that are perfectly common in the
Judaic milieu of the first century and which compel
the perushim to silence. The upshot of it all is that
the human, understood as human need, is what governs
the Sabbath (v.8).[74]

   Hill[75] argues that it is unlikely that Jesus used
Hos. 6:6. He offers the point that the citation is

unique to Matthew and may therefore be a redactional insertion.[76] This only begs the question, since one could counter that Mark might have dropped the verse and Luke might have followed Mark, or vice versa, or both followed a version other than Matthew. While Hummel[77] stresses the unity of vv. 5-7 and Barth[78] argues that 5-6 were found by Matthew in the tradition and are not from Jesus, to which Matthew also appends v.7, I am basing my discussion on the Aland texts and will therefore not digress to discuss the merits of these and similar critical notices. It will suffice here only to point out that Hill[79] is incorrect in his argument that because neither illustration used by the Matthean Jesus (vv. 4-5) deals with "preparing food on the Sabbath." Matthew is not interested in justifying the disciples' action of v.1. Matthew has no interest in the question of preparing food on the Sabbath. Matthew's interest is in establishing the teaching of Jesus concerning the Sabbath, and this he does masterfully. He points out that it is the view of Jesus that one must consider <u>hesed</u> above cult, of which the Sabbath is an integral part, and that despite its status of <u>kodesh</u> it is secondary to the preservation of human life and health. One must recall that, if the disciples had returned from their mission or had just had a Sabbath reunion during the mission and were very hungry, even if actual life was not at stake, the mere possibility that health will be endangered[80] was sufficient to allow a waiver of the Sabbath restriction. If Matthew, as form and redaction critics argue, were doing such a brilliant job of manipulating the text, he would have placed v.8 after v.12. Matthew has plentiful arguments to use. He uses very apt illustrations in which two varying types of <u>kodesh</u> are superseded by principles that take precedence. The illustrations are reinforced by a <u>kal vehomer</u>, and as is usual throughout proto-rabbinic and rabbinic literature, the principles and the hermeneutical rules are given greater reinforcement by a citation from scripture. Matthew could also have argued that the needs of "apostles of a mizvah"[81] supersede the requirements of the Sabbath (Num. R. 16:1).[82]

Matthew's pericope is quite coherent. Hunger supersedes the halakhic stringencies attached to holy food and, in turn, requirements of the cult supersede the holiness of the Sabbath. This in itself issues in a <u>kal vehomer</u>. If hunger supersedes an element of the cult, how much more so the Sabbath which is superseded

by the cult. Scripture supports this at Hos. 6:6
which is a pertinent support for the more general love
command, since it in effect raises the love command
specifically above the cult. There is also the strong
thrust here of cogently reinforcing all that has been
said. Sacrifice supersedes the Sabbath, but God
prefers hesed to sacrifice; how much more so, then,
will hesed supersede the Sabbath. The entire pericope
is a masterful proto-rabbinic exercise in the
application of hermeneutical rules and scriptural
exegesis. Scholars such as Kilpatrick[83] miss an
essential point in seeing the Matthean argument of
vv. 5-7 as merely "a recognized exception to the rule
in Pharisaic casuistry." This derives from confusing
Pharisees with proto-rabbis. Such arguments as the
Matthean Jesus offers may be casuistry, but they are
necessary proto-rabbinic efforts at ameliorating the
stringencies upheld by the various pietistic
(perushite-Pharisaic) circles such as those that
produced Jubilees and the Zadokite Document, which
brooked no exceptions to strict Sabbath observance.
There is no fundamental difference between the
Matthean Jesus' Sabbath halakhah and that of the
proto-rabbis once we eliminate the notion that
Christological implications are inherent at 12:6-8.[84]
F. F. Bruce[85] has astutely observed that there is
nothing to suggest that Jesus' kal vehomer is "that if
David could override the Law on occasion, so a
fortiori could the son of David."

    12.7. It is worth returning now to this
significant verse. Jesus is here reported to be
rebuking the fundamental outlook of the perushim. He
gives the love command, the divine request for hesed
over against cultic observance, a covenantal and near
sacramental importance. The practice of hesed
supersedes the Sabbath and cult, and in that sense
become soteriological, as at M. Ab. 1:2. For one
might argue that by violating the Sabbath one is
separating himself from the soteriological community,
the Sabbath being a sign of the covenant, its
observance a sign that one is among the elect. This
is of additional interest when one recalls that
Yohanan b. Zakkai uses the same verse to express the
idea that the practice of hesed replaces the
soteriological effect of the cult (Ab. de R.N. A, 4,
B, 8). In a commentary or expansion of M. Ab. 1:2 the
author of Abot de Rabbi Nathan has Joshua ask Yohanan
b. Zakkai whence expiation can be made since the
sacrificial cult is suspended. Yohanan's reply is

that expiation can be made through hesed, and he cites
Hos. 6:6. Hesed takes on this soteriological quality
again, as the commentator continues by observing that
Daniel's salvation in Babylonia was rooted in his
practice of hesed (ibid. A, 4). It is true that the
midrashic comment does not discuss violations of
serious institutions such as the Sabbath. But it does
begin by noting that Daniel did not observe cultic
requirements, and instead he benefited from acts of
hesed. The underlying philosophy can then be readily
applied by any proto-rabbi. Acts of hesed become so
important that by kal vehomer they supersede even the
Sabbath. Circumcision, the paschal offering, the
abodah in general, the needs of a mizvah apostle,
pikuah nefesh, cutting the ômer, and sundry other
situations or contexts allow for superseding the
Sabbath.[86] All of these are either related to the
cult or to humanitarian contexts. It is obvious to a
proto-rabbi that, if abodah supersedes the Sabbath and
hesed is more important than abodah, hesed will
supersede the Sabbath. If it is indeed true, as I
propose, that Jesus and Yohanan had a relationship in
Galilee between 20-30, it is of little surprise that
Matthew's tradition reported Jesus' use of Hos. 6:6,
and that the rabbinic tradition reported Yohanan's use
of the same verse, and in a semi-soteriological
context.

In view of the foregoing it becomes of little
consequence whether the correct reading at Mt. 12:1 is
tillein, picking, alone, or etillon. . .
psōkhontes. . . as at Lk. 6:1, picking and rubbing.[87]
The process involved in rubbing or crushing the grain
in one's hands to eat it is permitted (B. Shab. 128a;
T. Shab. 14:17; 16:22). This does not overcome the
need to explain tillein halakhically should tillein be
the correct reading. It is clear from our previous
discussion that: a) tillein may not refer at all to
plucking; and b) not all sages agreed on the question
of tolesh, plucking.[88] Therefore, there is little
difference halakhically whether we read tillein or
psōkhontes. In either case Jesus could argue that
there has been no violation and strengthen his
arguments with a series of principles and
hermeneutical rules.[89] And finally, while it is very
clear that the Matthean Jesus differs from the
Pharisees, even fundamentally, as Abrahams[90] puts it,
this is so for an entirely different reason than that
given by Abrahams. He sees Jesus as permitting the
abrogation of Sabbath halakhah for "man's ordinary

135

convenience," while the Rabbis (sic) "limited the
license to cases of danger to life." The Pharisees of
this pericope are not rabbis. And the Pharisees here
would not allow anything to supersede the Sabbath,
while Jesus is employing proto-rabbinic methodology
which was in direct conflict with the _perushim_ but in
full agreement with the later rabbis.

C. Healing on the Sabbath (Mt. 12:9-13)

Mt. 12:9-13 relates a second major Sabbath
incident. It is not explicitly stated, but implied
(vv. 1-8 and v. 14), that it too involved Jesus and
Pharisees. From the redaction which makes the second
incident contiguous with the first, it appears that
Jesus turned from his encounter in the field and
entered "their" synagogue (v. 9). "Their" in this
context could mean a synagogue frequented by _perushim_
and therefore one with which Jesus and his disciples
were reluctant to identify.[91] Jesus is now asked by
his opponents whether it is allowed to heal on the
Sabbath (v. 10). The redactor meanwhile lets us know
(v. 10) that the intention of the questioners is to
have proof with which to accuse him. Jesus uses a _kal_
vehomer from a sheep to a human (v. 11-12), and
stresses that it is certainly allowed to perform a
good deed on the Sabbath. He then heals the man with
the withered arm (v. 13).[92]

In the light of Herbert Loewe's statement[93] that
"Jesus did nothing that could have been regarded as
violating the Sabbath...he compounded no drugs,"[94] the
questions must perforce be raised whether Jesus was
guilty of Sabbath violation by proto-rabbinic norms,
and whether his reponse is to be seen as a legitimate
suggestion of norms by which to be governed.
Furthermore, one must precisely assess the problem.
Is the act of healing a violation, even when achieved
through prayer or through a word as at Mt. 12:13, or
only when achieved by applying drugs that are produced
on the Sabbath, as at Jn. 9? What precisely were the
proto-rabbinic norms? What were the halakhic
alternatives in first-century Judaism?

At the very outset we are confronted by a strange
situation. Unlike what occurred in the grain
incident, neither Jesus nor the disciples have done
anything which has been seen and challenged. The
healing of the man with the withered arm, therefore,

136

appears to be a separate incident that may have followed some other episode. It may have been after another theoretical torah discourse. Jesus had perhaps already given them a view on some question for which they could not fault him, and then he entered the synagogue. They saw the man with the withered arm there and decided here is a question he may falter on. The Pharisees (v. 14), after all, were consistently looking for a way to discredit Jesus in order that he not succeed in winning followers from among their pietistic ranks. The perushim were not at all at ease with Jesus' call to the masses at Mt. 11:28-30. The perushim knew their burden was heavy. Since the time of Ezra and Nehemiah, exacerbated by the tumultuous years of the Maccabee uprising and the consequent dissent of the ḥasidim, pietistic circles were expanding the restrictions and intensifying stringency. Jubilees and the Zadokite Document, as we will see, made earlier literature appear almost non-nomian in reference to the Sabbath. Jesus and the other proto-rabbis were all engaged in an effort to ameliorate the harshness of this halakhah.

12:11. When the Pharisees asked Jesus whether it is allowed to heal on the Sabbath, he replied with what appears to be an irrelevant illustration. He refers to a sheep that falls in a pit or cistern on the Sabbath and asks them whether any one of them ouki kratesei auto kai egerei, would not take hold of it and lift it out. Does Jesus base his question on an erroneous assumption? Does he or the redactor not know that the perushim will not lift out either an animal or a human from a pit on the Sabbath (CDC 11:13-14; 16-17)? Or indeed does my hypothesis that the people challenging Jesus are pietistic perushim falter at Mt. 12:11?

Perhaps we are to read v. 11 in a different light. There is no doubt in the gospel that for Matthew the teaching of the perushim has much validity (Mt. 23:2-3). This validity is confirmed after 70 when many of its views were incorporated into rabbinic Judaism in order to give the rabbis hegemony over a widespread consensus. But neither the rabbis after 70 nor Jesus and his contemporary proto-rabbis at 30 were inclined toward perushite stringency. The Matthean Jesus makes it clear that he considers a major weakness of this movement to be its stringency, which is clearly implied at 11:30, and that a second major weakness is the hypocrisy of which it is guilty

(Mt. 23:13-15). Jesus here attacks them with a vehemence similar to that of Mt. 23, but he is in a synagogue on a Sabbath morning, and he launches his attack on their hypocrisy with gentle halakhic irony. We must note that he stresses in his question _probaten hen_, one sheep.[95] His point is that if they were faced with serious economic consequences, the loss of their last or only sheep, they would give up their stringency and lift it out of the pit. Jesus is thus thrusting the dagger deep. He is saying they would do this despite the prohibition, for they have no provision for saving life, or for waiving or superseding the Sabbath in any instance. And yet, he says, "which man among you" would not violate Sabbath? Only his kind of near-mockery of their halakhic hypocrisy can explain the violence of their reaction at v. 14. In this regard Lk. 13:15-16 is of interest.

12:12. Here Jesus becomes more serious. He has made the point that no only he, but even they, would save the sheep. He then offers the _kal vehomer_ for a human and the conclusion that it is permitted to act beneficially on the Sabbath. Jesus is extending the current proto-rabbinic norm, clarifying the permission to provide support for the animal in this condition (T. Shab. 14:3). But while he may be intensifying the proto-rabbinic norm, the more important point is that he is rejecting _perushite_ stringency.

Then Jesus heals the man's withered arms. We are here in a rather awkward situation. Jesus has done nothing that can be considered a prohibited activity. He has performed a miracle. He has merely asked the man to stretch forth his arm. The man does so and is healed. On these grounds alone one could argue that Jesus is guilty of nothing. One almost finds oneself preferring the clear-cut story at Jn. 9 where Jesus mixes a compound and commits an actual act of healing. We are even in a worse situation than Jn. 5:1-9. Although there too Jesus is said to heal by the word, he may be accused by pietists of telling the man to carry his mat on the Sabbath (v. 8), and to instruct someone to violate a norm is in itself a violation(M. San. 11:2). This indeed is the concern of the "Jews" at Jn. 5:10. In both cases reported in the fourth gospel (Jn. 5:1-9; 9:1-12), the violation in question is not the healing but telling the man to carry (5:10), and making the paste (9:6, 11, 14f.). Pancaro,[96] following Haenchen, sees the episode at Jn. 5:1-9 as originally a healing story unrelated to

the Sabbath. But Raymond Brown[97] affirms it as a
Sabbath story. When Jesus defends himself
(Jn. 7:21-23), by a kal vehomer based on circumcision
which supersedes the Sabbath, we are on familiar
ground.

There are many halkhot that might reflect the
Matthean Jesus' position. Extinguishing a fire is one
of the thirty-nine prohibited activities
(M. Shab. 7:2), but one may extinguish it out of fear
of robbers or evil spirits, and most interestingly, to
allow a sick person to fall asleep (M. Shab. 2:5).
There is no obvious pikuah nefesh[98] in the last
instance, nor even safak nefashot.[99] Although there
is no pikuah nefesh or safek nefashot involved, one
may carry with him from a private domain into the
public domain an amulet which some people believed had
curative powers (M. Shab. 6:2). Bathing in the hot
springs of Tiberius was permitted (M. Shab. 22:5).
When cure or medicinal properties are involved, the
stringency of not carrying on the Sabbath is relaxed
(M. Shab. 6:6, 10). In the case of M. Shab. 6:10 we
find a difference of opinion, but it is not that the
anonymous sages oppose relaxing the rule of carrying
in health-related cases; it is because the amulets or
charms under consideration are regarded as heathen
superstition. Again at M. Shab. 8:1 we find a
difference of opinion regarding the carrying of
health-related objects. The very fact that the
difference of opinion exists is instructive. Among
the Pharisees who challenge Jesus in the New Testament
there are no options. This strongly indicates that
they are not the proto-rabbis whose teachings are
represented in the Mishnah. A comprehensive survey of
the entire corpus of Sabbath halakhah will reveal much
difference of opinion on whether certain
health-related objects and ingredients of potions may
be carried and what quantity or size may be carried.
There are stringencies and relaxations reflected, as
to carrying,[100] imbibing the various health-related
herbs, foods or liquids (M. Shab. 14:3-4), and for
whom one may perform healing processes, and the type
of processes one may perform (M. Shab. 18:3).[101]

The upshot of the complexity of the halakhah is
that it is an oversimplified generalization to
conclude that Jesus had violated the Sabbath by
healing. The essence of the argument may be that
Jesus has healed a man with a withered arm whose life
is not placed in danger by that withered arm either

immediately or in the foreseeable future. Thus Montefiore[102] asserts that "unrestricted permission" to heal is not granted in the rabbinic literature. But that is precisely what is the difficulty. Unrestricted permission is not granted in the rabbinic literature. But the rabbinic literature reflects decades of compromise between stringency and leniency. We have no way of knowing whether Jesus was the only proto-rabbi who apparently favored the unrestrictive right to heal a person who is within one's mizvah reach on the Sabbath. Perhaps he was. Perhaps his teaching stimulated the pro-unrestricted healing forces. In any event one must reckon with the halakhic facts. As late as the end of the second century, when the Mishnah was compiled, "healing" was not listed among the thirty-nine prohibited categories of work. Later authorities simply listed the grinding, pounding and mixing of medicines under the heading of "grinding."[103] But these derivative activities, known as <u>toladot</u>, were certainly not catalogued from the beginning. Efforts were made from time to time to list derivatives(B. Shab. 73b), and by the late third century 1521 derivative activities were computed by R. Yoḥanan and R. Simon b. Lakish (P. Shab. 9 b-c). That this process was an old one is evident from the judgement that the Sabbath halakhah is "like a mountain hanging by a hair" (M. Ḥag. 1:8; T. Ḥag. 1:9). This signified that there is little biblical support for the ever-increasing complexity of the Sabbath halakhah. But during the life of Jesus this was not yet the case. There was stringency on the part of pietists and there was leniency on the part of others. We have no way to state with certainty that healing, later prohibited as <u>toladah</u>, was actually forbidden in Jesus' time except by Pharisees, that is, the <u>perushim</u>, the pietistic separatists. Jesus opposed their stringency.

Healing was not listed among the prohibitions at Qumran (CDC 10:14-11:8), but it was prohibited to deliver an animal of its new-born, without qualification (11:13), and to save an animal from a pit (11:13f.), or a human from a cistern (11:16f.). One may derive the prohibition of healing by a <u>kal vehomer</u>. The Pharisees who would not save a life would naturally oppose Jesus' healing. Jesus, a proto-rabbi who would not only save a life in a clear and present danger, but also one that might only possibly be in a degree of danger later on, advocated unrestricted healing on the Sabbath. A first-century

proto-rabbi, Matyá ben Ḥeresh permitted one to treat a
sore throat on the Sabbath   (M. Yom. 8:6).   Jesus
was not violating a halakhah. He was creating one in
opposition to the <u>perushite</u> extremism.   Rabbinic
literature no longer preserves documentable sources to
tell us how many like Matyá might have agreed with
Jesus, but it preserves a wide array of material in
Mishnah and Toseftá that points to the great flux in
the halakhah and the strong thrust toward the
preservation of both human and animal life.
Unrestricted healing was simply the natural result of
all of the principles applicable to Sabbath halakhah,
and above all the ultimate response to Is. 58:13.

We might now inquire as to the nature of Jesus'
statement that "How much more valuable is a man than a
sheep; consequently it is permitted to act beneficially
on the Sabbath."   Jesus is saying that one would not
only help a sheep in danger of losing its life, but
simply to make it more comfortable (B. Shab. 128b).[104]
How much more, then, shall one make a human
comfortable!   Treating a sore throat is a parallel
case.   It is not a matter of saving life, but of
making one comfortable.   Among the many halakhic
principles Jesus could fall back upon is the one that
was based upon Ex. 23:5, that one must not allow a
living creature to suffer.[105]   He need not offer a
comprehensive discourse. On the other hand, however,
perhaps Matthew's pericope is the precis of a
lengthier lecture on the subject of healing on the
Sabbath. Even if curing a man with a withered arm is
only to give him comfort, that would suffice.   And
considering the halakhah related to animals it is a
<u>kal vehomer</u> that one may heal a human.   One violates
no prohibition by doing so, and one fulfills a great
miẓvah. Jesus says <u>Kalōs poiein</u>, to act beneficially,
to do that which benefits one's fellow-human, a
miẓvah, is permitted on the Sabbath.

12:14. The violent reaction of the Pharisees,
<u>symboulion</u> elabon <u>kat</u> <u>auton</u> hopōs <u>auton</u> apolesōsin,
("they took counsel against him how to destroy him")
should be properly understood.   The word <u>apolesōsin</u>
commonly translated as "destroy"[106] or "kill,"[107] need
not be so understood.   It might be a Greek rendering
of <u>lemahrim ōto</u>, "to renounce him," or "to place him
under the ban," "to excommunicate him."   A Greek
translator might conceivably have taken the Hebrew
term in its earlier biblical meaning of "destroy,"[108]
with the sense of "to cut off," and its continued

141

later sense of being "doomed to destruction."[109] The
Pharisees, that is, the pietistic separatists, the
perushim, sought to obviate Jesus' influence and to
isolate him in order that he not win adherents from
among the masses. The misunderstanding of the use of
mahrim went so far as to impel the author of Mark some
decades later to add the Herodians to the account
Mk. 3:6). The author of Mark could see no way that
Pharisees could put Jesus to death and so he brought
the royal power into the picture. In effect, the
pietists sought to set Jesus utterly apart because
they recognized in him a total threat to their
halakhah. Until that time they were willing to give
him the benefit of the doubt, having regarded both
John the Baptist and Jesus as similar to them. John
was dead. Now they decided that Jesus must be
ostracized so that no followers of the pietist trends
would listen to his lectures or sermons and
conceivably be influenced by him. This was an
application of strict pietist principles as recorded
for at least one group know to us in the Qumran Manual
of Discipline (1 QS 5:18).[110]

D. Pentateuchal and Extra-Pentateuchal
Sabbath Halakhah

1. The Pentateuch

The Sabbath halakhah of the Pentateuch is sparse
despite the many references to sanctifying and
observing the Sabbath, and the injunctions to perform
no melakhah.[111] There are references to cultic
activities on the Sabbath (Lev. 24:8; Num. 28:9-10).
There is a specific halakhah at Ex. 35:3 not to kindle
a fire on the Sabbath. The manna episode may or may
not imply that baking and cooking on the Sabbath are
forbidden (v. 2), or that one must not leave his home
or settlement on the Sabbath (v. 29). This whole
section, however, is best taken as part of the
wilderness tradition narrowly relevant to a saving
miracle, with no halakhic implications for the future.
There is the implication again at Num. 15:32-34 that a
gatherer of sticks or firewood is violating the
Sabbath. Philo connects this with the prohibition on
lighting a fire.[112] But there is no specific
injunction. The sin is not explicated, despite the
death sentence being pronounced (v. 35). Ploughing
and reaping is explicityly forbidden at Ex. 34:21,
indicating at least tentatively that a possible
definition of melakhah is one's gainful occupation.

One is not permitted to order one's family, slave, animal or <u>ger</u> to "work" on the Sabbath, but again there is no definition and no specifics of what is permitted or forbidden (Ex. 20:10; Deut. 5:14), or what is the meaning of "rest" (Deut. 5:14).

2. The Prophets

The reference at Amos 8:5 is taken by modern commentators to mean that the merchant impatiently anticipates the end of the Sabbath in order to engage in grain sales which enable him to further profiteer from the poor.[113] This would imply that buying and selling or trade and commerce were prohibited on the Sabbath. But there is no explicit prohibition indicating that these activities are encompassed under <u>malakhah</u>. It appears that, if it is a reference to the Sabbath, it is of a piece with Is. 58:13 which calls for a quiescent form of observance in which the person does not discuss or anticipate the business of the weekdays. The history books [114] report on cultic activity that took place on the Sabbath. Ezekiel[115] refers to the Sabbath as a sign (20:12-13), deplores its profanation (22:8), and points to the cultic activity related to the Sabbath (45:17). But in none of these instances do we receive any new information on the halakhah of the Sabbath.

When we turn to Jeremiah we find something different. Jeremiah admonishes both the leaders and the people of Jerusalem and Judah (17:20), that they are not to transport wares through the gates of Jerusalem on the Sabbath (v. 21), nor take parcels or baggage (<u>masâ</u>, "a burden") out of their houses (vv. 22, 24, 27), nor do any <u>melakhah</u> (vv. 22, 24, 27). Again there is no expanded definition of <u>melakhah</u> except insofar as transporting or carrying appears as a prohibited activity.

3. The Writings[116]

From Nehemiah[117] we receive a clearer halakhic picture which helps us envision the Sabbath halakhah circa 400 B.C. This enables us to better understand the catalogue of Sabbath halakhah found in one of the next major works in Judaism, Jubilees, which undoubtedly followed closely upon Ben Sira. Nehemiah (13:15) reports that people treaded winepresses, loaded up the pack-animals with produce and other baggage, and transported these products into

Jerusalem, and that he cautioned them against this. He reports that non-Jews brought their wares into Jerusalem and sold them to Jews (v. 16). But Nehemiah had the police power to close Jerusalem on the Sabbath, and he ordered that no masã be brought into Jerusalem on the Sabbath (v. 19). We cannot be certain what became generally prohibited. All we can say is that the "school" of Nehemiah, which also means Ezra, seems to have followed the halakhah advocated by Jeremiah. This may reflect a halakhic trend of two centuries which had expanded upon the relative Pentateuchal silence. Put another way, in deference to modern critics who date the Pentateuch to the exilic period, the Sabbath halakhah of Jeremiah and Nehemiah specifies what was probably encompassed within the more general statements of the Pentateuch. The assumption would be that to do no melakhah signified not to kindle fires, not to transport wares, not to pursue agriculture or the production of agricultural goods, and not to engage in trade and commerce. There is nothing in Jeremiah (17:22) that indicates a person must carry nothing on his person when he leaves his house. The entire Sitz im Leben of Jer. 17 and Neh. 13 relates to gainful occupation, to business, gainful agriculture, production and transportation, not such private acts as plucking grain (Mt. 12:1), carrying a mat (Jn. 5:8), healing (Mt. 12:13) or even preparing a medicine (Jn. 9:6).

The foregoing indicates that there is no specific prohibition in the Pentateuch, Prophets or Writings that was violated by Jesus or his disciples. Nevertheless, the evidence points in the direction of an expanding Sabbath halakhah in which the command to hallow the seventh day and to rest on it as a sign of the covenant between God and Israel was gradually being defined. At 400 B.C., this effort to define it was only in its infancy. The exegesis on the contiguity of Ex. 35:2-3 to the report concerning the building of the portable sanctuary (Ex. 35:4-39) was still in the distant future. Ultimately this exegesis resulted in the cataloguing of thirty-nine prohibited forms of work based on the type of activity related to the building of the sanctuary (M. Shab. 7:2). But these prohibitions were not yet formalized. We begin to see the product of the acceleration of restrictions in the Book of Jubilees.

4. The Book of Jubilees

From Josephus[118] we learn that a second-century B.C. writer, Agatharcides of Cnidos, reported that "those who are called _Youdaioi_" abstain from work every seventh day and do not engage in agricultural operations, other forms of public service, or bear arms, but rather spend the day in their _hierois_ (synagogues?). This indicates that by 200 B.C. the prohibitions were still largely interpreted as related to the question of engaging in one's occupation. And now bearing arms and warfare is added to the list. The notice that they spend the day in their holy centers (_hierois_) implies they basically observed a quiescent day oriented to prayer and piety. This type of observance is projected back to circa 300 B.C. when Ptolemy I is said to have taken advantage of the Sabbath to occupy Jerusalem.[119]

The natural by-product of spending the day in a place of worship and study is quietism. The attitude present at Is. 58:13 which discourages one from engaging in one's own activities or interests in order to achieve a day which can be called "a delight," grew into the halakhah of Jubilees. In every society the desirable often becomes the communal objective to which an individual is obligated. As piety increased among certain circles after the establishment of the Ezraic-Nehemian community of the elect, the Sabbath restrictions on the individual increased in order to bring about the envisioned quietistic Sabbath. Ultimately we find a catalogue or digest of such Sabbath halakhah in the Book of Jubilees (2:17-33; 50:6-13). "All work" (2:17; 50:7), is to be eschewed, but work is defined only by the specifics listed thereafter. Here too the Isaianic "day of delight"[120] is emphasized (2:21), but this delight is something one would forego only at the pain of death (2:25; 50:8), as well as at the risk of the loss of immortality (2:27).[121]

The specifics in Jubilees include: 1. not to pursue private interests; 2. not to prepare any solid or liquid food on the Sabbath; 3. not to draw water; 4. not to transport goods; 5. not to carry burdens into or out of one's house; 6. not to engage in sexual relations; 7. not to plan trade and commerce; 8. not to take a journey; 9. not to engage in agricultural labor; 10. not to light a fire; 11. not to ride upon an animal; 12. not to travel by a ship; 13. not to strike or kill a living creature; 14. not to hunt, trap or fish; 15. not to fast; 16. not to make war.122 A report at B. Nid. 38a concerning "early pietists" informs us of their effort to mathematically compute the time of birth from the time of conception so that birth should not take place on the Sabbath. It is apparent from this that they were not in favor of the waiving of Sabbath restrictions such as lighting a fire and boiling water in the interests of the preservation of life (M. Shab. 18:3). If pietists had believed the Sabbath could be waived in such cases, they would not have been so anxious lest there be a birth on the Sabbath. Indeed, in the entire roster of Sabbath halakhah in Jubilees there is no provision for anything to supersede the Sabbath except the cultic requirements (Jub. 50:10). A close examination of the details reveals that this has already become more restrictive than the earlier halakhah,123 escalating a trend that began with the late prophetic period and was formalized by Nehemiah.

The foregoing indicates that the halakhic leniency of Jesus could only lead to serious controversy with the advocate of the halakhah of Jubilees. While Jubilees set the cult above the Sabbath, it did not set human concerns above it. The very emphasis at 50:10 that specifies the rest is to be complete except for the needs of the cult, and the reiteration at 50:11 that only atoning cultic operations may be performed on the Sabbath, point to the lack of a concept of pikuah nefesh among these early pietists. There were many opportunities, such as at vv. 10-13 to add "except for the need to preserve life." The absence of this waiver is not only duplicated at Qumran, but opposition to it is made even more explicit.

5. Philo

The biblical and apocryphal material point to a conservative tendency which may relate to fear of a "domino theory" after the Ezraic-Nehemian restoration. There was a turning inward by the small Judean community. This is reflected in the quietism of Deutero (or Trito),124 Isaiah's approach to the Sabbath and in Nehemiah's strict response to laxity, both building upon earlier attitudes expressed by Amos and Jeremiah. This trend moves through Jubilees to reach a peak of severity and restrictiveness in the pietistic separatism of Qumran. We must also in this

146

regard take not of the emphasis in Jubilees upon the idea that gentiles have no portion in the Sabbath (2:31), a reaction to the ecumenical spirit of Is. 56:3, 6.

Turning to Philo, we find that this strict attitude toward the Sabbath halakhah penetrated the diaspora as well. Philo corroborates the prevalence of an attitude favoring a quiescent Sabbath in his various references to the Sabbath as a day of rest, contemplation, pursuit of wisdom, and meditation on one's deeds with a view to correcting them.125 To supplement this basically agadic view of the Sabbath, Philo also reports on a rather restrictive catalogue of halakhah. At a very minimum we can assume this is the halakhah Philo advocated for Alexandrians, if not all Graeco-Roman diaspora communities. It is apparent that Philo's halakhah, however, was not even universal in Alexandria when he rejects the antinomian attitude of the extreme allegorists.126

It is certainly impossible to determine whether we have a relatively comprehensive picture or only a rather sparse one of Alexandrian Sabbath halakhah. We are unable to make a judgment on whether Philo is only very general even in his particulars, or is conveying the basic halakhah as he saw it. In sum, it is less extensive than that of Jubilees and considerably less so than that of Qumran.

In addition to the positive elements referred to above, such as enjoying the Sabbath, spending it in enriching contemplation and the pursuit of wisdom, the halakhah of Philo details a number of restrictive specifics. These include: 1. to abstain from activities that help one seek or obtain a livelihood;127 2. not to light a fire; 3. not to till the ground; 4. not to carry loads; 5. not to institute court proceedings; 6. not to serve as jurors; 7. not to recover deposits or loans;128 8. not to cut any shoot, branch or leaf from a growing plant; 9. not to pluck fruit from its plant or tree; 10. not to engage in any profit-making tekhnai (mental or manual acts); 11. not to engage in activities that provide the means to perform a forbidden activity, such as gathering firewood.129

It is clear from a careful scrutiny of the Sabbath halakhah of the pietists who adhered to Jubilees and from that of Philo that there are differences. The scope of this dissertation does not require that a talmudic-type commentary be here employed either to harmonize or explain the discrepancies.130 Philo reflects the existence of a halakhah that specifically prohibits plucking from a plant. According to some interpretations of Mt. 12:1 this is precisely the activity engaged in by the disciples. On the other hand, if it is correct that what the disciples did was to pick seeds out of an ear of grain, this activity is not specified as prohibited by Philo, nor would it fall under the category of "agriculture." Furthermore, Philo writes131 that the reason one is not to pluck vegetation on the Sabbath is because one must demonstrate that on the Sabbath all of nature is set free. He does not characterize it in and of itself as an activity which is prohibited because of the prohibition on manual activities, such as those that require excessive energy or are unseemly. This might lead to the conjecture that Philo would so interpret the halakhah as to allow plucking in order to feed a hungry human. It has been noted earlier132 that Philo saw the Torah as given in order to teach gentleness, but it cannot be determined with certainty that he would favor superseding the Sabath stringency.133

Noticeably absent from Philo is any specific statement concerning when one is exempt from Sabbath prohibitions, or whether there is any general principle of when an act may supersede the Sabbath. Like Jubilees and Pentateuch, he affirms the death penalty for violation of the Sabbath.134 From the vehemence of Philo's language, "But to dare to debase and deface the stamp of things consecrated shews the utmost height of impiety,"135 it appears doubtful that he would allow anything to supersede the Sabbath. The one exception may be in cultic requirements, an exception already anticipated in the Torah and in Jubilees. It may not have been as necessary to provide this exception in the diaspora, however, as it was in the Jerusalem Temple.136 It should be noticed, therefore, that Philo's halakhah was of a pietistic order. Put another way, it is possible that both Jubilees and Philo reflect an older halakhah, the product of the Ezraic-Nehemian retrenchment. We can understand, therefore, the allegorists' rejection of this stringent approach to the Sabbath. Jubilees condemned a person to death for riding on an animal (50:12), but in the rabbinic literature we find that there was no tendency to do this, and condemning one to death on this basis was seen as an exceptional case that took place under very unusual crisis-conditions (B. San. 46a). In this regard Philo appears to have no prohibition on riding at all. Jubilees and Philonic halakhah are probably incomplete, but they demonstrate how Sabbath restrictions advanced beyond the generalized prohibition on work that we find in the Pentateuch, and even beyond the more expanded particulars of Nehemiah. The Philonic halakhah reflects an independence in diaspora thought and practice, however, insofar as certain Jubilees stringencies are not specified by Philo, such as sexual relations, riding, sailing, and fasting.

In sum, Philo evinces an emphasis upon restraint from activites through which one plans business, trade and commerce, how to make a living or profit. He stresses the freedom of all of nature which gives the human, animal and vegetable segments of the world the freedom to rest on the seventh day, as God proclaimed at the beginning. But as a function of his polemics with allegorists he is unrelenting in the strict demand for a committed observance with no provision for exemption, waiver or supersession except perhaps for cultic purposes. It nevertheless remains of interest that neither Jubilees nor Philo any more than the Pentateuch, Prophets or Writings, mentions healing on the Sabbath.

b. Qumran: The Zadokite Document

The foregoing provides a picture of an escalating Sabbath stringency from the pre-exilic period to the first century. We have also incidentally learned that some Jews did not observe this halakhah.[138] Some probably adhered to Jubilees, others practiced according to Philo, and yet others were more pious than both these groups. It is logical to surmise that there were those who stood somewhere between the antinomian allegorists and the stringent Sabbatarians, the most exreme of which we find at Qumran. These middle-of-the-roaders were followers of proto-rabbis, and among them one of the most articulate was Jesus.

A review of the Sabbath halakhah of Qumran[139] reveals that the pietistic separatists who had produced this literature, reached a peak in restrictiveness for Sabbath observance. No real purpose can be served at this point to detail the twenty-nine items I calculate to be on the Qumran roster. It must be pointed out that CDC contains all of the prohibitions found in the Bible and in Jubilees with only two exceptions.140 But it adds fourteen new ones. This can only be interpreted to mean that at least one segment of perushim were in the process of developing a rather complex system of Sabbath halakhah to govern all possible exigencies. The scope of the dissertation allows no more than to comment on those items that are of direct concern to the questions at Mt. 12:1-8, 9-13.

At the very outset it must be restated that to compare the halakhah of Mt. 12 with that of any group other than pietists who follow a stringent halakhah of the Jubilees-Qumran type would lead us astray. It is true that Qumran would have radically altered the halakhah of the Torah if it is correct to conclude that it abrogated the death penalty (CDC 12:3-5), a matter too complex and diverting to go into here. But despite this apparent amelioration it is still hardly supportable to say that the Torah is "no less severe and precise" than CDC.141 The Torah, like Philo, provided the death penalty, and to this extent may be adjudged "severe." But the Torah was hardly precise at all on the Sabbath violations that might make one culpable for the death penalty. Kimbrough142 concludes that the "Sabbath halakhah at Qumran may be nearer authentic Jewish halakhah prior to A.D. 70, free of the system of ̆erubin."143 All that is proven from the absence of ̆erubin from the Qumran halakhah is that it was more rigid. It possessed no loopholes, no alleviations or ameliorations. Just as it had no ̆erubin it did not permit the Sabbath to be superseded for saving life, and it considerably narrowed the right to waive Sabbath restrictions for the needs of the cult. While Jubilees (50:12) prohibits a "journey" which implies a long trip, Qumran prohibits a very short expedition of over 1000 cubits beyond one's city (CDC 10:21), an exceedingly strict construction placed upon Ex. 16:29. An echo of Qumran's lack of the ameliorating ̆erub system is found among the Samaritans who rejected it when it was devised by the rabbis (M. Ned. 3:10).

Pertinent to our discussion is the halakhah at CDC 11:4f. This reads ̆al yitareb ish merezono bashabat. Schiffman144 translates "No one shall enter partnership by his own volition on the Sabbath." He interprets it to mean that one should not declare his private property to be communal property on the

Sabbath. He concedes, however, that this is redundant following CDC 10:17-19 which prohibits all forms of business, commerce, financial transactions, and even the planning thereof. He then discusses the following alternative. Shechter[145] translates as "mingle," but in his note to the text[146] he suggests reading àl yiràb, one is not to go hungry voluntarily, and conjectures that yitàreb is a corruption of yiràb or yitàneh, that one should not fast voluntarily on the Sabbath. Ginzberg[147] agrees with Schechter's view that it means one is not to go hungry, citing support from P. Taan. 67a (cf. P. Ned. 40d), that one should not fast later than the sixth hour on the Sabbath, a view corroborated by Josephus.[148] But Ginzberg incorrectly stated that Schechter's "reading" is yitràeb, one should not starve himself. Schechter's text[149] reads yitàreb. Rabin[150] translates "let no man starve himself," and provides an alternative reading of yitràeb. But Rabin says nothing further in his notes. It appears to me, therefore, that if yitràeb is the correct reading, our form, yitàreb was the result of a metathesis with the àyin and resh transposed by the scribe. In any event this is a prohibition against fasting and supports the desire of the disciples to pick the seeds of grain as food. The perushim, however, had no provision for superseding the Sabbath on any grounds, and therefore objected to their action.

At CDC 11:13-14, 16-17, the Qumran community prohibited saving both an animal and a human from a situation of immediate peril. This is pertinent to the opposition by "Pharisees" to healing on the Sabbath. At line 13 there is a difference of opinion whether to read tapil, when the animal delivers her young she drops it into a pit, or tipol, an animal falls into a pit.[151] The reading tipol makes this into the precise halakhah cited by Matthew at 12:11. The perushim oppose saving the animal or helping it in any way. Proto-rabbinic halakhah presupposed by the Matthean Jesus is more lenient (T. Shab. 14:3).[152] The permission granted by the Toseftà is to succor the animal in order that it not die. This means that if it were confronted by drowning this succor could be extended to helping it out of the pit, and this was the interpretation placed upon the passage in rabbinic Judaism.[153] The leniency in rabbinic literature is also reflected in the permission to save even two animals at once on a festival (P. Beẓ. 62a). Actually the phrase at T. Shab. 14:3 is òsin lah parnasah,

151

which need not be tranlated "provide her with food" as does Schiffman.154 Both the verb _pirnes_ and the noun _parnasah_155 mean more than succoring with food. It signifies support in general, the necessities for life, or in modern terminology, the Toseftà is saying that life-support techniques can be provided for the animal.

The _perushim_ had no provision to save human life (CDC 11:16-17), and would therefore reverse Jesus' _kal vehomer_ to argue that, if one cannot violate the Sabbath to save human life, how much more so is it prohibited to save an animal. The _perushim_ simply did not recognize the principle of _pikuah nefesh_. This idea is difficult fo modern scholars to accept. Thus Rabin156 and Ginzberg157 make emendations to reverse the meaning. Other scholars such as Kimbrough,158 Dupont-Sommer,159 Gaster,160 Jean Daniélou161 all labor at restoring humanity to the halakhah of Qumran. But taking Qumran halakhah at face value, it is apparent that it was quite harsh, the normal consequence of extreme pietism, and points to the _perushim_ as having been the opponents of Jesus. They possessed a monolithic halakhah with no options for leniency or humanitarian concern, such as a waiver for _pikuah nefesh_. It was with the halakhah of _perushim_ of this variety that Jesus struggled, and not with that of a handful of proto-rabbis laboring away in their schools.162

It is possible that Qumran abolished the death penalty for Sabbath violation (CDC 12:3-5), in favor of the ostracism of the offender and close scrutiny of the offender for seven years. It is possible, however, with Ginzberg163 to read the text to exclude the death penalty only for those who teach improper halakhah, and to include it for those who perform an act in violation of the Sabbath. Rabin164 and Schiffman165 maintain that Qumran abolished the death penalty. But whether we accept the Rabin view or the Ginzberg hypothesis, Ginzberg's statement in this context, that, as regards the Sabbath halakhah, the Qumran people are ". . . in full harmony with the [rabbinic] halakhah. . ." is wide of the mark. Particulars of the two systems resemble one another, but the underlying philosophy is different.

Summary

The foregoing has demonstrated that the Sabbath

halakhah constantly grew in quantity and in restrictiveness. After explicating this halakhah I contended that the halakhah of the Matthean Jesus was in conflict with that of pietistic Jews who are represented as <u>Pharisaioi</u> in the New Testament. They maintained a stringent code of Sabbath behavior similar to that represented in Jubilees and the Zadokite Fragment. No exemptions from restrictions were allowed except for cultic purposes (Jub. 50:10f.). Others interpreted even this more narrowly to allow deviations from the restrictions only for the Sabbath offering (CDC 11:18).166 For such pietists the right to save life, as has been noted, did not supersede the Sabbath. Therefore, certainly the right to preserve health in cases where danger to life was not overt or immediate, <u>a fortiori</u> did not supersede the Sabbath. There was, therefore, no provision to heal a person on the Sabbath. All such acts performed by Jesus or his disciples were not in accord with the halakhah of those pietists who had begun their dissent in early Hasmonean times and ultimately became extremist and separatist. Finding even the norms of Jubilees insufficient for their piety they moved beyond that to the Zadokite Document and the halakhah we now know to be in the Temple Scroll.167 In all instances rabbinic halakhah seeks to ameliorate the more stringent halakhah of Qumran and Jubilees. The Matthean Jesus was of this proto-rabbinic stream which rejected the <u>perushite</u> extremism. He allowed his disciples to pick grain to assuage their hunger on the Sabbath, and he practiced healing on the Sabbath. For him the love command dictated that humanitarian concerns supersede the Sabbath and amply demonstrated that this theory can be sustained by the traditional methodology.

On the halakhah index between the Pentateuch and the Mishnah, Jesus was in the vanguard of the Mishnaic teachers in a studied effort to relax the growing complexity and restrictiveness of Sabbath halakhah.168 It is possible that ca. 30 A.D. he still stood relatively alone.

VI. SUMMARY AND CONCLUSIONS

A. Summary

The Matthean Jesus frequently made demands of his disciples and followers that were stricter and more taxing than the commonly observed Judaic norms of the first century. In such cases he expected those who sought entry into the coming world in which Divine Sovereignty[1] was to manifest itself to submit to norms that were <u>lifnim meshurat hadin</u>. But this did not make of him spiritual kin to the <u>perushim</u>, pietists and separatists who proliferated all over Palestine (and Egypt at least[2]) during the first century B.C. and the first century A.D. Instead, he applied a variety of principles to questions of halakhah as did other <u>hakhamim</u> of the era, in order to alleviate the burden they imposed upon those who followed them. The Matthean Jesus was neither what is commonly called a Sadducee, nor a Pharisee. Among proto-rabbis he was neither a follower of Bet Hillel nor of Bet Shammai. He undoubtedly had some contact with Yoḥanan b. Zakkai, but was not part of his circle. He may have had early affinities with a segment of <u>perushim</u>, the Essenes, as did possibly John the Baptist. But when we come to know Jesus at his baptism by John, he is entering the stage of history as a <u>hakham</u>, a proto-rabbi, who has become spiritually converted and transformed into a charismatic prophet-figure. Like a prophet he preached fearlessly of awesome things, but like the <u>hakham</u> he taught halakhah along with his àgadic preaching. In this function he employed the freedom of interpretation, the independent authority and the methodology that was the style of proto-rabbinism.[3]

It was argued in the second chapter that the New Testament does not define <u>Pharisaioi</u> and that the term "scribe" does not necessarily refer to proto-rabbis. The sayings of proto-rabbis of which we have knowledge, from Simon the Righteous through Yoḥanan b. Zakkai, have little affinity with the material presented by Josephus on the <u>Pharisaioi</u>. Josephus does not mention significant proto-rabbis and he does not describe the halakhah we know to be proto-rabbinic. Though writing after 70 A.D. Josephus does not use the title "rabbi." His statement that <u>Pharisaioi</u> are "exact" exponents of the laws and "excel the rest of the nation" in observance[4] applies more to <u>perushim</u> than to proto-rabbis. It was the <u>perushim</u> who were precise, meticulous and zealous in their religion. This fastidiousness toward ritualistic minutiae is also characteristic of the Pharisaioi of the New Testament. When Jesus demands greater piety of his followers over that of Pharisaioi (Mt. 5:20) he is not saying that Pharisaic halakhah is not stringent enough, but that Pharisaioi are hypocrites (6:2, 5, etc.).

Considering the diversity reflected in proto-rabbinic halakhah the thesis argued by Morton Smith[5] is unsupportable. He asserts that Jesus' halakhic divergences "...which set him sharply against his contemporaries, contributed to the hostility which led to his death..." More to the point is the statement by T. W. Manson[6] that the so-called legalistic deliberations recorded in the rabbinic literature should not be dismissed as "pettifogging." Manson writes,

> It is, in fact, much easier to denouce the scribal system than to do without it: ...any criticism we may pass upon Jewish legalism will be perilously like the rebukes which Satan administers to Sin.

Indeed, as argued in Chapters Three, Four and Five, the Matthean Jesus uses precisely the same "scribal" (read: proto-rabbinic) system. On the other hand, the characteristics found in the rabbinic literature that are attributed to perushim neatly fit the pietistic, separatist and ascetic features of Essenes and Qumranites.[7] Women are accused of preferring sexual relations with their husbands even if that prevents their husbands from making economic strides by working more hours or travelling on business. In that context (M. Sot. 3:4) sexual abstinence is referred to as perishut. That sexual abstinence was a major feature among perushim (whether Essenes or Qumranites) is well-known. On the other hand we are also aware that there were women at Qumran[8] and among the Therapeutae,[9] and R. Joshua of the Yoḥanan b. Zakkai circle, names the female parushah as a highly undesirable type (ibid.).

The beraitá at B. Sot. 22b (cf. P. Ber. 14b), which enigmatically described seven types of perushim indicates a definite tension between proto-rabbis and perushim, a tension which is paralleled in the

155

relationships between Jesus and the _perushim_. The very fact that Jesus uses Hos. 6:6 against them is very telling, for it emphasized precisely the difference between him and _perushim_ as the same type of difference that obtained between proto-rabbis and _perushim_. The refusal to see this, and the insistence upon a Christological approach to the life of Jesus of Nazareth during what all will concede to be his human ministry, becomes a stumbling block to scholars.[10] Thus Guelich[11] becomes entangled in internal confusion over whether Qumran does or does not use Hos. 6:6. At first he argues that IQS 9:3ff. uses Hos. 6:6, but then concedes it is not explicit. It is not even implicit. If Jubilees and the Qumran halakhah are representatives of the type of halakhah followed by _Pharisaioi-perushim_, then for the _perushim_ hesed played no role in halakhah. Fastidious observance of the harshest stringencies was an absolute requirement. Guelich,[12] reluctant to approach the matter in this way, adjudges the Temple at Mt. 12:6, to signify Jesus as the new Temple, and because love comes before sacrifice the disciples may violate the Sabbath in the service of the new Temple. Guelich thus sees Mt. 12:6-7 as "a Christological issue" and not a question of transgressing the Sabbath. This unsubstantiated assertion is made without consideration for the lack of logic inherent in it. Hos. 6:6 declares love precedes sacrifice, not the Sabbath. Love supersedes the Sabbath as a result of exegesis. The correct analogy would be between Temple sacrifice and the crucifixion. When the disciples pick the grain it is for themselves, not in the service of "the new Temple" (Jesus). But the Matthean Jesus makes the point clearer than Guelich: the disciples may pick the grain because they are mizvah apostles in the service of the Kingdom. But what is greater than the Temple is the obligation of love, because hesed takes precedence over sacrifice, and certainly over the Sabbath, and therefore if the _perushim_ understood Hos. 6:6 they would allow the picking of the grain.

In the matter of divorce the Matthean Jesus was not as rigorously opposed as was the halakhah of Qumran. Although many varying interpretations of Deut. 24:1-4 were current, the Matthean Jesus had an independent approach. He opposed divorce as contrary to God's will, but pragmatically allowed it in the one instance of adultery. At variance with the Judaic approach at the time, except for those who followed the halakhah of Qumran, or similar stringencies, he abolished the right of polygamy. Contrary to all proto-rabbinic circles, he made a married man subject to charge of adultery when others would have considered the married man's union with a second female rightful polygamy. The Matthean Jesus did not abolish the halakhah of divorce. He narrowed it to the one case of adultery. But he did abolish the right of a man to practice polygamy, thereby acting with ultimate proto-rabbinic independence even of the Torah. With a Jesus-like _egō de legō_, R. Ammi[13] said _sheani ōmer_, "But I say," that polygamy is to be rejected (B. Yeb. 65a). This was not the halakhic reality, however, and polygamy remained an option in Judaism until modern times among, for example, Yemenite Jews.

In the matter of Sabbath healing Jesus had no tradition against healing. The pietistic inference from the absence of any rationale for violating the Sabbath, that healing was forbidden, was unacceptable to him. When he healed on the Sabbath he performed _kalōs_, something good, an act of _hesed_, and this indirectly again invoked Hos. 6:6.

B. Conclusions

The above study leads to the following conclusions.

1. The Matthean Jesus was not in controversy with the men who were the immediate predecessors of the rabbis of Yaḅneh, a scholar group that I call "proto-rabbis." The _Pharisaioi_ of the New Testament constitute a variety of pietistic and separatist extremists in the Jewish community, who adhered to a Sabbath and divorce halakhah best exemplified by the Book of Jubilees and the writings of Qumran. The "scribes" are functionaries among both the _perushim_ and the priests, and are not proto-rabbis. That scribes are so frequently mentioned with _Pharisaioi_ is not surprising when one considers the vast literary output of Qumran and dares to speculate on what has not yet been discovered, and upon what has perished. The Sadducees are priests or followers of the priests. Since Jesus is addressed as "rabbi" there is much reason to wonder why the evangelist-redactor never refers to the antagonists as such, if indeed that is what the _Pharisaioi_ are, since he does accuse them of desiring the title (Mt. 23:7). Mark more accurately

157

omits that charge at 12:38-40.

2. On the subject of divorce the Matthean Jesus has a wholly independent viewpoint which stands alone in the first century. His halakhah against polygamy became the Christian norm, albeit often breached, but did not gain a position of authority in Judaism until the Middle Ages. His view that adultery alone is grounds for divorce was early reinterpreted by Christians. The more rigid the Christian community grew in the abolition of the right of divorce, the more permissive the halakhah became until the Hillelite-Akibian "easy divorce" became the talmudic norm. R. Ammi[14] stands as an example of a strand within Judaism which may have been influenced by Jesus' arguments against polygamy rooted in the order of creation.

3. On the subject of the Sabbath the Matthean Jesus stands out as an articulate dissenter from the Ezraic-Nehamian quiescent Sabbath which turned into a day on which the stringencies often defeated the healing purpose of a Sabbath. In effect Jesus' healing on the Sabbath, as a sign that hōste exestin tois sabbasin kalos pōiein, "it is permitted to act beneficially on the Sabbath" proclaimed the very purpose of the Sabbath as a redemptive-healing day. His arguments concerning picking grain seeds for food was of a similar order: love and human benefit are of primary concern, and are not in conflict with Sabbath halakhah. Rabbinic Judaism that grew out of Yabneh and Usha after 70 A.D. consistently devised halakhic limitations upon Sabbath stringency, seeking ways to alleviate the harshest effects of pietism which had strongly influenced the masses. Most significantly, rabbinism applied the proto-rabbinic waivers utilzed so expertly by Jesus, in order to reduce the potency of perushite stringency which Yabneh inherited. While excluding the writings of Qumran, Yabnean Judaism was unable to exclude the Sabbath conservatism, just as the exclusion of the hellenistic and apocryphal writings did not succeed in excluding the theosophical speculations that turn up again and again in midrash and later kabalah. In sum, there may be more to the apocryphal tradition than Christianity has conceded. The Gospel of Thomas, 27,[15] records in the name of Jesus, "If you do not observe the Sabbath as a Sabbath, you will not see the Father."[16] What Jesus did was not to transcend the Sabbath or spiritualize its observance, an effort combated by Philo.[17] He

acted as a proto-rabbi by applying hermeneutics and other principles in the normal course of interpreting the requirements of the Sabbath.

4. During his brief ministry Jesus was a proto-rabbi whose views influenced his contemporaries and possibly entered tannaitic literature as the views of others.[18] If there is any truth at all to the tradition at Lk. 2:46, the precocious Jesus enjoyed the company of proto-rabbinic scholars (<u>didaskaloi</u>), and his maturation in this regard is observed at Lk. 2:52.[19] A classic example of a view enunciated by Jesus which is attributed to later tanna, R. Simon B. Menasia, is Mt. 12:8, "For man is the lord of the Sabbath."[20] Had Christian Jews not been expelled from the synagogues after 90 A.D., but remained a segment of Judaism, it is well within the realm of possibility that Jesus would have secured a place in the proto-rabbinic pantheon. He would have been a source to whom Sabbath leniency would have been attributed, while at the same time he would have been looked to as the source of stringency in divorce and a heavy yoke in a wide variety of questions touching upon civil law and personal ethics.

I. Notes

[1]The following constitute a sampling of works both undertaking and questioning form-critical and redaction-critical examinations of Matthew: R. Bultmann, The History of the Synoptic Tradition, trans. J. Marsh (Oxford: Basil Blackwell, 1963); M. Dibelius, From Tradition to Gospel Rev. 2nd ed. trans. Bertram Lee Woolf, (New York: Scribner, 1965); G. Bornkamm, G. Barth, and H. J. Held, Überlieferung und Auslegung im Matthäus-evangelium (Neukirchen: Buchhandlung des Erziehungs-vereins, 1960); English edition, Tradition and Interpretation in Matthew, trans. Percy Scott (London: SCM Press, 1963); K. L. Schmidt, Der Rahmen der Geschichte Jesu, 2nd ed. (Darmstadt: Wissenschaftliche Buchgesellschaft, 1964); V. Taylor, The Formation of the Gospel Tradition (London: Macmillan & Co., 1933); H. Riesenfeld, The Gospel Tradition and Its Beginnings: A Study in the Limits of 'Formgeschichte' (London: A. R. Mowbray, 1957); B. Gerhardsson, Memory and Manuscript, trans. Eric J. Sharpe, (Uppsala: Gleerup, 1961);W. D. Davies, "Reflections on a Scandinavian Approach to 'The Gospel Tradition'," Appendix XV, The Setting of the Sermon on the Mount, (rpt. Cambridge: Cambridge University Press, 1977); K. Koch, The Growth of the Biblical Tradition, trans. from 2nd ed. S. M. Cupitt, (New York: Scribner, 1969).

[2]Davies, op. cit., p. 480.

[3]The following constitutes a representative, but by no means exhaustive bibliography: G. Strecker, Der Weg der Gerechtigkeit (Munich: Kösel-Verlag, 1946); E. Schweizer, "Observance of the Law and Charismatic Activity in Matthew" NTS, 16 (1969-70), 213-230; Das Evangelium nach Matthäus (Göttingen: Vandenhoech and Ruprecht, 1973); G. Kilpatrick, The Origins of the Gospel According to St. Matthew (Oxford: Clarendon Press, 1946); G. Bornkamm, "Enderwartung und Kirche im Matthäusevangelium" in Überlieferung, op. cit.; and "Der Auferstandene und der Irdische," ibid.; B. W. Bacon, Studies in Matthew (New York: Holt & Co., 1930); "Jesus and the Law," JBL, 47 (1928), 203-231; K. Stendahl, The School of St. Matthew (Uppsala: Gleerup, 1954); G. Barth, "Das Gesetzesverstandnis des Evangelisten Mattäus", Überlieferung op. cit.; R. Hummel, Die Auseinandersetzung zwischen Kirche und Judentum im Matthäus-evangelium (Munich: Kaiser, 1966); W. D. Davies, op. cit.; A. Sand, Das Gesetz und

die Propheten (Regensburg: Pustet, 1974);
D. R. A. Hare, The Theme of Jewish Persecution of
Christians in the Gospel According to St. Matthew
(Cambridge: Cambridge University Press, 1967);
E. von Dobschutz, "Matthäus als Rabbi und Katechet"
ZNW, 27 (1928), 338-348; M. Goulder, Midrash and
Lection in Matthew (London: SPCK, 1974); D. Rossler,
Gesetz und Geschichte (Neukirchen: Neukirchener
Verlag, 1960); K. Berger, Die Gesetzesauslegung Jesu.
(Neukirchen: Neukirchener Verlag, 1972); the latter
pp. 3-11 provides a review of the research done on the
theme of "Jesus and the Law"; A. von Harnack, "Hat
Jesus das alttestamentliche Gesetz abgeschafft?," Aus
Wissenschaft und Leben II (Giessen: Topelmann, 1911);
G. Bornkamm, Jesus of Nazareth, trans. Irene and
Fraser McLuskey with James M. Robinson (New York:
Harper and Row, 1960).

4Asher Finkel, The Pharisees and the Teacher of
Nazareth (Leiden: E. J. Brill, 1964).

5R. J. Banks, Jesus and the Law in the Synoptic
Tradition, (Cambridge: Cambridge University Press,
1975).

6John P. Meier, Law and History in Matthew's
Gospel (Rome: Biblical Institute Press, 1976).

7Among Christians stands out W. D. Davies, op.
cit., and his other writings, e.g., Paul and Rabbinic
Judaism (rpt. New York: Harper and Row, 1967);
E. P. Sanders, Paul and Palestinian Judaism
(Philadephia: Fortress Press, 1977). Among Jewish
scholars perhaps greatest objectivity is found in
David Daube, The New Testament and Rabbinic Judaism
(London: Athlone Press, 1956).

8The scope of this dissertation does not allow
for a careful examination of the term "Pharisaism" or
of the nature of the religious thought and life that
goes by that name. It will have to suffice to note
that the working hypothesis of this study is that
Pharisaioi in our New Testament text represents a
broad spectrum of the Jewish community in the first
century, a wide variety of people who went by the name
of perushim because they were pietists or separatists
or both. They were not necessarily the predecessors
of the post-70 "rabbis." The predecessors of the
latter I call "proto-rabbis." Josephus speaks of the
Pharisaioi at several places, but his evidence does

not contradict the views expressed here.

[9]E. P. Sanders, op. cit., p. 62, "The question of who the Pharisees were and of how they saw themselves vis a vis the rest of Judaism appears quite wide open." Cf. p. 61 and notes 7, 8, 10 for references to recent doubts raised on this identification. Cf. also the discordant skepticism of E. Rivkin, "Defining the Pharisees: the Tannaitic Sources," HUCA, 40-41 (1969-70), pp. 205-249; Jacob Neusner, Development of a Legend (Leiden: E. J. Brill, 1970), and in other writings, most notably The Rabbinic Traditions About the Pharisees Before 70, 3 vols. (Leiden: E. J. Brill, 1971).

[10]Translation by H. St. J. Thackeray, War, I, 5.2. (110). For Josephus's passages on Pharisaioi see War II, 8.2 (119); 8.14 (162 ff.); Ant. XIII, 5.9 (171-72); 10.5 (288); 10.6 (297 f.); 15.5 (401); 16.1 (405 ff.). The main statement is found at Ant. XVIII, 1.2 (11) - 5 (23).

[11]The possible references to proto-rabbis as distinct from Pharisaioi in Josephus are at Ant. XVII.6.2-4 (149-167); 9.3 (214, 216)(logiōtatoi); War I, 33.2 (648 ff.)(punthanomenoi); II, 8.1 (117f.); 17.8 (433); 17.9 (445). The term sophistai is used a number of times and is used for persons described in rabbinic style as lecturing to large audiences (War I, 33.2 (648)); the other terms are always distinct from any indentity with Pharisaioi in their contexts. The translation that follows in the text is by Ralph Marcus except that I have changed his "laws" for nomōn to "norms."

[12]Translation by Louis Feldman, Ant. XVIII, 1.3 (12).

[13]See, for example, the writings of G. F. Moore, Judaism of the First Centuries of the Christian Era: the Age of Tannaim, 3 vols. (Cambridge, Mass.: Harvard University Press, 1950); Travers Herford, The Pharisees (Boston: Beacon Press, 1962); Louis Finkelstein, The Pharisees: The Sociological Background of Their Faith, 2 vols. (Philadelphia: Jewish Publication Society, 1962); and many other writings on the subject.

[14]See notes 8 and 9 above.

15Mt. 22:35; Lk. 10:25; 11:45f.; 52f.; 14:3; 7:30; it is clear that in each case the use of nomikos implies not all the Pharisaioi present were nomikoi and indeed, as at Lk. 7:30, it is evident that the terms designate different groups. The term nomikos refers to a proto-rabbi. As over against a Sadducee, he too may be taken as a parush in colloquial idiom, but not all perushim are proto-rabbis. And the nomikoi are never hostile. As for the term peirazon, (Lk. 10:25; Mt. 22:35) translated as "tempting" or "to disconcert," it is my conviction that it can equally well mean "test" and not have a conspiratorial nuance. While Jesus attacks the nomikoi at Lk. 11:45-52, they hold their silence and it is "pharisees and scribes" who are hostile at v. 53. Space forbids a thorough discussion of the use of nomikoi and grammateis by Lk., but a careful scrutiny of his references shows they are not synonymous. Thus at 11:53 the grammateis are coupled with Pharisaioi as at 6:7 while the separate "alas" for nomikoi at 11:46 indicates they were separate from Pharisaioi. Again at Lk. 14:2 nomikoi are silent but at 15:2 grammateis coupled with Pharisaioi again complain against him, as they do with high priests at 19:47. Nothing like the anger of grammateis at 20:19 is ever related of nomikoi. There is no nomikos involved in the Passion narrative.

16I Tim. 1:7; Acts 5:34; Lk. 5:17. At Acts 5:34 the author is careful to identify Gamaliel I as a proto-rabbi and not as an ordinary "pharisee"-parush. This is interestingly corroborated at M. Sot. 9:15, "When Rabban Gamaliel the Elder died...perishut died." Obviously the meaning is that the very special type of acceptable pietism coupled with expertise in Torah and halakhah saw its last ideal representative in Gamaliel I.

17At M. Yad. 4:6 where Sadducees are represented as disputing halakhah with "Pharisees," the reference to perushim is accepted by Ellis Rivkin, op. cit. p. 209, as one to what I would term a proto-rabbi. But it should be carefully scrutinized, for Yoḥanan b. Zakkai immediately disassociates himself, the proto-rabbi and post-70 rabbi par excellence, from perushim. In all the other "controversy" sources listed by Rivkin there is no evidence that the perushim are those we know as pre-70 proto-rabbis, or post-70 rabbis. In some texts, e.g., T. Yom. 1:8 where hakhamim, a term applicable to proto-rabbis, appears to be used "as synonymous" (Rivkin's word, p. 214) with _perushim_, it only proves that the _hakhamim_ and _perushim_ agreed on a particular halakhah. As in the case of the N.T. the _hakhamim_ (_nomikoi_) are distinct from _perushim_ (_Pharisaioi_), although like Gamaliel the Elder they may concur with _perushim_ in aspects of piety as _perushim_ concur with _hakhamim_ in aspects of halakhah. This similarity in aspects of halakhah led to Louis Ginzberg's early conclusions, now supported by Chaim Rabin, that the Damascus Covenant indicates the Dead Sea sect to have been a "pharisaic" branch. It is interesting that Rivkin does not see at all that the _perushim_ are similar to Qumranites and/or Essenes and does not refer to them in his article. See   L. Ginzberg, _An Unknown Jewish Sect_ (New York: Schocken, 1975). The scope of this dissertation does not permit more exhaustive critique of Rivkin or other scholars on this subject. See Chapter Six, n. 7 below. A separate monograph is still a desideratum. See also Jack Lightstone, "Sadducees versus Pharisees: The Tannaitic Sources," _Christianity, Judaism and Other Graeco-Roman Cults_ ed. Jacob Neusner, 4 parts, (Leiden: E. J. Brill, 1975), IV, 206-217.

[18]See n. 16.

[19]All translations of Hebrew, Greek or Aramaic are my own unless otherwise noted.

[20]It is clear that the people at large, consisting of a medley of _ammei haarez_, _perushim_, Zealots, _sicarii_, Boethusians, Morning Bathers, etc. and those who were known without labels, were not avid supporters of the priests. Some priests were _perushim_, but those who held the power were in disrepute. See Josephus, _Ant._ XX, 8:8 (181, 207); B. Pes. 57a; T. Men. 13:21. See also _Ant._ XX, 10.5 (247-251) where Josephus indicates that the priestly line had been considered invalid since the days of Herod; _War_ II, 17.2 (409 f.); 10.4 (197). As a Hasmonean he does not include the Hasmonean line among invalid priests.

[21]This traditional approach to Judaism as "legalism" can be followed in a large variety of works in different languages deriving from an assortment of backgrounds. See a sampling of these works in the subsequent notes. A complementary fault in this evaluation of Judaism is that the period of Ezra and

Nehemiah is termed "early Judaism" and the period of Jesus "later Judaism" as if nothing has occured within Judaism since then.

[22]*Paul and Palestinian Judaism*, pp. 33-60.

[23]F. F. Weber, *Jüdische Theologie auf Grund des Talmud und Wernwandter Schriften* (Leipzig: Dörffling, 1897); E. Schürer, *A History of the Jewish People in the Time of Jesus Christ*, 5 vols., trans. John Macpherson et al. (New York: Scribner, 1897-1898); rev. ed. G. Vermes, F. Millar, I (1973); W. Bousset, *Die Religion des Judentums im Neutestamentlichen Zeitalter* (Berlin: Reuther and Reichard, 1903); R. Bultmann, *Theology of the New Testament*, 2 vols. in 1, trans. K. Grobel (New York: Charles Scribner's Sons, 1951-1955); *Primitive Christianity in its Contemporary Setting*, trans. R. H. Fuller (London and New York: Meridan Books, 1956); H. Strack and P. Billerbeck, *Kommentar zum Neuen Testament aus Talmud und Midrasch*, 5 vols. 4 med. (Munich: Beck, 1965); *Theological Dictionary of the New Testament*, ed. Gerhard Kittel, G. Griedrich, trans. Geoffrey W. Bromiley (Grand Rapids, Mich.: Eerdmans, 1964-1977).

[24]See n. 22.

[25]G. F. Moore, "Christian Writers on Judaism," *HTR*, 14 (1921), pp. 197-254; *Judaism*.

[26]See also the discussion of some aspects of this question in Davies, *Setting*, Appendix VI, 447-450.

[27]Not all priests were Sadducees. John the Baptist's family of rural priests may have been of the ̂ammei haărez or of the *perushim*, although manifestly John's father Zekhariah remained loyal to the Temple. The opposition of Jesus to what was happening in the Temple was probably one of the reasons *perushim* looked for the subordination of Jesus to them. But nevertheless Jesus did not ally himself with the *perushim*. Although his parents took him to the Temple as a youngster, there is no evidence Jesus supported the Temple priesthood once he embarked on his mission. At Mt. 8:4; Mk. 1:43f.; Lk. 5:14, he tells the cured leper to make the Mosaic offering, because he did not want him to reveal the source of his healing, not because he supported the priesthood. It only indicates political prudence before he was ready for the Passover denouement ("so as not to offend them").

Since temple worship stood under protection of the Roman government and the overseeing of the temple finances was carried out by Roman authorities during 6-41 A.D., the payment of the temple tax was no longer strictly devotional, but part of the "tribute to Caesar." This explains Jesus' reference to tolls and tribute (v. 25) when asked about the temple half-shekel. See Emil Schürer, A History of the Jewish People in the Time of Jesus, ed. Nahum Glatzer (New York: Schocken, 1975), p. 195.

[28]For a brief sketch of the shift of Judaic leadership from Jerusalem to Yabneh, to Yohanan b. Zakkai and then to Gamaliel II, see Jacob Neusner, A Life of Rabban Yohanan b. Zakkai (Leiden: E. J. Brill, 1962), pp. 147-171.

[29]See J. Z. Lauterbach, "Ordination," JE IX, 428-430; T. San. 1:1; P. San. 19a; M. San. 4:4; B. San. 5a-b; 13b. In the first stage Yohanan b. Zakkai ordained his own disciples, as did other rabbis according to the implications of the text at P. San. 19a. Later it was reserved as a prerogative of the collegium of Nasi and his court. There is much difference of opinion, however, precisely how much authority the Nasi had. See the discussion by Hugo Mantel, Studies in the History of the Sanhedrin (Cambridge, Mass.: Harvard University Press, 1965), pp. 206ff.

[30]See below II, C, 1.

[31]Typical examples of the stress on Jesus' "uniqueness" which raises him out of the realm of proto-rabbis is G. Bornkamm, Jesus of Nazareth; Banks, Jesus and the Law, and others.

[32]Sif. Num. 112; P. Ned. 36c; B. San. 90b, and others.

[33]Op. cit., 255.

[34]Op. cit., 9-10. It should be noted that I use Christian Jew and Christian Judaism for the same people and phenomena for which others employ the term Jewish Christian and Jewish Christianity. This is not the place for me to discuss my reasons, a task I hope to undertake elsewhere.

[35]K. Stendhal, op. cit.

[36] Op. cit., 15-35

[37] O. Lamar Cope, Matthew a Scribe Trained For The Kingdom of Heaven (Washington, D. C.: Catholic Biblical Association, 1976), p. 10.

[38] J. P. Meier, op. cit. 20f.

[39] I use the term "Law" when citing others who use it, as a concession to literary convention. When I speak for myself I will use the words Torah and halakhah.

[40] H. S. Reimarus, The Goal of Jesus and His Disciples, trans. G. W. Buchanan (Leiden: E. J. Brill, 1970); D. F. Straus, Das Leben Jesu 4th ed. (Bonn, n.p. 1877); F. C. Bauer, Vorlesungen über Neutestamentliche Theologie (Leipzig: Fues, 1864); A. Harnack, "Hat Jesus des alttestamentliche Gesetz abgeschafft?" op.cit.

[41] M. Kahler, Jesus und das Alte Testament (Leipzig: A. Deichert, 1896); B. H. Branscomb, Jesus and the Law of Moses (New York: Smith, 1930); T. W. Manson, "Jesus, Paul, and the Law," Judaism and Christianity III, ed. E. I. J. Rosenthal (rpt. London: KTAV, 1967), 125-141.

[42] T. W. Manson, The Teaching of Jesus (Paperback rpt. Cambridge: University Press, 1967); The Sayings of Jesus (London: SCM 1949); Ethics and the Gospel (London: SCM Press, 1960).

[43] G. Bornkamm, op. cit.; E. Percy, Die Botschaft Jesu (Lund: Gleerup, 1953).

[44] H. S. Schoeps, "Jesus und das jüdische Gesetz," Aus Fruhchristlicher Zeit (Tubingen: Mohr, 1950) pp. 212-220.

[45] G. F. Knight, Law and Grace: Must a Christian Keep the Law of Moses? (Philadelphia: Westminster Press, 1962).

[46] J. Wenham, Our Lord's View of the Old Testament (London: Tyndale Press, 1953).

[47] B. H. Streeter, The Four Gospels (London: Macmillan, 1953) pp. 500-504; G. Hebert, "The Problem

of the Gospel According to Matthew" SJT, 14 (1961)
403-413.

48Kilpatrick, op. cit.

49B. W. Bacon, op. cit.; B. H. Branscomb, op.
cit.

50Petrine; Bacon; Hellenistic: Branscomb. I see
Matthew as on the same wave-length as James, a
Christian Jew who continues to emphasize the
observance of halakhah, albeit a new Christian
halakhah.

51G. Bornkamm, in Überlieferung, pp.
13-47;G. Barth, ibid., pp. 54-104; R. Hummel, op.
cit.;   pp. 34-75; W. D. Davies, op. cit.
pp. 387-401. Davies refers to the "Christian
rabbinism of Matthew," p. 401.

52Op. cit. pp. 130-175, especially pp. 146f.
where he argues that Matthew's Jesus revokes the Law.

53K. Berger, op. cit. Divorce is dealt with
comprehensively at pp. 508-575; R. Banks, op. cit.,
pp. 146-159.

54Asher Finkel, op. cit.

55Erich Klostermann, Jesu Stellung zum
Alten Testament (Kiel: R. Cordes, 1904).

56Finkel, 134.

57Gen. 2:3; Ex. 20:8; 11; Deut. 5:12, 15.

58The generation of the exile, distant from the
Jerusalem cult emphasized the inherent sacrificial
nature of circumcision. It was a sacramental act
performed in lieu of sacrifice. The blood of
circumcision was seen to have an atoning power as is
reflected in the Targum to Ez. 16:16. The expiatory
nature of the rite is also clear from the Targ. to
Ex. 4:24-26. See PRE 29; Phillip Sigal, The Emergence
of Contemporary Judaism (Pittsburgh: Pickwick Press,
1977), II, 187, 210f., 503f.

59See Sir James George Frazer Folklore in the Old
Testament 3 vols. (London: Macmillan, 1918) II,
passim, on circumcision among East African tribes;

III, 96, 239ff. on diffusion of the rite in the Pacific and Australia (p. 262). At II, 329 he tells of the Nandi tribe where the foreskins are presented as an offering to God, reminiscent of the narrative at Ex. 4:24-26. See n. 58.

60This is a classical pericope and has been included in the liturgy in several different locations. It is recited in Sabbath eve maariv worship at the conclusion of the shemá portion of the liturgy, again in the ámidah of Sabbath morning worship, and is used as a portion of the afternoon kiddush, the proclamation of the sanctity of the Sabbath before the second Sabbath meal. These may be located in their respective berths in any standard prayerbook. See, for instance, The Authorized Daily Prayerbook, ed. J. H. Hertz (New York: Bloch, 1948) pp. 372ff. (Heb.) 373f. 456-457; 564-565 (Eng.).

61E. Neufeld, Ancient Hebrew Marriage Laws (London: Longmans Green Co., 1944), 185-188.

62Ibid., p. 37.

63The divorce passages in the O. T. are at Deut. 24:1-4; 22:19, 29 (restrictions on divorce); Jer. 3:1, 8: Is. 50:1; Mal. 2:16; possibly Ex. 18:2 (taken as such by Onk.). None of the divorce passages provide for how the writ is to be composed, its wording, who is to preside, whether to require witnesses or how many, whether there is any liturgical element, and so forth.

64Banks, op. cit., pp. 14f.

65Ibid., pp. 52-55. See Test. Reub. 3:8ff.; Test. Jud. 18:3ff.; Jub. 36:3ff.; I En. 94:6ff. for examples of nomos as not to be equated with what might be termed "legal."

66Ibid., pp. 39f., 42f.

67The phrase is used many times, e.g., Deut. 1:5; 4:8; 44; 17:18-19.

68Deut. 1:5 refers to narrative, "this corpus of learning," and to no law at all. 4:8 obviously refers again to this corpus and does not pronounce any "law" or collection of laws as absolute. To take 4:44 as referring only to the establishment of three refuge

169

cities and to call this administrative fiat "Torah" is
rather inadequate. At v. 41 as so often in the N.T.,
"at that time" serves as a connective phrase which
tells us very little and does not introduce a separate
unit at 41-43. 4:44 seals the whole previous section
which began with 1:5 and stands as part of 4:44-49.
17:18-19 again gives no evidence of an absolutism.
These verses refer to the same "corpus" to which, as
we have already seen, Banks conceded "flexibility."
It is "limited," but is subject to historic growth and
supplementation.

[69]Banks, op. cit., p. 55.

[70]Ibid., 56.

[71]Ibid., 57f.

[72]Ibid., p. 59.

[73]Ibid., p. 58.

[74]Ibid., p. 59. P. Bläser, Das Gesetz bei
Paulus, (Munster: I. W. Aschendorff, 1941), p. 39,
estimates that five O. T. passages on the Sabbath
become 39 articles and 1521 passages in the Mishnah.
Cited by Banks, p. 59. But Banks appears unaware that
this count is at P. Shab. 9c and refers to a later
computation of secondary acts forbidden on the
Sabbath, toladot, and not to the acts forbidden in the
Mishnah.

[75]M. Ḥag. 1:8 indicates that the proliferation of
Sabbath halakhah has little scriptural support.
M. Er. 10:15 refers to the fact that much can be
permitted on the Sabbath because it was only forbidden
by rabbinic interpretation. Cf. also the extensive
non-scriptural prohibitions debated before the war of
66-70, at M. Shab. 1:4-8.

[76]Op. cit., pp. 60f.

[77]Ibid., pp. 60-64.

[78]A good example is the approach of Alexander
Ross, Pansebeia: A View of All the Religions in
the World, 6th Ed. (London: 1653). Judaism was
discussed in the first section of the book, issued
again in 1656 as a pamphlet with the title A View of
the Jewish Religion.

[79]Op. cit., p. 64.

[80]The term _minim_ can signify Christian Jew or some other sectarian. At times it must mean gnostics. It is not necessary for the purpose of this study to do a word analysis. This text portrays people who denied a future life and the word must there signify Sadducee as some texts attest, rather than _minim_, since that term can refer to Christians, Essenes, Qumranites or gnostics, all of whom believed in a "world to come."

[81]Op. cit., pp. 60ff.

[82]M. Shebi 10:3-4; Git. 4:3; Sif. Deut. 113. The _prozbol_ is a document which is deposited with the court. It states that the lender, under the judges' authority, may collect any debt due to him at any time. This legal instrument actually takes precedence over the biblical tradition. Another example of a proto-rabbinic abrogation of a Torah norm is the suspension of intensive inquiry of witnesses in civil cases. Here, at B. Yeb. 122b we find Deut. 15:7 pitted against Lev. 24:22.

[83]Mt. 22:34-40; Mk. 12:28-34; Lk. 10:25-28.

[84]Op. cit., p. 165.

[85]Mt. 22:35. The Greek Testament, ed. Kurt Aland et al, (New York: American Bible Society, 1966), note 5 on the text, where _nomikos_ is given a rating of "considerable degree of doubt" (p. xi). Cf. B. M. Metzger, A Textual Commentary on the Greek New Testament (London and New York: United Bible Societies, 1971), p. 59.

[86]J. W. Doeve, Jewish Hermeneutics in the Synoptic Gospels and Acts (Assen: Van Gorcum, 1954), pp. 122f.

[87]Op. cit., p. 170f.

[88]Sifra, ed. Weiss, 89b; P. Ned. 41c; Gen. R. 24:7. Paul, at Gal. 5:14 sounds like Akiba, as he does at Rom. 13:8-10; the same tradition is at James 2:8.

[89]Test. Iss. 5:2; Test. Dan 5:3; 7:6;

Sif. Deut. 323. The last cited could very well be the source for Jesus' citation of Deut. 6:4 which is the taking upon oneself the "yoke of the kingdom of heaven" in Judaic liturgy. The "yoke" is thus subsumed under the love command. At Sif. ibid. we also hear that receiving the yoke of God's sovereignty is attested by acting toward one another with benevolence. For Hillel: B. Shab. 31a.

[90]See note 89, and in addition: Test. Zeb. 5:1; Test. Gad 4:2; Test. Jos. 11:1; Test. Benj. 3:3; Philo, The Spec. Laws II, 15(56)-16(70); at 63 Philo stresses that duty to one's fellowman in Judaism is expressed through one's humanity and justice to all humans, and at 69 he emphasizes that all humans are by nature free. He lists these ideas as objects of Sabbath study. Moses II, 31 (163); Abr. 37 (208).

[91]At Rom. 13:8 and Gal. 5:13 the terms allēlous and ton heteron need mean no more than "one another," confined to Christians.

[92]For a very recent review see Meier, op. cit., pp. 41-124.

[93]A. Merx, Matthäus, pp. 73ff., cited by Banks, op. cit., p. 207. For its usage for "abolish" see II Macc. 2:22; IV Macc. 5:33, and with nomos, cf. II Macc. 4:11; Philo Spec. Laws III, 33M (182) uses it in the sense of "subvert."

[94]Banks, op. cit., 208ff.

[95]Op. cit., p. 74, n. 77.

[96]Ibid., p. 85.

[97]Ibid., pp. 87-89.

[98]Ibid., p. 42.

[99]Ibid., p. 43, especially n. 12.

[100]H. Baltensweiler, Die Ehe im Neuer Testament (Zurich: Zwingli-Verlag, 1967) p. 80.

[101]H. J. Holtzman, cited by Meier, p. 44, n. 15.

[102]Meier, p. 121.

[103]Ibid.

[104]Ibid., pp. 46-123.

[105]Ibid., p. 123.

[106]Section A.

[107]Meier, p. 124.

[108]See III, B,[1] below.

[109]Meier, p. 124.

[110]From ca. 500 B.C.

[111]Phillip Sigal, New Dimensions in Judaism (Jericho, New York: Exposition Press, 1972), pp. 58-115. It should be noted that for the purposes of this dissertation only those factors that can be reasonably shown to be operative before 70 A.D. will be utilized.

[112]Taking a variety of verses in conjunction, such as those telling of the zekenim of Jer. 26 who are identified with the sofer Shafan whose son saves Jeremiah and the zekenim who consulted Ezekiel, leads me to the conclusion that an emergent non-establishment group of scholastics constituted the circles out of which came Ezra the Sofer and the predecessors of proto-rabbis.

[113]The earliest rabbinic tradition considering the hellenistic sages as proto-rabbis, that is, as forerunners and "types" of themselves, is M. Ab. 1:1ff.

[114]Mt. 23:7-8 either anticipates or reflects the same attitude as that of M. Ab. 1:10, "U'senah et harabanut," which is said in the name of a 1st century B.C. teacher, Shemáyah, who urged his disciples to eschew a formal position of status and power. At Ab. de R. N. A, 11, B, 22, ed. Schechter, p. 46, the saying is related to status derived from expertise in Torah.

173

II. Notes

[1]The term Mishnah signifies teaching which is recited orally, the term being etymologically derived from shanah or shani, "to repeat," (Jastrow, II, 1605 a), from which it came to signify the repetition of teaching, recital. In Aramaic the root teni, tena, has the same signification, accounting for the Aramaic term for Mishnah, matnitā, and the term by which the teachers of this material are known, tannaim. The Mishnah is a digest of selected halakhah (norms of conduct) covering all phases of socio-economic life, personal religious and public cultic ritual, personal ethics, domestic relations, and civil and criminal law. It contains both the results of expository treatment of scriptural texts as well as usages handed down as historic custom and enactments of both a positive (takanot) and negative (gezerot) thrust. Originally the term Mishnah included what was later distinguished as beraitā, the material later kept "outside" of the "canonical" collection. It also signified halakhic midrash (see note 3). The Mishnah as a corpus of halakhah more or less as we have it today, was edited ca. 200 A.D. See Saul Lieberman, Hellenism in JewishPalestine (New York: Jewish Theological Seminary, 1950), pp. 83ff.; B. Gerhardsson, Memory and Manuscript pp. 28, 79-84, and variously throughout the book; Moses Mielziner, Introduction to the Talmud, 4th ed. (New York: Bloch, 1968), pp. 4-16; Herman L. Strack, Introduction to the Talmud and Midrash, trans. from 5th ed. (New York: Meridan Books, 1959), pp. 3f.

[2]Toseftā is a collection of beraitot, of halakhic norms omitted from the Mishnah. It contains matter of the same nature and is produced in a similar style. The term means "supplement" or "appendix" and is a halakhic collection supplementary to the Mishnah. It is thought by some that the Toseftā in its present form belongs to a time as late as the fifth or sixth century. See Zekhariah Frankel, Maybo Hayerushalmi (Breslau: H. Skutsch, 1870), p. 22a; Strack, op. cit., pp. 75f.; Mielziner, p. 17. I think Tosefta embodies the earliest halakhah.

[3]Midrash signifies both the process of exposition of a text and the resultant corpus of material in which the exposition is collected. Tannaitic midrashim include Mekhiltā to Exodus, Sifrā (also called Torat Kohanim) to Leviticus, Sifre to Numbers and Deuteronomy. These are considered halakhic

midrashim because they contain the expository material from which Mishnah and Tosefta are in part extracted. But they are by no means limited to halakhah. Each contains agadah, non-halakhic material. Modern scholars date the Mekhilta to the 4th or 5th century, Sifra and Sifre to the 4th. Nevertheless, current Judaic scholarship recognizes that these midrashim contain material that was composed before the Hasmonean era. See Louis Finkelstein, <u>Pharisaism in the Making</u> (New York: KTAV, 1972), pp. 13-120. The ăgadic midrashim are many, and are expository of scripture on a non-halakhic level, offering homilies, parables, and folk-lore, although they include some halakhic matter. The oldest is believed to be Genesis Rabbah, dated to the fifth century, except for later accretions. The other ăgadic midrashim are generally dated from the seventh to the ninth centuries. See Strack, op. cit., pp. 201-234; Mielziner, op. cit., pp. 18-20.

[4]Talmud is a term signifying both the midrash-expository process and the corpus of literature resulting from the process. The Palestinian Talmud came into its present form in the 4th cent., the Babylonian Talmud in the 6th cent. with some modifications continuing into the 7th cent. by teachers known as Saboraim. The post-tannaitic teachers of the Talmud are called Ămoraim (sing. Ămoră), interpreters or expounders. Another term often encountered for the expository material that follows a Mishnah pericope in the text of the Talmud, is gemară. The term is derived from the root gamar, to complete (Jastrow, I, 255), and signifies "completing" the Mishnah by virtue of expounding it to its logical conclusions or ramifications; perhaps it has the significance of "consummate." In any event, in its various grammatical forms it came to mean study, teach, derive teaching, be well-versed, and as a proper name, to refer to the Talmud. See Strack, 65-74; Mielziner, 41f., 52-62.

[5]See E. P. Sanders, <u>Paul</u>, pp. 59-69; Davies, <u>The Setting</u>, 256-315.

[6]The term "rabbinic Judaism," of necessity can derive only from the title "rabbi" used by its protagonists. The tradition is that the ordination which bestowed this title upon certain individuals began with Yohanan ben Zakkai's ordaining of his disciples at Yabneh: P. San. 19a.

[7]See now the proposals for early dating presented by John A. T. Robinson, Redating the New Testament (Philadephia: The Westminster Press, 1976).

[8]More attention should be given to Louis Finkelstein, New Light From the Prophets (New York: Basic Books, 1969). Much expanded study along these lines is a desideratum.

[9]Adequate consideration must be given to the relative authenticity of the written texts as faithful testimony to earlier oral tradition as well as "reprints" of earlier notes, pamphlets, testimonies, catechetical collections, etc. See B. Gerhardsson, Memory and Manuscript, Part Two. This thesis and its conclusions have been severly criticized by Morton Smith, "A Comparison of Early Christian and Early Rabbinic Tradition," JBL, 82 (1963), 169-176. In my opinion Smith is without warrant in the manner in which he takes Gerhardsson to task. Thus, while Smith (p. 171) is correct that there was no rabbinic "doctrinal center" as Gerhardsson claims (p. 131), and that there is more miracle material about Jesus, underscoring the difference in content and form of transmission between the material of the N.T. and rabbinic literature, Smith tends to shrug off the rabbinic material that contradicts the absolutism with which he expresses himself. See Smith, p. 172f. and n. 10. Smith also overlooks the fact that the N.T. is not necessarily a rabbinic-style midrash or mishnaic form, but a "new O.T." and therefore its form and content, while reflecting proto-rabbinic ideas, would have greater affinity with biblical literature in form and style.

[10]See D. A. R. Hare, The Theme of JewishPersecution.

[11]At Ex. R. 46:4 we find kyrie, mari, abi as synonyms: "my lord, master, father." This is found to be the same usage at B. Taan. 23b in Aramaic where abba is a term of respect. See Genesis Apocryphon 2:24, abi, mari, cited by Joachim Jeremias, The Prayers of Jesus (Naperville, Ill.: Alec R. Allenson, 1967), p. 58, n. 31. Elijah is called kyrios at LXX III Ki. 18:7, as is Ahab at v. 10, and passim.

[12]I leave the term sofer untranslated throughout because I believe the term "scribe" is inadequate and

"scholastic" or "scholar" which it means often would be confusing to the reader who finds "scribe" everywhere.

13For the kohen, see Aelred Cody, A History of the Old Testament Priesthood (Rome: Pontifical Biblical Institute, 1962); for the nabi see J. Lindblom, Prophecy in Ancient Israel (Philadelphia: Fortress, 1962); for the hakham see O. S. Rankin, Israel's Wisdom Literature, (New York: Schocken, 1969). Rankin, among others, such as R. B. Y. Scott and Robert Gordis, refers to "wisdom-schools" (p. 3) and indicates the later ones were continuations of such from prophetic times.

14His important role as the learned man at court, the King's "intellectual," is seen e.g., at II Ki. 22:8.

15The Dabar of the nabi, the word of God given by the prophet, is parallel to the Torah of the kohen and carries the same weight in the saying of Jeremiah. That dabar is revelatory by God is evident at Jer. 18:1, and frequently in the prophetic writings.

16At M. Ab. 1:1 Moses receives torah (i.e., "instruction") not The Torah (i.e., the Pentateuch). See also Finkelstein, New Light, pp. 3, 5, 13, 77, 132f. for further comments; Pharisaism, for the early dating of rabbinic material.

17Morton Smith, Palestinian Parties and PoliticsThat Shaped the Old Testament (New York and London: Columbia University Press, 1971) pp. 82-125.

18Ancient Near Eastern Texts, ed. James B. Pritchard, 2nd ed. (Princeton, N.J.: Princeton University Press, 1955), pp. 491f. The papyrus cited here indicates the Temple existed long before Cambyses conquered Egypt in 525 B.C., despite the Deuteronomic reform.

19Ez. 11:18; 33:23f.; Zekh. 10:2; 13:2f.; Mal. 1:6-2:9.

20The scope of this dissertation does not require a discussion of all of the enigma concerning the dating and the priority of Ezra and Nehemiah. I adopt the priority of Ezra. For this period in general and for some of the problems of literary and historical

177

criticism see Peter R. Ackroyd, Exile and Restoration
(Philadelphia: The Westminster Press, 1968); Toledot
Am Yisrael, ed. H. H. Ben Sasson, 3 vols. (Tel Aviv:
Devir, 1969); Ezra-Nehemiah, The Anchor Bible, trans.
Jacob M. Myers (Garden City, N.Y.: Doubleday and Co.,
1965).

[21]II Ki. 19:2; 22:14; Neh. 8:1, 4, 9, 13; 12:26,
36; Ben Sira 38:24-39:11.

[22]Since Ben Sira was not included among the
sacred writings and dropped out as an authority in
Judaism he is not listed in M. Ab. But there is no
reason to deny him the potential status of a
proto-rabbi. He conducted a beth midrash (Ben Sira
51:23) perhaps best translated as a "research
institute" which he also terms a yeshibah, "a session"
(51:29) both terms are known to us as rabbinic; Ben
Sira 51:23-30. He is cited extensively in talmudic
literature: B. San. 100b; B. B. 98b; P. Hag. 77c; and
at over twenty-five other places. At times his verses
are introduced with the same term as scripture, ketib,
"it is written," e.g., P. Ber. 11b. The term Tanu
rabbanan introducing tannaite teaching is used for Ben
Sira at B. Pes. 113b.

[23]M. Ab. 1:1, the proto-rabbi was to be prudent
in his scholarly deliberations, set up many disciples
and create a hedge for the Torah, that is, ornament it
with interpretation and application. Ben Sira is
already supporting what we know to be the later
rabbinic notion of contemporary authority as over
subjection to past authority as greater or more sacred.
Thus at 39:6-8 there is emphasis: "He himself pours
forth wise sayings...He himself directs counsel and
knowledge...He himself declares wise instruction and
glories in the nomos of the Lord..." The beth midrash
of Shemayah and Abtalion mentioned at B. Yom. 35b is
of a period little over a century removed from Ben
Sira. See n. 22. There are also times when Ben Sira
is quoted by another rabbi in the style of a rabbi:
"R. Lazar said in the name of Ben Sira," P. Hag. 77c.

[24]The great task of a comprehensive re-evaluation
of Ben Sira is still ahead of us. The scope of this
dissertation does not permit further exploration. I
have adumbrated a few lines of research in my The
Emergence of Contemporary Judaism (Pittsburgh:
Pickwick Press, 1979), Vol. I, Chap. 5. On Torah and
Wisdom see 1:26; 19:20; 24. Robert Pfeiffer saw this

to some measure when he wrote "...Sirach marks the transition from the Bible to the Talmud, from the authority of inspiration...to the authority of learning," History of the New Testament Times (New York: Harper & Row, 1949) pp. 369, 381ff.

[25]Pfeiffer, p. 371.

[26]For an excellent recent study of the question of Hellenism and Judaism in this early period see Martin Hengel, Hellenism and Judaism, trans. John Bowden, 2 vols. (Philadelphia: Fortress Press, 1974); Ben Sira is discussed at various points, but especially at I, 131-153, 157-162, although Hengel sees him as no more than a "wisdom teacher" (I, 132). Saul Lieberman's classic works, Hellenism, and Greek in Jewish Palestine (New York: Jewish Theological Seminary, 1942) dealt with the early rabbinic period.

[27]No attempt can here by made to settle the very complex question of which Simon was Simon the Righteous of the Mishnah and when he lived. See n. 29.

[28]The collection of sacred writings: B.B.B. 15a; P. Meg. 70d; liturgical matter: B. Ber. 33a; Meg. 17b; P. Ber. 4d; educational curriculum; P. Shek. 48c; establishment of Purim: B. Meg. 2a. For a recent survey of the sources see Ira J. Schiffer, "The Men of the Great Assembly," Persons and Institutions in Early Rabbinic Literature, ed. William S. Green (Missoula, Mont.: Scholars Press, 1977).

[29]See a brief survey of the literature and views concerning The Great Assembly of M. Ab. 1:1 in Moore, Judaism, III, 7-11; Henry Englander, "The Men of the Great Synagogue" HUCA, Jubilee Volume (1925), 145-169. Englander sees Simon as Simon I, ca. 270 B.C. and interprets the "great assembly" to signify the community as a whole. Israel as a body is called "The Great Community," a reference to the higher religious life of the post-exilic community until the mid-3rd cent. when Hellenism began to affect it. It is an interesting, albeit unconvincing, thesis, but whether correct or not does not affect this thesis. See also Louis Finkelstein, Haperushim VeAnshei Keneset Hagedolah (New York: Jewish Theological Seminary, 1950).

[30]A gathering mentioned at M. Shab. 1:4 which is

given as the locus of "eighteen decrees" cannot be
included as a "great assembly" notwithstanding Solomon
Zeitlin who incorrectly sees this as such a conclave.
See his The Rise and Fall of the Judean State 2 vols.
(Philadelphia: Jewish Publication Society, 1968-69)
II, 358f. Many rabbinic sources refer to these
"eighteen" with exasperating variants, contradictions
and omissions. Actually the most that should be said
for it is that it was a "joint session" of members of
the schools of Hillel and Shammai. See Alexander
Guttmann, Rabbinic Judaism in the Making (Detroit:
Wayne State University Press, 1970), pp. 102f.

31Finkel, p. 17.

32Ibid., p. 18.

33B. Er. 13a; Ecc. R. 2:17. Joachim Jeremias,
Jerusalem in the Time of Jesus, trans. F. H. and C. H.
Cave; (Philadelphia: Fortress Press, 1969) is in
error in his view of the "scribes." He thinks they
are rabbis, p. 236; and thinks the title was a formal
title of ordinations even before the time of Jesus.
His work requires much correction in general, pp.
233-267 on both "scribes" and "pharisees." It is
clear that he confuses "Pharisees" with hakhamim (p.
264). See also M. Sot. 9:15, B. Sot. 49a; Git. 67a.

34For a discussion of the function of the sofer
in rabbinic times see Saul Lieberman, Greek, pp. 20-48.
That hakhamim were regarded as more significant than
sofrim is evident at M. Sot. 9:15 where it is said
that since the destruction of 70 the hakhamim are no
better than sofrim. See B. A. Z. 9a where sofer and
tanna (a "rabbi") are distinct and P. Ber. 7c where
sofer and rabbi are distinct, and T. San. 2:6. See
also P. Maas. Sh. 56a for the pre-70 sofer as having a
distinctive profession. Cf. B. Gerhardsson, Memory,
pp. 45-55. At P. San. 18d Gamaliel I is distinct from
his sofer.

35For an evaluation in form-critical style of the
traditions of Simon the Righteous see Jacob Neusner,
The Rabbinic Traditions About the Pharisees Before 70,
3 Parts, (Leiden: E. J. Brill, 1971), Pt. I, 24-59;
Finkelstein, New Light, pp. 77-90; Guttmann, pp. 9-11.
Guttmann sees Simon as Simon I, ca. 270 B.C. and as
head of the innovative Great Assembly, but personally
conservative and therefore connected with no halakhic
change. Actually Simon was not said to be "head" of
any specific assembly, innovative or otherwise, but

rather a survivor of a recent assembly. In the light
of B. Meg. 11a where he is chronologically connected
with the Hasmoneans it appears to me that it is best,
on balance, and upon consideration of all of the
scholarly debate on Simon which cannot be reproduced
here, to see him as Simon II, ca. 200 B.C. See n. 29
above.

    ³⁶Finkelstein, New Light, p. 78, using Ab. de R.
N. A 1, p. 2, B 1; p. 2 argues somewhat differently
and concludes that neither Simon nor Antigonus was
originally in the list of tradents. I do not accept
this. The nature of midrash, which is what Ab. de R.
N. is, is to interpolate much material and produce
disconnected results. A, 4-5 and B, 5, 10, pick up
the Abot list again with Simon and Antigonus. What is
different in the list of Ab. de R. N. A, is
theinclusion of shoftim after zekenim and the
separation of Haggai, Zekhariah and Malakhi from the
other nebiim. Then "the men of the great assembly"
are said to have received the tradition from Haggai,
Zekhariah and Malakhi. The same list is offered by
Version B. But both versions come back to Simon,
after midrashically dealing with the apothegms of Ab.
1:1; and then list Antigonus, after expounding Simon's
maxims. Ab. de R. N. B, offers a third list which
incorporates Eli and Samuel between the shoftim and
the prophets. It is not possible here to deal
comprehensively with these variant lists, but I want
to suggest that they reflect varying schools of
thought. The list that includes Eli and Samuel, as
Finkelstein, p. 79, indicates, is undoubtedly the
original one, and I believe it is anti-Samaritan since
the Samaritans accused Eli of perverting the priestly
line. Samuel is sui generis and therefore not
included among the judges or the prophets, and Haggai,
Zekhariah and Malakhi are listed separately because,
as post-exilic heralds and teachers of the new age
they represent the beginning of the
soferic-hakhamic-proto-rabbinic form of teaching and
authority. Neither Ezra nor Nehemiah is in the list
because the rabbis identified the "Great Assembly"
with them, and telescoped the whole Persian period
into thirty-four years, (B.A.Z. 9a). Since all of the
dating by the rabbis is aberrant it is hardly
necessary to attempt to solve the chronological
problems relating to Simon II. See n. 56 below.

    ³⁷Cited by Charles Taylor in "An Appendix" to his
Sayings of the Jewish Fathers, "Prolegomenon," Judah

Goldin, 2nd ed. (New York: KTAV, 1969), p. 135, from a 17th century version (ibid., p. 114). For another discussion of Ab. 1 see David Hoffman, Die erste Mischna (Berlin: H. Itskowski, 1851), pp. 26-37, trans. into Hebrew as Hamishnah Harishonah by S. Grunberg, Berlin; 1913 rpt. Jerusalem, 1967; The First Mishnah, trans. Paul Foxheimer (New York: Maurosho, 1977).

38M. Sot. 9:14 records that in reaction to the "war with Titus" (the closing period of the revolt of 66-73 including the capture and burning of the Temple in 70) a gezerah, a prohibiting enactment, was issued against teaching Greek culture. This did not succeed, however, and Greek continued to be a vehicle of learning.

39One need but read the Epistles to verify the climate of those years.

40The Gospel According to Matthew and the Gospel According to John serve as our best sources, although at times one must read the polemic into or out of the text. Yet, the famous birkat haminim, the 12th paragraph added to the daily amidah, asking God's imprecation upon nozrim (Nazarenes, as Christians were then known), testifies to this polemical era.

41We also see this in the Epistle of Barnabas.

42This we can verify by reading Origen and the whole range of literature going under the rubric Adversus Judaeos. See also Robert L. Wilken, Judaismand the Early Christian Mind (New Haven: Yale University Press, 1971), 9-38.

43On the correct meaning of "make a hedge for the Torah," see Sigal, New Dimensions, pp. 47f.; 202f.; 215f.; n. 11, 221f.; Louis Finkelstein, "Introductory Study to Pirke Abot" JBL, 57 (1938), 13-50, p. 30, also in Pharisaism, 121-158, p. 138; 159-173; "The Maxim of the Anshe Keneset Ha-Gedolah," JBL, 59 (1940), 455-469.

44See further the form-critical study of Abot. 1 by Neusner, Rabbinic Traditions, Pt. I.

45M. Ed. 1:4; P. Hag. 77d; Shek. 47b.

46For the following dates see for example,

Travers Herford's commentary <u>Pirke Aboth</u> (New York:
Jewish Institute of Religion, 1945): 'The two Yosis:
200-160 B.C. (p. 25); Joshua b. Peraḥyah, in the time
of John Hyrcanus, the last quarter of the second
century B.C. (p. 27); Nittai the Arbelite, undated (p.
28); Judah b. Tabbai and Simon b. Shetah; during the
reign of Alexander Jannaeus, ca. 100-80 B.C. (pp.
29f.); Shemàyah and Abtalion: ca. 50 B.C. (p. 31);
Hillel and Shammai: from 30 B.C. into the first
decades of the first century A.D. (p. 32); Simon (M.
Ab. 1:17) may be a son of Hillel (belonging before
1:16) first quarter of the first century B.C. See
Herford's discussion of his identity at pp. 36f.
Gamaliel I (1:16) and his son Simon (1:18) then follow.
They are proto-rabbinic leaders on the eve of the
destruction of Jerusalem and witness the rise of
Christianity. Simon b. Gamaliel is dated 1-66 A.D.
(p. 38).

⁴⁷Josephus, <u>The Life</u> 38 (190f; 309). Josephus'
Simon described at 309, who is the object of a bitter
riot by the people in defense of Josephus against him,
hardly sounds like the Simon of Ab. 1:18. The Simon
at 191 said to be of a very illustrious family and of
the sect of the Pharisees, who have the reputation of
being unrivalled experts in their country's laws,
sounds more like Simon b. Gamaliel. The Jesus b.
Gamaliel of <u>Ant</u>. XX, 9.4 (213, 223), 211-215, 223, may
be Joshua b. <u>Gamala</u> of M. Yeb. 6:4, Sifra 95a, M. Yom.
3:9, B. Yom. 18a, B.B. 21a, who is a priest and not a
proto-rabbi contra Neusner, <u>Rabbinic Traditions</u>,
396f., who lists him among the pre-70 scholars.

⁴⁸Josephus, <u>Ant</u>., XV.1.1(3); 10.4(370). Josephus
refers to "Pollion the Pharisee and his disciple
Samaias" (1.1(3)) which can just as well imply that
Samaias was not a Pharisee. See n. 49.

⁴⁹Solomon Zeitlin, "Samaias and Pollion,"
<u>Journalof Jewish Lore and Philosophy</u> ed. David
Neumark, (rpt. New York: KTAV, 1969), p. 62, citing
Graetz and Dernbourg as seeing Shemàyah and Abtalion
in the first passage (XV.1.1(3)) and Shammai and
Hillel in the other (XV.10.4(370)). Shemàyah was not
a disciple of Abtalion nor was Shammai a disciple of
Hillel, so XV.(370) where Samaias is a disciple of
Pollion, points to neither pair. Zietlin cites Lehman
and Isaac Halevy as identifying them both times as
Hillel and Shammai. Zeitlin himself goes through
acrobatic exegesis to come up with one Samaias as

Shammai and the other as Shemáyah. I cannot here
enter into a detailed analysis of all these views, but
I think Josephus refers to none of our four
proto-rabbis, but simply to two men by the name of
Pollion and Samaias who were perushim-Pharisaioi. See
further Section 2 below.

[50]M. Maas. Sh. 5:15; Sot. 9:10; Par. 3:5; Yad.
4:6; T. Sot. 3:10; and a number of times in the
Babylonian Talmud.

[51]M. Taan. 3:8; B. Ber. 19a; Taan. 23a; and
elsewhere.

[52]M. Hag. 2:2; B. Hag. 16b. Josephus, War
II,17.8(433)17.9 (445) tells of a Manahem whom he
calls a sophistes, indicating he was a proto-rabbi.
This Menahem was a zealot and is an example of
proto-rabbis who opposed the pacifism of Yohanan b.
Zakkai and continued in a nationalist mood until the
denouement with Bar Kokhbah.

[53]Their names and where they are referred to in
the texts are collected by Neusner, op. cit. I,
389-419. I do not mention Hanina b. Dosa here because
no halakhah is given in his name. The sources
indicate, however, that as a healer, miracle worker
and teacher of wisdom he was Jesus-like. See M. Ber.
5:5; B. Ber. 34b (to which cf. Jn. 4:46-53); B. Taan.
24b; M. Ab. 3:9f.

[54]M. Ab. 2:9 indicates Yohanan received the
tradition from both Hillel and Shammai. If so, he was
at least an adolescent before the years 10 A.D. and
therefore born before the year 1. This would make him
roughly the same age as Jesus. After Hillel and/or
Shammai died, Yohanan settled in Arav, in Galilee, as
we see at B. Shab. 146a; M. Shab. 16:7; 22:3; at P.
Shab. 15d it is specified that he was there for 18
years; ibid. 17d; B. Ber. 34b; the latter source also
specifies that Yohanan taught in Arav where the famous
pietist Hanina b. Doas came to study with him.
According to some scholars Arav was not far from
Sepphoris, and therefore not far from Nazareth. In
any case, Yohanan would have been in Galilee for about
two decades from 20-40 or 25-45, in either case,
during the ministry of Jesus. Then he returned to
serve in Jerusalem while Gamaliel I was still alive
and a leading figure, about 35-50.

55T. San. 2:6; B. San. 11b; P. San. 18d.

56It is clear that something went wrong in the editorial process of M. Ab. Obviously 2:5-8, sayings by Hillel, should have followed 1:14 as a Hillel-complex. 1:15, quoting Shammai might then either follow the Hillel block, or even precede it, as Shammai precedes Hillel at the end of M. Hag. 2:2. Louis Ginzberg, "The Midrash Tamid," Journal of JewishLore and Philosophy 1 (1919), p. 288, n. 108, has brought attention to the fact the Ab. de R. N. B, 23-24, pp. 47-48, preserves Shammaite precedence. We would then have Shammai at 1:14, Hillel would follow with 1:15 and 2:5-8; 2:9 would follow with Yohanan b. Zakkai "receiving" from both Hillel and Shammai and closing the chain of tradition which is now self-evidently ensconced at Yabneh. In his commentary to Abot (pp. 6f.) Herford takes note of the "discontinuous" nature of the section 2:1-4, but not of the whole of 1:15-2:4. According to my conjecture, the textual order would be 1:1-13; 14, (Shammai); (Hillel) then the Hillel block 1:15; 2:5-8; 2:9 for Yohanan b. Zakkai; 1:17, Simon son of Hillel; 1:16, Gamaliel I; 1:18, Simon II son of Gamaliel I. Then 2:10 would pick up the threads of the new era, the disciples of Yohanan b. Zakkai: 2:1-4, as Herford indicates (p. 7) was undoubtedly added after the completion of the Mishnah within the cycle of Hillel family sayings.

57At M. Peah. 2:5-6 he cannot answer a question and consults another scholar.

58His view, at Ab. de R. N. A, 40, p. 127 that favors study by the sons of the rich coincides with the saying given in the name of Bet Shammai, ibid., 3 and B, 4, p. 14. His halakhah agrees with Bet Shammai, M. Bez. 2:6-7. It is possible that R. Gamaliel in the latter source is Gamaliel II, but nevertheless when he cites his father for support, he is giving a Shammaite stamp to the whole House of Gamaliel. See also M. Er. 6:2, Suk. 3:9; B. Ber. 43a; Yeb. 15a; T. Shab. 1:22.

59Neusner, Rabbinic Traditions I, 364-367, collects a number of halakhot which he attributes to Gamaliel I. Some of these may belong to Gamaliel II, as Neusner concedes, p. 314, noting also that the periocopae in which he is found are primarily stories. In any case, his halakhot are not very numerous considering the mystique of Rabban Gamaliel the Elder. The major halakhot are: the right of a woman to remarrry on the testimony of one witness that her husband is dead, M. Yeb. 16:7; B. Yeb. 115a; an ordinance allowing witnesses of the new moon freer movement in Jerusalem while waiting to give testimony, M.R.H. 2:5; ordinances related to divorce, M. Git. 4:2-3; permission to drink from vessels used for gentile wine, T. A. Z. 4:9; a number of halakhot given by other scholars are approved by him. The second example listed above is the one most likely to date to Gamaliel I but is more of an administrative procedure than a halakhah.

[60]Ibid., p. 375.

[61]Ibid., p. 387.

[62]There are three version of Yohanan's withdrawal: Ab. de R. N. A, 4, pp. 22-24, B, 6, p. 19f.; B. Git. 56a-b; Lam. R. 1:31. At Git. 56b he asks Vespasian for "Yabneh and its sages," which implies there already was a school there with anti-war proto-rabbis and their disciples. On Yohanan b. Zakkai see W. Bacher, Agadot Hatannaim, trans. A. Z. Rabinowitz (Jerusalem: Devir, 1921) I, 17-33; Neusner, A Life of Rabban Yohanan BenZakkai; Gedalyahu Alon, "The Patriarchate of Rabban Yohanan Ben Zakkai," in his Jews, Judaism and the Classical World, trans. Israel Abrahams (Jerusalem: Magnes Press, 1977). Josephus, Ant. XIII.15(395) calls Jamnia (Yabneh) a maritime city, and at XIV.4(75); War I.7(156) he calls it an inland city.

[63]S. G. F. Brandon, Jesus and the Zealots (New York: Charles Scribner's Sons, 1967) pp. 214f. rejects the tradition that Jerusalem Christians withdrew to Pella. See also pp. 208-212 and notes. The main case against the patristic tradition of the flight to Pella is made by Brandon in his The Fall of Jerusalem and the Christian Church (London: S.P.C.K., 1951). But see also a critique of his views by Barbara C. Gray, "Movements of the Jerusalem Church During the First Jewish War," The Journal of Ecclesiastical History, 24 (1973), 1-7.

[64]This is a subject beyond the purview of this dissertation and is therefore not being entered into.

[65]Life, 38-39 (190-196).

[66]Taylor, in his Commentary to M. Ab. at 1:18 (Herford, 1:17) p. 24, n. 37, following other modern scholars such as Jost, maintains that Simon was of the peace party. Taylor also considers the Simon of 1:18 to be the son of Gamaliel I but it is my view that, with Herford, (pp. 36f.), he should be taken to be the son of Hillel, and that various editorial adjustments are needed for the arrangement of the first two chapters of Ab., as noted earlier. In any event it is the question of Simon ben Gamaliel I which is before us now, and whether he was pro-war or anti-war. See also Alon, op. cit. p. 335 who sees Simon b. Gamaliel as pro-Zealot. But Alon rather confuses the issue when he attempts to prove that Simon b. Gamaliel I was put to death by the Romans by citing sources that manifestly speak of Simon b. Gamaliel II, pp. 336f., n. 70. At Ab. de R. N. A, 38 and B, 41, p. 114, R. Simon b. Gamaliel is arrested along with R. Ishmael b. Elisha and this undoubtedly refers to the Hadrianic period, as a reference to Betar (p. 115) confirms. This is very clear at B. San. 11a. Furthermore, at Makhiltá de Rabbi Ishmael, trans. Jacob Z. Lauterbach. (Philadelphia: Jewish Publication Society, 1949), III, 141f., the R. Simon who goes to his death with R. Ishmael is not specified as "ben Gamaliel." AtB. San. 11a, further, Samuel the Small at Yabneh, prophecies their deaths. Cf. Sem. 8. The textual references dispose of much of Alon's support for the idea that Simon b. Gamaliel I, was executed by the Romans. It would also appear that if Simon b. Gamaliel I was executed by the Romans, Josephus would not fail to tell us this. But this does not solve our enigma. For Simon b. Gamaliel II, (Simon III), was still alive at the reorganization at Usha after 140. B. Git. 58a, Sot. 49b; 83a. The solution of the problems in these texts, however, is not germane to our theme.

[67]See n. 66.

[68]Eusebius, The Ecclesiastical History, trans. Kirsopp Lake, 2 vols. (Cambridge, Mass.: Harvard University Press, 1953) III, 12, pp. 232f.

[69]Descent from the Davidic line was claimed by both the Palestinian Patriarch and Babylonian Exilarch. P. Kel, 32b; Taan. 68a; B. Ket. 62b; San 5a; Hor. 11b. See Geza Vermes, Jesus the Jew (New York: Macmillan, 1973) p. 157.

[70]The "chain" requested by Yohanan is usually taken as the family of Gamaliel (Rashi, ad. loc; Neusner, A Life, p. 121; Alon, op. cit., p. 338).

[71]See notes 66 and 70.

[72]Alon, pp. 323ff. provides a number of names of proto-rabbis who chose not to associate with Yohanan. Ab. de R. N. A, 14, B, 15, p. 59 indicates R. Eliezer b. Arakh went to Emmaus. He was a major disciple(M. Ab. 2:12), and undoubtedly the sources reflect that others too did not choose to accompany Yohanan to Yabneh. At T. Hag. 2:1 we have an elaborate eulogy by Yohanan b. Zakkai of Eliezer b. Arakh. See alsoB. Hag. 14b. Despite the close relationship between Yohanan and Eliezer indicated in these sources, Eliezer left him. See B. Shab. 147b. Dr. D. R. A. Hare brought to my attention the article by E. Trocmé, "Le Christianisme Primitif un Mythe Historique?" ETR, 49(1974), 15-29. Trocmé argues that Yohanan b. Zakkai launched an "orthodoxy" after 70 which affected the independent development of Christianity (pp. 20f.). But Trocmé does not give the necessary space to the problem of the animosity occasioned by Christian political withdrawal from Jewish national aspirations since Pella.

[73]Adolph Büchler, Die Priester und der Cultus im Letzten Jahrzehnte des Jerusalemischen Tempels (Vienna: Israel Theologische Lehranstalt, 1895) p. 17, lists a number of priests, but apparently anachronistically includes Yosi b. Yoezer who lived over two hundred years earlier. Büchler, p. 23, assumes R. Simon b. Nathaniel and R. Yosi hakohen (M. Ab. 2:10) joined Yohanan at Yabneh, but Alon, p. 327, suggests they were not there. Neither scholar provides persuasive evidence in either direction. Similarly it is not clear whether the prominent R. Zadok the Priest who later joined Gamaliel II at Yabneh, had gone with Yohanan. Yohanan is reported to have asked for Vepasian to provide a doctor for him (B. Git. 56b), and this may have been a gesture to pacify him. Undoubtedly, if Yohanan could have won over Zadok, he may have won over most of the priests. But he failed.

[74]At M. Shek. 1:4 and Ed. 8:3 we have examples of halakhic differences between Yohanan and priests, and the implication that he was not able to govern them.

[75]M. Yad. 4:6; T. Yad. 2:9. See Büchler, p. 25.
M. Par. 3:5-8, has Yoḥanan in its parallel at T. Par.
3:8. See also B. Men. 65a where we read "Boethusians"
instead of Sadducees; B. B. B. 115b.

[76]Alon, p. 320 on Büchler, p. 18.

[77]At Ab. de R. N. A, 20, p. 72, Ḥananiah (as his
name is given there, p. 70) uses S of S 1:6 "My
mother's sons have turned their anger on me," to refer
to the Jews who have taken a human king and set aside
the yoke of God, a typical position of the Zealots.
He follows this up with a positive view of Moses'
militancy in Egypt, similarly a view to be expected of
Zealots. At M. Ab. 3:2 he favors support of the
government. It is possible that he turned from
Zealotry to pacifism when he realized the debacle that
was about to come upon them. Therefore, unlike Alon,
I see his latter words as referring to a time later in
the war, probably even after Yoḥanan left Jerusalem.
For militant priests see Josephus War II, 17.2(409).

[78]Alon, p. 321.

[79]Above, B, 3.

[80]Neusner, Rabbinic Traditions III 239f. While I
concur with Neusner in certain broad conclusions on
the subject of Pharisees, I by no means agree with him
in detail. Above all, I do not regard the
proto-rabbis as a class as constituting "The
Pharisees." This is not the place for a critique of
his detailed research. This has already been done by
Solomon Zeitlin in a devastating critique of Rabbinic
Traditions in JQR, 65, pp. 127-135. See Neusner's
conclusions, "History of the Traditions" in Rabbinic
Traditions, pp. 239-319. I do not agree that a
so-called "Pharisaic party" which is to be equated
with so-called "Pharisees" who in turn are equated
with the proto-rabbis as a class, constitute "an
important force in Hasmonean politics." Had they done
so, we would find them of some consequence in
Hasmonean literature. The phenomenon termed
"Pharisee" arises only in Josephus and the New
Testament. Neither intertestamental literature nor
Philo refers to this phenomenon. The Qumran
literature di not have to. It was composed by real
Pharisaioi-perushim, pietistic separatists. I also do
not accept Neusner's implications, at III, 306f., that

189

the rabbinic tradition invented the relationship of Gamaliel to Hillel, and the discipleship of Yoḥanan b. Zakkai.

[81]Mt. 6:2, 5; 15:7; 23:13-26

[82]These issues are given here only in a sampling: Sabbath: Mt. 12:1ff.; ritual purity: 15:1ff.; divorce: 19:3; Mt. 23 mentions the talit and tefilin; there are references to oaths and tithings. Mark discusses the Sabbath, washing hands before eating, and refers to the levirate marriage. Lk. too deals with the Sabbath and tithes, and John too has the Sabbath theme in prominence.

[83]See above II, C, 1.

[84]M. Ab. 2:9, in telling us that Yoḥanan received from both Hillel and Shammai makes it quite plausible he was both eclectic, and independent and original. Certainly his efforts at Yabneh, which are beyond our horizon show an effort to create a substitute for Jerusalem and to transmogrify the theology that was territorially centered, and Temple-oriented, and subjected to a hereditary priesthood.

[85]Op. cit., p. 305. He draws a dividing line between the Pharisees of Josephus and those of the rabbinic tradition with Hillel; and maintains that with Hillel the politically-oriented Pharisees who sought to control Palestine were transformed into a religious sect. On the surface this would help explain why rabbinic literature never refers to the proto-rabbis as "Pharisees." It seeks to create a new identity. On the other hand, if such a transformation took place after 50 B.C., why does not Josephus reflect it, and why, 100 years later and more, would New Testament writers still call these post-Hillel circles "Pharisees?" It appears rather that Pharisaioi might simply be a way to describe all non-Establishment separatist sects, a hebraic counterpart of the term haeresis or a less pejorative term than minim. In this view, when Josephus refers to Sadducees, Essenes and Pharisees he lumps together under "Pharisees" all who were neither Sadducees nor Essenes. They numbered in their ranks some of the proto-rabbis who were closer in piety and disposition to the perushim than to the Sadducees and to those perushim who were specifically Essenes. The New Testament too possibly refers to these groups

indiscriminately as Pharisaioi, including the Essenes, excluding only the Sadducees who were of the Establishment in Jerusalem.

[86]Ibid., p. 306.

[87]See Joachim Jeremias, The Eucharistic Words of Jesus, trans. Norman Perrin (Philadelphia: Fortress Press, 1977), pp. 36-41.

[88]The Neusner view, op. cit., p. 307, that the Yosis originated the sect and that each pair has thirty years is a schematic without warrant. On the methodology and leniency of the proto-rabbis see Chap. 3 below.

[89]Ibid., p. 317.

[90]Julius Kaplan, The Redaction of the Babylonian Talmud (Jerusalem: Makor, 1973), pp. 261-288. The prohibition against writing oral torah was relatively late and without formal authority for it is never mentioned in the Mishnah. Furthermore, it only applied to permanent, authoritative works that would be set up as rivals to scripture. One tannaitic reference opposed to writing halakhah is found at B. Tem. 14b citing a beraita from the school of Ishmael. See Gerhardsson, op. cit., pp. 71-189. It is not necessary here to cite the references to written rabbinic materials as both Gerhardsson and Kaplan have collected a number of examples. See Lieberman, Hellenism, p. 84.

[91]Neusner, op. cit., pp. 315f.

[92]T. Ber. 3:25; M. Yad. 4:6, 7, 8; T. Yad. 2:20. At M. Ab. 2:5 Hillel is quoted as saying "al tifrosh min hazibur" "separate not, [do not be a parush] from the community." The pejorative comments on perushim are found at B. Sot. 22b; P. Ber. 14b.

[93]War I, 33.2(648ff.); Ant. XVII 6.2(152). Thus even Josephus may not mean to identify Pharisees-Rabbis. He may have used the term to signify dissenters from the Sadducee-supported Establishment priesthood and all others who so dissented. Some of these were "abstainers," true pietist perushim, and not proto-rabbis. Some were only dissenters and were proto-rabbis. Some proto-rabbis were also pious abstainers. See

"Introduction," above.

94The scope of this chapter precludes my
engagingin a detailed and technical research
enterprise into the question of the meaning and
constituency of Pharisees, Pharisaism and Sadducees
and Sadducaeism. Such a study would also require a
careful critique of the earlier literature and
deserves more than a monograph of its own. The
following literature represents a selection from the
past fifty years for background to this subject. All
of these writers identify the Pharisees as the Rabbis
no matter how they may differ over particulars. I
limit the selection to books and articles not listed
in the notes above.   G. Alon, Mahkarim Betoledot
Yisrael, (Tel Aviv: Hakibutz Hameuhad, 1957-58); G.
Alon, ToledotHayehudim beEretz Yisrael Bitekufat
Hamishnah Vehatalmud (Tel Aviv: Hakibutz Hameuhad,
1952-1955); "The Attitude of the Pharisees to Roman
Rule and the House of Herod," Jews, Judaism and the
Classical World; G. H. Box, Judaism in the Greek
Period (rpt. Westport, Conn.: Greenwood Press, 1971);
Adolph Büchler, Types of Palestinian Jewish Piety From
70 B.C.E. to 70 C.E. (London: Jew's College, 1922);
Henri Daniel-Rops, Jesus and His Times, trans. Ruby
Millar (York: Dutton, 1958); Hyman G. Enelow, "The
Modern Reconstruction of the Pharisees," in Selected
Works of Hyman G. Enelow (Kingsport, Tenn.: Kingsport
Press, 1935) IV, 117-134; J. N. Epstein Mevoot
Lesifrut Hatannaim, ed. Ezra Melamed (Tel Aviv:
Devir, 1957); Z. Frankel, Darkhe HaMishnah (Lipsiae:
H. Hunger, 1860); B. Z. Katz, Perushim Zedukim,
Kannaim, Nozrim (Tel Aviv: N. Twersky, 1947); J. Z.
Lauterbach, Rabbinic Essays (Cincinnati: Hebrew Union
College Press, 1951).

III. Notes

[1]Above, Chap. 2. Whoever the men were, and whatever the Great Assembly was, they and it were pre-first century. See also my New Dimensions, Chap. 2.

[2]B. Er. 21b; B. K. 82a; Shab. 14b; R. H. 31b, and elsewhere.

[3]Ruth R. 2:9 commenting on the text of Ruth 1:4; cf. 4:6; 7:7; 7:10. At 2:9, the sage in whose name the tradition is cited is R. Meir who refers to a previously well-known tradition. This can easily signify a pre-first-century tradition. So too atB. Yeb. 69a scholars at Usha during the 2nd cent. refer to the tradition as an old well-known anonymous saying. Cf. B. Yeb. 76b and parallels; P. K. 16:1, Louis Ginzberg, Legends of the Jews, 7 vols. (Philadelphia: Jewish Publication Society, 1946) IV, 88-89; VI, 191, n. 53; M. Yeb. 8:3. The rabbis believed that this exegesis had such high antiquity that they attributed it to the time of Ruth, and sometimes as an innovation made by Boaz. Again, this suggests that innovations contrary to the Torah were made in the pre-Christian period, that the rabbis knew this and not only accepted it, but turned to it in order to stabilize their own authority.

[4]Yosi b. Yoezer was a member of the first zug, the "pairs" of scholars listed at M. Ab. 1:4-15. He is thought to be one of the sages put to death by Alcimus, at I Macc. 7:16, ca. 160 B.C. See Gen. R. 65:2; Midrash to Ps. 11:7.

[5]Mekhiltá, Sifra and Sifre.

[6]See Lauterbach's essay "Midrash and Mishnah" in Rabbinic Essays, in its entirety.

[7]The Hellenistic Age, J. B. Bury et. al. (Cambridge: University Press, 1925; rpt. New York: Kraus Co., 1968); Moses Hadas, Hellenistic Culture (New York: Columbia University Press, 1959); W. W. Tarn, Hellenistic Civilization rev. 3rd ed., with G. T. Griffith (London: Edward Arnold & Co., 1952).

[8]See Chap. 2 above. See also B. A. Z. 37a; Ned. 19a; Pes. 16a, 17b. We find Yosi's halakhah

incorporated at M. Kel. 15:6, that while all liquids are susceptible to impurity, those of the Temple slaughterhouse are not. Cf. M. Makh. 6:4 for all the liquids, and Lev. 11:34, 38 for the basis of this halakhah.

[9]After a long interval of decline, first, imported glassware, and later, locally produced products appeared in Palestine from the 7th cent. B.C. 2nd-1st cent. B.C. wares have been found at Ashdod, Jerusalem and Samaria. See Encyclopedia Judaica 7, 603-606.

[10]See my discussion of this and references in my New Dimensions pp. 110ff. and p. 234, notes 8-9.

[11]At P. Shab. 3d the same decree is attributed to Judah b. Tabbai, somewhat later, but still first century B.C. He may have reissued an earlier gezerah. See B. Ḥul. 6a. See also the discussion of this question by Louis Ginzberg, On Jewish Law and Lore (Philadephia: The Jewish Publication Society, 1955), pp. 79ff. Cf. P. Pes. 27d; Ket. 32c.

[12]See the discussion of this at B. Shab. 15b.

[13]In my notes on the lectures of Professor Saul Lieberman (1951) on the tractate Abodah Zarah, I have a record of an extended discussion in which Lieberman preferred the ritualistic explanation to the economic which was stressed by Ginzberg (n. 11 above).

[14]B. B. M. 59b; Git. 60a; Tem. 16a; Er. 13b; Ber. 5a; Meg. 19b; Num. R. 19:6; Yeb. 62a; P. Peah. 15b. A perusal of these references will yield two very revolutionary ideas. One is that no heavenly voice can overrule the decision of a sage, for the Torah was given at Sinai and no other heavenly voice can supersede it. The revealed Torah means only that which the sage says it means. The second is that the Torah can be violated in order to enact takanot that will better serve the will of God.

[15]Neusner, Rabbinic Traditions I, 61-81.

[16]Ibid., p. 62. Cf. Sifra 55a. There we have a report on one of the three items recorded as testimony of Yosi b. Yoezer, that the liquids of the Temple slaughterhouse are pure, offered in the school of Akiba. Again, while the authority here, (R. Eliezer)

is post-1st cent., there is no reason to doubt that
when he cites Yosi he is citing a well-known historic
tradition.

[17]Ibid., p. 65.

[18]Ibid., p. 66.

[19]Ibid., p. 80.

[20]See B. Shab. 23a; B. Ber. 54a; San. 46a. For
an early study of this period and the methodology of
the proto-rabbis, see I. H. Weiss, Dor Dor Vedorshov
5 vols. (Wilna: Joseph Zawadzki, 1911), Vol. I. And
see II, 49-65 where Weiss offers ten principles by
which the sages were guided when they instituted
takanot and gezerot.

[21]Contrary to Deut. 4:2; 13:1. A beraita at
B. Yeb. 21a, reflects the tradition that Lev. 18:30
gives the sages the right to add injunctions to those
of the Torah. Thus they believed Lev. 18:30 gives
them the right to prohibit incest in a 2nd degree,
superseding Deut. 4:2. This was based upon the
premise of their exegesis of Deut. 17:11 which they
took to allow them to insist upon contemporary
authority. See New Dimensions, index entry
"Contemporary Authority." It is noteworthy that they
applied a statement addressed to priests (Lev. 18:30)
to themselves.

[22]Cf. the beraita of B. R. H. 25a-b, and how
first-century scholars are listed at B. San. 31b, 32b,
as examples of what the Torah means at Deut. 17:8-11
for one to take the decisions of the court of his time.
The Tosefta reference is found in Erfurt Ms. 2:3,
cited by Zuckermandel, p. 211 and Lieberman, p. 311f.,
B. Yeb. 21a.

[23]See Finkelstein, New Light and Gerhardsson,
Memory, on this in general. For older modern works on
the development of the Mishnah and the dating of early
rabbinic material see David Hoffman, Die erste
Mischna, Hamishnah Harishona (Hebrew), The First
Mishnah (English); C. Albeck, Untersuchungen über die
Redaktion der Mischna (Berlin: C. A. Schwetshke,
1923); Mavo La Mishnah (Hebrew)(Jerusalem: Mosad
Bialik, 1959); J. N. Epstein, Mavo Lenusah Hamishnah
(Hebrew) (Jerusalem: n.p., 1948); Zekhariah Frankel,
Darkhe Hamishnah; Louis Ginzberg, "The Mishnah Tamid"

Journal of Jewish Lore and Philosophy, pp. 33-44;
197-209; 265-295; A. Guttmann, "The Problem of the
Anonymous Mishnah" HUCA, 16 (1941), 137-155. See also
M. Schachter, TheBabylonian and Jerusalem Mishnah
Textually Compared (Jerusalem: Mosad Harav Kook,
1959).

[24]Cf. Mt. 23:34; Lk. 11:50. See also The Lives
of the Prophets, trans. C. C. Torrey (Philadelphia:
Society of Biblical Literature, 1946), p. 47. Both
Torrey and Douglas R. A. Hare, who has produced a new
edition of the Lives to be published in the
forthcomoing Doubleday edition of the Pseudepigrapha,
date this work to the first century.

[25]Rabbinic Traditions I, 72.

[26]Ibid., p. 80.

[27]In speaking of the transmission of oral
tradition, Daniel Patte writes, "Suffice it here to
say that modern critics often underestimate the
accuracy of the transmission of those traditions."
See his EarlyJewish Hermeneutic in Palestine SBL
Dissertation Series 22 (Missoula, Mont.: Scholars
Press, 1975) p. 13, and in general, especially his
chapter on Targum, pp. 49-86.

[28]New Light, pp. 26-29.

[29]Gen. R. 22:8; Ex. R. 30:17; P. Targ. to
Gen. 4:8.

[30]Geza Vermes, Post-Biblical Jewish Studies
(Leiden: E. J. Brill, 1975), p. 112. See in general
on this, Vermes, Scripture and Tradition in Judaism
(Leiden: E. J. Brill, 1961).

[31]This theme is more fully developed in my New
Dimensions, Chap. 5, but there it is not in any way
related to the halakhah of Jesus or to the identity of
Pharisaioi-perushim.

[32]The conjuction of nomos amd prophētai occurs
four times in Mt., at 5:17; 7:12; 11:13; 22:40. See
Sand Gesetz, 33-45; 183-193, for a recent discussion
of the phrase. Berger, Gesetzesauslegung, 209-226,
has an excursion on the phrase, where he rejects the
notion that nomos in these contexts refers to a
canonical division. I agree with Berger's formulation

that that phrase connotes the total tradition but supplement this with my conviction that it denotes the tradition in the light of the prophetic spirit. The only difficulty with this interpretation is at 11:13.

[33]I translate daȁt (usually taken as "knowledge" in the sense of intimate knowledge or "love") as at Gen. 4:1; 18:19; Ex. 2:25 etc.

[34]Gesetz, 125-167, sees the importance of the prophets in the interpretation of the nomos.

[35]Gesetz, 188-217.

[36]I am not unmindful of the arguments that critics offer for and against the reading hoi prophētai kai ho nomos at Mt. 11:13, but a decision on this is not relevant here since the evidence does not warrant departure from the text used for this dissertation. See Meier, Law and History, pp. 86f. Meier is burdened by his conviction that Mt. is making a "canonical" statement and therefore would be standing the canon on its head if he followed this order in the phrase.

[37]Ibid., p. 86, n. 98.

[38]I expand on the question of Elijah-Phineas in my Emergence, I, published in 1979. A selection of sources for the tradition: P. Targ. to Ex. 4:13; 6:18; Num. 25:12-13; Sifre Num. 131, among others. At times the references are allusive and oblique, and at times the result of exegesis, but quite pervasive in early and late sources. For example, Lev. R. 1:1 reflects a tradition that the angel at Judg. 2:1 refers to Phineas upon whom rested the holy spirit. See further on the Elijah-Phineas tradition my Emergence, I, Chap. 6, notes 104, 138. Michael Goulder, Midrash, fails to note these midrashic allusions in his discussion of Mt. 11:7-19, pp. 355-359. On the other hand, C. H. Dodd, According to the Scriptures (New York: Charles Scribner's Sons, 1953), p. 126, indicates that frequently a verse was quoted from scripture as a pointer to a whole context. One can take this further to suggest that a word, in this case, heshib with its double entendre, points to a whole context. Although Mal. 3:23 names Elijah as the eschatological figure, Mt. 17:10 refers to the "scribal" tradition that Elijah will herald the eschaton. This may reflect his awareness of a

post-Malakhi midrashic tradition of Phineas-Elijah,
which is now applied to John (17:12f.). On the basis
of what I have here said I reject the view of Meier
concerning Mt. 11:13, op. cit., pp. 165, 169 that the
"Law" is "prophetic" and "...pointed forward to the
life and teaching of Jesus...the Law, like prophecy,
had a prophetic task within a given period of
salvation-history." This is not what Matthew meant at
11:13 where he was very specific. Matthew Black, An
Aramaic Approach to the Gospels and Acts, 3rd ed.
(Oxford: Clarendon Press, 1967) did not call
attention to any Aramaic or targumic allusions at
Mt. 11:14.

[39]For Rab. see Abba Arekha, JE I; Herman Strack,
Introduction, p. 121.

[40]On the Virtues, 161; in speaking of a variety
of pentateuchal commandments, Philo writes, "With such
instructions he tamed and softened the minds of the
citizens. . . and set them out of reach of. . . evil
qualities. . . ." He goes on to say that it is vital
to live by this Revelation, "For as when the sun has
risen. . . and all things are filled with light, so
when God, the spiritual sun, rises and shines upon the
soul, the gloomy night of passions and vices is
scattered. . . ." (164). Again at 165 he says it is
all "to repress and destroy pride."

[41]One example is at B. Suk. 30a where we are told
one cannot discharge his obligation to carry the lulab
and etrog (palm branch and citron) at Sukot
worship-processionals if he has stolen them. See also
B. Ber. 47b; B. K. 94a; San. 6b.

[42]Sigal, New Dimensions. At p. 218f., n. 2, I
list twenty-two criteria by which the proto-rabbinic
and rabbinic scholars governed their halakhic
transactions. Under the rubric of the "humanitarian"
one might place kavod hamet, to do honor to the
deceased; mipnai tikun haolam, for the welfare of
society; mipnai shalom bayit, for domestic harmony;
mipnai darkei shalom, for the promotion of
peace,(M. Git. 4:2-7, 9; B. Git. 32-48; 59b). There
was also a tendency toward leniency in the
decision-making process. This criterion was expressed
in various ways, such as m'shoom agunah akiloo, they
were lenient in order to relieve a woman trapped in
marriage; or mekil beavelut, one is lenient in matters
related to bereavement (B. Git. 33a; Yeb. 114b; 122b;

M. K. 18a, Bekh. 49a etc.). See Section 4 below. Perhaps the most suggestive criterion was <u>ain gozrin gezerah sheain yakhol rov zibur laamod bah</u>, for which see the text and notes 44ff.

[43]See n. 42.

[44]Ishmael b. Elisha lived during the first and second centuries, perhaps ca. 60-140 and became the mentor of many rabbis in his own school; Strack, Introduction, p. 112; Herford, <u>Aboth</u>, p. 83. On the basis of a description of his personality the rule could have been stated by him, or if it is an older rule, reinforced by his teaching. See <u>JE</u> VI, 649.

[45]It is difficult at times to know which Simon b. Gamaliel is meant. Simon b. Gamaliel I was a leader in Jerusalem during the early part of the Judean revolt against Rome in 66; mentioned by Josephus, <u>Life</u> 38 (190); <u>War</u> IV, 3.9 (159). Simon b. Gamaliel II was a second-century rabbinic leader. Strack, pp. 110, 116; Cf. Herford, <u>Aboth</u>, p. 38. In the light of Simon b. Gamaliel II's consistent leniency in halakhic matters, as seen throughout the Talmud, he too could have been the author of it, or have reinforced his grandfather's principle.

[46]Eleazer b. Zadok is another who is difficult to date since there were two by that name. Eleazer b. Zadok I was a first-second century scholar and had a grandson of the same name who was active during the latter half of the 2nd century; Strack, pp. 112, 115.

[47]This principle affected much halakhah. See B. B. K. 79b; B. B. 60b; Hor. 3b. M. Git. 4:2-7, 9; B. Git. 32-48.

[48]Joshua (b. Hananiah) was a first-second century scholar of the circle of Yoḥanan b. Zakkai; at M. Ab. 2:16 he teaches that "hatred of people" is an evil that "drives one from the world," and thereby reflected his pacifistic views which led him to be a peace-party leader and at constant odds with Gamaliel II. See Herford, <u>Aboth</u>, pp. 57f.; Strack, p. 111.

[49]Sukah is the hut set up as a temporary dwelling for use during the festival of Sukot in accordance with Lev. 23:42.

[50]M. Suk. 2:7; Bez. 1:5; Hag. 1:2.

[51]The source cited relates to Gamaliel I. But this only means that the specific burial halakhot are early first century. The formula upon which revision was based reflects an even earlier condition.

[52]Salo Baron, A Social and Religious History of the Jews 16 vols. (New York: Jewish Publication Society, 1952-76) II, 288. Cf. T. Nid., 9:17. See Louis Ginzberg, A Commentary on the Palestine Talmud (New York: KTAV, 1971) III, 63ff.; P. Ber. 6a.

[53]M. Demai 3:1 states the poor may eat food suspected of being untithed. M. Shab. 18:1 indicates one may clear away such grain on the Sabbath to make room for visitors. Since it is permitted to the poor it is not considered to be an unusable article which is forbidden on the Sabbath. Cf. B. Shab. 127b recording a beraita in which a difference of opinion between the Bet Shammai and Bet Hillel on whether the poor may eat demai, is expressed, again providing an early date. Cf. B. Pes. 35b; Suk. 35b; Ber. 47a; Er. 17b; 31a.

[54]Test. Jud. 26:3, "let no one bury me in costly apparel." The translation is by R. H. Charles, Apocrypha and Pseudepigrapha 2 vols. (Oxford: Clarendon Press, 1908). It is true that the words "in costly apparel" are not found in the Armenian version, but are in the Greek and Slavonic Mss. See The Greek Versions of the Testaments of the Twelve Patriarchs, ed. R. H. Charles, (Oxford: Clarendon Press, 1908), p. xvi, where Charles concludes that the main weakness of the Armenian is that it omits words and phrases too frequently.

[55]See also M. Ber. 4:4; B. Ber. 29b; P. Ber. 36. Simon b. Nathanel was a first-century scholar of the circle of Yohanan b. Zakkai, a son-in-law of Gamaliel I. See T. A. Z. 3:10.

[56]Eliezer b. Hyrcanus was a leading 1st-2nd century scholar of the circle of Yohanan b. Zakkai. At B. B. M. 59b and P. M. K. 81d it appears he was excommunicated for denying the authority of the majority opinion over that of an individual. For a current study of Eliezer based upon form-criticism see J. Neusner, Eliezer Ben Hyrcanus 2 vols. (Leiden: E. J. Brill, 1973).

[57] Cf. B. Ber. 29b, P. Ber. 30.

[58] Mekh. to Ex. 31:14, ed. Lauterbach, III, 198f.; B. B. K. 9ab.

[59] B. San. 74a; Cf. B. Pes. 25a; Yom. 82a.

[60] See Chap. 2, n. 20 for literature on the Ezra-Nehemiah question.

[61] Jer. 29:4-23. "Seek the welfare of the city whither I have exiled you" (v. 7), implies obedience to the requirements of law and social order.

[62] B. Git. 10b; B. K. 113ab; Ned. 28a; B. B. 54b, 55a. I reject the notion expressed by Leo Landman, Jewish Law and the Diaspora (Philadelphia: Jewish Publication Society, 1968), p. 24, that Samuel originated the rule as "a modus vivendi for the Jew." See also Isaac Herzog, The Main Institutions of JewishLaw 2 vols. (2nd ed. London: Soncino Press, 1967), pp. 24-32. This modus vivendi was needed far earlier and explains Jeremiah's letter. Jeremiah applied Sam. 10:25 which teaches that the valid law of the state is binding, as obligatory to any state's law. That is, it is a function of "royal prerogative." (Herzog, p. 26). This was needed in Palestine as well where Persian and Graeco-Roman laws were in effect. Jewish "autonomy" in those periods when the occupying power allowed Judaic religious practice to function freely as the law of the province, was not based one-hundred percent upon Jewish halakhah alone. The autonomy meant only that the extant Judaic law was operative, not that the State could not impose its own law as well. This is clear from Ezra 7:26 where the king imposes both his law and the Torah's. Furthermore, Landman, pp. 124, 207, n. 1, and Chap. 10 and notes in general, following Herzog, p. 26f., argues that the principle d.d.d. applied only to civil law and not to ritual. It is true that our present state of research only yields talmudic examples of d.d.d. applied to civil cases, but the silence of the Talmud is not to be taken as a limitation upon its function. The fact is that post-talmudic scholars understood it as having universal application. In any event the N.T. episode is one of civil law. See my discussion of this in New Dimensions, pp. 89-92. Furthermore, far from militating against high antiquity, the fact that the principle is never

questioned and is simply cited by Samuel as a well-known concept implies that it was of long-standing validity. The principle is never cited in the Palestinian Talmud because in Palestine the authorities would not concede that the law of the conquerer is valid. Although they followed the law of the sovereign power they would not embody its validity in the halakhah. This makes the Jesus episode even more interesting.

[63]See Schürer, History, ed. Vermes, I, 357-398; sacrifices were offered daily on behalf of Caesar and the Romans (p. 379f.). Cf. Josephus, Ag. Ap. II, 6 (77); War II, 10.4 (197) 17, 2 (409f.); 17, 3 (412-417). Josephus reflects the accomodation made by Judaic authorities over the centuries against opposition within Judaism.

[64]See J. Duncan M. Derrett, Law in the New Testament (London: Darton, Longman and Todd, 1970) pp. 313-338.

[65]Ibid.

[66]This is the meaning of the Hebrew lo takir panim, "do not recognize a face (person)" when adjudicating a case, at Deut. 16:19; cf. Lev. 19:15.

[67]David Daube, "Rabbinic Methods of Interpretation and Hellenistic Rhetoric," HUCA, 22 (1949), 239-264. However, while Daube, p. 240 dates the adoption of the hellenistic methods to about 100-25 B.C. some of the hermeneutical rules were used considerably earlier.

[68]The kal vehomer was indigenous, present already within the Old Testament and in the Apocrypha. See Louis Jacobs, "The Qal Va-Homer Argument," BSOAS, 35(1972). An example of kal vehomer used by Moses is given at Ab. de R. N. A, 2, p. 9f. cf. Ex. 6:12; Deut. 31:27; Ab. de R. N. B, 44 lists five kal vehomer examples in the Pentateuch. Cf. Ben Sira 10:31.

[69]The School of St. Matthew.

[70]The Use of the Old Testament in St. Matthew's Gospel (Leiden: E. J. Brill, 1967).

[71]Ibid., pp. 205-215.

[72]Richard N. Longenecker, Biblical Exegesis in the Apostolic Period (n.p. William B. Eerdman's Publishing Co., 1975), p. 28. This book has a useful bibliography, pp. 221-230.

[73]B. Ber. 28a; B. Yeb. 69a, 76b; Kid. 67b; Ket. 7b; Ḥul. 62b.

[74]Op. cit., pp. 28f.

[75]Ibid.

[76]Ibid.

[77]The seven middot, or hermeneutical canons, are listed also in the Introduction to Sifra on Leviticus, and at T. San. 7:11, sometimes with variations. See Doeve, Jewish Hermeneutics, pp. 65-74; Strack, Introduction, pp. 93ff.

[78]At Prov. 23:20 sovẻi is defined by wine and zolel by meat.

[79]See F. F. Bruce, Biblical Exegesis in the Qumran Texts (London: Tyndale; Grand Rapids, Mich.: Wm. B. Eerdmans, 1960); R. Loewe, "The 'Plain' Meaning of Scripture in Early Jewish Exegesis," PIJSL I, ed. J. G. Weiss (Jerusalem: Hebrew University, 1964) 140-185; S. G. Sowers, The Hermeneutics of Philo and Hebrews (Richmond, Va.: John Knox, 1965); G. Vermes, Scripture and Tradition in Judaism; Daniel Patte, Early Jewish Hermeneutic in Palestine; R. Williamson, Philo and the Epistle to the Hebrews (Leiden: E. J. Brill, 1970).

[80]Jacob Z. Lauterbach, "Peshat," JE IX, 653.

[81]See Chapters 4 and 5 below.

[82]Op. cit. See also Sowers, op. cit.

[83]Op. cit., pp. 172ff.

[84]Op. cit., pp. 66-70.

[85]p. 69.

[86]Bornkamm, Barth and Held, Tradition, pp. 31, 35, 79f., 81ff., 91f.; Barth, p. 92, n. 2 fails to perceive this although he recognizes that the Qumran

halakhah was stricter. See further on the entire Sabbath pericope in Chap. 5.

[87]Op. cit., pp. 106f.

[88]It appears Ãkiba was Nahum's disciple for twenty-two years, Gen. R. 1:14. Ãkiba was even more ingenious according to B. Men. 29b. Cf. Daube, op. cit., p. 241, n. 7.

[89]Cf. T. Pes. 4:1, B. Pes. 66a. See Lieberman, Hellenism, pp. 60f.

[90]At Sifra 22b this rule is attributed to zekenim harishonim, "the early elders." It is rule 5 of Hillel's rules at T. San. 7:11, and of R. Ishmael's at Sifra, 1a. On the rule's antiquity see also Lauterbach, Rabbinic Essays, pp. 221f.

[91]Tannaitic midrash to Lev. See the edition of J. H. Weiss, (Vienna: Schlossberg, 1861 rpt. New York: OM, 1946), p. 2.

[92]Finkelstein, New Light will help cast some light on how there was a free flow from Deuteronomic halakhah to the first century. Finkelstein has also shown how our extant texts incorporate older material which had once been the source for texts developed in the two post-70 schools of Ãkiba and Ishmael: "The Sources of the Tannaitic Midrashim" JQR, 31 (1941), 211-243.

[93]See The Zadokite Documents, ed. Chaim Rabin (Oxford: Clarendon Press, 1954), p. 19 (Hebrew text), p. 18 (Eng.).

[94]See p. 19, n. 2 to line 9. But I do not think, as Rabin does, that the issue here is merely euphemism. The issue here is probably the use of a different version of the Torah. True the Mishnah denounces one who "uses a euphemism," but refers to using the text which cites the rule in a euphemistic manner.

[95]Michael Fishbane, "The Qumran Pesher and Traits of Ancient Hermeneutics," Proceedings of the Sixth World Congress of Jewish Studies (Jerusalem: Magnes Press, 1977).

[96]Jewish Hermeneutics, pp. 92f.

[97]Doeve refers to Rengstorf's article "didaskō," The Theological Dictionary of the New Testament, 10 vols., ed. Gerhard Kittel, trans. Geoffrey W. Bromiley (Grand Rapids, Mich.: Wm. B. Eerdmans, 1964-1976) II, 135-165.

[98]Ibid., p. 140.

[99]Ibid., p. 142.

[100]See Chap. 1 on the presuppositions which are obstacles to the correct understanding of the relationship between Jesus and the New Testament on the one hand, and rabbinic Judaism on the other.

[101]The same passage is also found at B. Kid. 40b with some textual variations, but none of substance. Cf. B. B. K. 17a, Meg. 27a, P. Pes. 30b, Hag. 76c, for halakhic illustrations where study is given halakhic advantage because it leads to practice. Exemplary conduct is always the goal.

[102]See Chap. 2 above for my discussion of the arrangement of Chap. 1 of Abot and the identification of Simon at 1:17 as the son of Hillel and not of Gamaliel I.

[103]Unfortunately Doeve, p. 94, also misapplies some sources. He sees B. Hag. 14a, San. 38b, where Akiba's agadic views are resisted and he is told to attend to complex halakhah, as indicating "some rabbis concerned themselves only with halakhah, like Akiba for instance," utterly overlooking the fact that Akiba engaged with some degree of expertise in mysticism and esoteric speculation, and is famous as one of the four who delved deeply into esoteric subjects, and alone emerged unscathed. Cf. B. Hag. 14b; Mekh. ed. Laut. I, 108 where Akiba offers an esoteric interpretation for a place-name. Doeve, pp. 94f., is also misreading the halakhic literature when he states that halakhah countenanced divergent opinions, "but not divergent practice," and compounds this misreading at p. 95, n. 1 with the statement that although "dissentient views regarding the halakhah are transmitted. . . no doubt is allowed to subsist as to how the practice should be." A cursory reading of any tractate of the Mishnah would provide prolific refutation of this notion.

[104]See references at n. 20 above.

[105]See for instance L. Goppelt, <u>Typos. Die Typologische Deutung des Alten Testaments im Neuen</u> (Darmstadt: Wissenschaftliche Buchgesellschaft, 1969), pp. 68f.

[106]Op. cit., p. 207.

[107]There were two ways of reckoning the night-span: according to three watches, which meant each watch was four hours; according to four watches, each composed of three hours. Depending upon how the night was reckoned when this view was stated by R. Eliezer, the latest permissible time for reciting the evening Shemá was either 9 or 10 p.m.

[108]Chap. 2, above.

[109]For a historical discussion of this era, see Victor Tcherikover, <u>Hellenistic Civilization and theJews</u>, trans. S. Applebaum (Philadelphia: Jewish Publication Society, 1969) pp. 80-89. Tcherikover, p. 437, n. 112, accepts the second Simon, called "the Just" as the one of M. Ab., ca. 200 B.C.

[110]See Chap. 2 above for the discussion of the list of sages of M. Ab. 1. It is evident from Ab. de R. N. A, 5 that Antigonus was a teacher who upset the traditionalists in his classes so that some are reported to have dissented and organized new groupings.

[111]That something very revolutionary happened in the time of Yosi b. Yoezer, and involved him, is clear from M. Sot. 9:9 which reports that when the two Yosis died the <u>eshkolot</u> ("clusters") ceased. This term refers to them as men of great scholarship. Cf. B. Sot. 47b; Tem. 15b, 16a. It is extremely uncertain as to what this statement meant precisely, but apparently later sages perceived that a watershed had occurred. See also T. B. K. 8:13. Alexander Guttmann, <u>Rabbinic Judaism</u> discusses these puzzling passages (except for T. B. K.) and cites S. Krauss (p. 33) to the effect that <u>eshkalot</u> is related to the Greek <u>skholē</u>, a school, and therefore signifies "schools of thought." The meaning of the statement at M. Sot. 9:9 would then be that, after the Yosis died, the <u>eshkolot</u> system of the pre-Maccabee era came to an end; and what they had introduced became a new trend, namely the tolerant accomodation between leniency and

206

stringency.

112Chap. 5 below.

113On the whole question of the development of the mishnah-form of halakhah and its replacement of the midrash-form of exposition, see Lauterbach, "Midrash and Mishnah," in Rabbinic Essays, especially p. 188, n. 32; pp. 213-224.

114In his discussion, ibid., Lauterbach, failed to note that zekenim harishonim, "the early sages" at Sifra 22b might be a reference to Yosi himself. It is common in tannaitic literature for a plural term to conceal the identity of an individual. Thus often hakhamim, "sages," refer to one scholar. Sifra, some generations later, is corroborating Yosi's halakhic position and attributes it to "early elders" (i.e., Yosi).

115This is explicated at Sifra 22b, in a comment to Lev. 5:2: "If anyone touches any impure thing, the carcass of an impure beast, or the carcass of an unclean animal, or the carcass of an unclean insect. . . ." The kelal or general principle is expressed in "any impure thing," and the delimiting perat in the particulars enumerated. Impurity is then contracted only by touching that which partakes of the same quality as the particulars specified, namely, by touching a "father of impurity," that is, an original or primary source of impurity, a carcass.

116"Studies in Tannaitic Jurisprudence," Journal of Jewish Lore, I (1919), 297-311. This is now also accessible in Solomon Zeitlin, Studies in the Early History of Judaism (New York: KTAV, 1978), IV, 57-71. At n. 4 Zeitlin indicates that the famous first-second century Roman schools of Sabineans and Proculians, were actually founded by Ateius Capito and Antistius Labeo during the period of Augustus. This would be only one more affinity between Roman jurisprudence and the directions taken in proto-rabbinic halakhic evolution. See Boaz Cohen, Jewish and Roman Law (New York: Jewish Theological Seminary, 1966), I, 15; Saul Lieberman, "Roman Legal Institutions in Early Rabbinics and in the Acta Martyrum" JQR, 35 (1944), 1-57.

117See a recent analysis of this material by Alexander Guttmann, Rabbinic Judaism, pp. 59-124, where all the relevant primary sources are catalogued.

[118]B. Ber. 60a; Bez. 2b; Kid. 60b; Git. 41b; 74b; Nid. 59b.

[119]See n. 118.

[120]I am reading Mt. 15:10-20 as an episode separate from that of 15:1-9. As a matter of fact the text may here be redacted to combine two separate units. 15:20 is a proper closing for the first unit.

[121]Op. cit., p. 150. See his n. 62, p. 151 for an extensive bibliography on the fourth antithesis (oaths).

[122]Ibid., p. 152. Meier also cites Ex. 22:6-7 but unlike 5:10 there is no explicit evidence there that an oath is to be taken.

[123]Ibid.

[124]See above.

[125]See on this, S. Lieberman, Greek, pp. 115-143. Meier is innocent of any reference to Lieberman's work in his entire monograph.

[126]Ibid., p. 137.

[127]Meier, p. 156, and n. 74. It is not germane here to analyze Mt. 23. But it is clear that in the seven "Alas" passages the attack is made on "scribes and pharisees" six times. Once it is made against "blind guides" (23:16). (At vv. 24, 26, the term blind guide is secondary to Pharisee.)

[128]Op. cit., p. 134f.

[129]The following are a selection of Talmudic sources for the principle of lifnim: B. B. M. 24b; 30b; 81a; 88a; Ber. 7a; 45b; Ket. 97a; B. K. 99b. The principle of lifnim is supplemented by the category, midat hasidut, an act done out of piety beyond the requirement of the halakhah, as at B. B. M. 51b-52a, 52b; M. Shab. 16:3; B. Shab. 120a; Hul. 130b.

[130]Boaz Cohen, Jewish and Roman Law, pp. 46-52.

[131]Op. cit., p. 165.

132Saul J. Berman, "Lifnim Mishurat Hadin," JJS, 26 (1975), 86-104; 28 (1977), 181-193. See 28, pp. 186f.

133Mekh. III, 182.

134See Berman's discussion of whether to tranlate the term lifnim "within" or "beyond," op. cit., pp. 26, 86f.

135Josephus, Ant. XX. 10.5 (251).

136Examples of Sadducean halakhah are easily accessible in J. Newman, Halakhic Sources (Leiden: E. J. Brill, 1969) pp. 76ff.

137See for example the analysis of Morton Smith, Tannaitic Parallels to the Gospels (Philadelphia: Society of Biblical Literature, 1951) especially pp. 122-124; Finkelstein, Sources, p. 241.

138E.g., M. Ed. 7:3. This diversity exhibited throughout Eduyot contradicts the spirit in which Eliezer b. Hyrcanus was excommunicated (n. 56 above). The excommunication further reflects the autocracy with which Gamaliel II directed his administration at Yaḅneh. In contrast with Gamaliel II's attitude post-80, we find the discussion of an incident involving Akabya b. Mahalalel to which I refer in the text. See also   n. 139.

139Herford, Aḅ. p. 64, dates Akabya very early for a variety of sound reasons. Frankel, Darkhe haMishnah, pp. 56f. also adduces several arguments to date him as a younger contemporary of Hillel. This makes of him a contemporary of Jesus. See also Weiss, Dor, I, 166.

140The title Aḅ Bet Din occurs at M. Ḥag. 2:2; Ed. 5:6; P. Ber. 7d; Taan. 67d; each time, and in other references, it signifies second in authority. See the discussion of the problems attendant upon this office by Hugo Mantel, Studies in the History of the Sanhedrin, 104-118, for the period prior to 70.

141See Schachter, Babylonian and Jerusalem Mishnah, p. 295 where he cites the reading of the Babylonian Mishnah text for the word used by Akabya as duḡmá and the Palestinian text as dikmah. But both terms convey the same meaning, that Akabya ruled in the case of one "like himself." See P. M. K. 81d; Jastrow I, 307. This is contra Mantel, op. cit. p. 115 who rejects the theory that Akabya was excommunicated for insulting sages, but he does not convincingly expound the text.

[142]Frankel, Darkhe haMishnah, 37; B. Git. 57b; San. 96b. Herford, Aboth, p. 31 cites B. Pes. 70b where Shemáyah and ʿAbtalyon are called "great expositors" and correctly says this is not proof against their being proselytes, pointing to the obscure origin of Akiba and Meier. But he fails to cite the reinforcing Git. and San. passages. These show that the beraitá tradition that Shemáyah and Abtalyon were proselytes is given with a sense of pride that such miracles can occur. Pes. 70b is in accord with this notion. There Judah b. Durtai and his son separate themselves from the Jerusalem cult because they believed there was an inadequacy in the rites when the festival offering was omitted on the Sabbath, and were astonished that Shemáyah and Abtalyon never taught what to them was the correct view, that a festival sacrifice, like the paschal offering, supersedes the Sabbath. Judah and his son are described as perushim after the act of separation. They are examples of separatists who followed neither the proto-rabbis nor the Jerusalem priestly Establishment. They are also examples of halakhic dissenters who were not excommunicated. Neusner, Rabbinic Tradition III, 256, is at a loss to explain the Judah b. Durtai story. But I believe that the Judah b. Durtai passage is a significant relic of an old tradition that preserves the varying attitudes towards the cult in Jerusalem. Qumran and Essenes rejected the cult. Some Jerusalemites who were not perushim to begin with, and thus accepted the cult, became perushim when certain proto-rabbinic halakhic views gained ascendancy in Jerusalem and subsequently rejected the cult. Judah and his son are examples of this. It is further evidence that perushim were not the proto-rabbis, even if proto-rabbis occasionally were pietists in matters of semi-ascetic abstention and purity practices.

[143]Arndt-Gingrich, Lexicon, pp. 465, h, and 778, on lambanō and poieō, suggests that both symboulion elabon (Mt. 12:14) and symboulion epoioun (Mk. 3:6) can share the meaning of "deliberating," "holding a consultation."

[144]The messianic idea of Qumran is confusing and too complex to enter into here. The Essenes appear not to have had one. It is safe to say that a broad spectrum of the populace of pietistic Jews would look to a Davidic figure. See the "Midrash on the Last Days" in Geza Vermes, The Dead Sea Scrolls in English, 2nd ed. (England: Penguin Books, 1975) 245-246, for a belief in a Davidic messiah at Qumran.

[145]Gesenius Lexicon, trans. S. P. Tregelles, pp. 305f.; Jastrow, pp. 503f. Matthew Black, An Aramaic Approach to the Gospels and Acts, does not discuss this verse.

[146]See the discussion by David Daube, The New Testament and Rabbinic Judaism pp. 55-62. Daube, however, makes no mention of the sources I have cited, and discusses an entirely different rabbinic expression. Strack-Billerbeck op. cit. do not discuss the phrase egō de legō, although they discuss the term "amen" at length, I, 242ff. See also Smith, Tannaitic Parallels, 27-30.

[147]See for example, Plato, Apology, ed. John Burnet (Oxford: Clarendon Press, 1924) p. 22a, line 2.

[148]E. Stauffer, "egō," in T.W.N.T. II, 345f.; in the English Version, T.D.N.T. II, 348. Even if Jesus pioneered the use of egō legō to contradict earlier teaching it came to be used by rabbis, as e.g., by R. Judah haNasi who uses the Hebrew equivalent of ōmer ânee at B. B. B. 124a to contradict T. Bekh. 6:15 on whether a firstborn receives a double inheritance from profit accruing from the estate after the death of a father. The Tosefta rejects the notion; R. Judah insists that the firstborn receives the double portion.

[149]M. Kil. 2:2; P. Kil. 27d indicates beêmet signifies a halakhah of high antiquity and of great authority, "a halakhah of Moses from Sinai." The use of amen and beêmet in their context is undoubtedly similar. Jesus uses amen to suggest alternative halakhah and designate this as the equal of Sinaitic halakhah. Cf. M. Ter. 2:1, P. Ter. 41a; M. Shab. 10:4, P. Shab. 12c.

211

IV. Notes

[1] The literature on the divorce texts was summarized by U. Holzmeister, "Die Streitfrage über Ehescheidungstexte bei Matthäus 5:32, 19:9," Biblica, 26 (1945), 133-146; and again by Bruce Vawter, "The Divorce Clauses in Mt. 5:32 and 19:9," CBQ, 16 (1954), 155-167. Since then there have been many articles and monographs which are listed throughout the notes and in the bibliography, e.g., a more recent one, A. Sand, "Die Unzuchtsklausel in Mt. 5:31-32 und 19:3-9," MTZ, 20 (1969), 118-129.

[2] R. Bultmann, The History of the Synoptic Tradition, pp. 135f.

[3] J. Jeremias, New Testament Theology, trans. John Bowden (New York: Scribner, 1971), I, 251ff.

[4] J. Suggs, Wisdom, Christology and Law in Matthew's Gospel (Cambridge, Mass.: Harvard University Press, 1970), pp. 110-115.

[5] R. Guelich, "The Antitheses of Mt. 5:21-48: Traditional and/or Redactional?" NTS, 22 (1976), pp. 444-457. See p. 445ff.

[6] Law and History, pp. 125-161. He discusses the divorce pericope at 140-150, and provides extensive bibliography at n. 38.

[7] Jesus and the Law, pp. 146-159, 182f., 191-193.

[8] The Pharisees, p. 164.

[9] The purported citation from Deut. 24:1 is not precise, neither according to the Masoretic text nor the Greek Bible Deut. 24:3. It is either the author's own paraphrase based upon another Hebrew text current at that time, or upon a Greek paraphrase of the text. See Robert Gundry, The Use of the Old Testament, p. 108; Stendahl, School, p. 137. Both Gundry and Stendahl regard the "quotation" as an allusion.

[10] The Greek New Testament, ed. Kurt Aland, Matthew Black, Bruce Metzger, Allen Wikgren (Stuttgart: Württemberg Bible Society, 1966). See also Strack-Billerbeck, Kommentar I, 303-321, 501-805, for the divorce periocopae.

[11]Eighth century Ms., Regius, at Paris, identified as L 019 in the Aland apparatus (p. xiv).

[12]Sixth century Ms., Bezae Cantabrigiensis, at Cambridge is identified as D 05 ibid., p. xiii.

[13]See Bruce M. Metzger, A Textual Commentary on the Greek New Testament (n.p.: United Bible Societies, 1971), pp. 13f.

[14]The word porneia is left untranslated at this juncture pending a discussion of its meaning below. See n. 16.

[15]The word autēn is regarded as having "dubious textual validity." See Metzger, p. 47.

[16]The Aland apparatus suggests here that there is "some degree of doubt" concerning the form of the exceptive clause, but although Metzger, p. 47 indicates there is "a considerable degree of doubt," nonetheless he concludes that the variant readings which are the same as 5:32 were assimilated to the latter. The form of the exceptive clause of 5:32 is found in Ms. B 03, the fourth century Vaticanus, and D 05, 6th cent. Bezae Cantabrigiensis, and other ancient witnesses.

[17]Variant readings for the end of the verse are also adjudged by Metzger (p. 48) to be influenced by 5:32. We retain the Aland text.

[18]See the Biblia Hebraica, ed. Rudolf Kittel and P. Kahle (Stuttgart: American Bible Society, 1952). The one correction suggested is innocuous.

[19]See Gerhard Von Rad, Deuteronomy A Commentary (Philadelphia: The Westminster Press, 1966), pp. 150f.; S. R. Driver, Deuteronomy A Critical and Exegetical Commentary, International Critical Commentary (New York: Charles Scribner's Sons, 1895), pp. 269f.

[20]As in the case of porneia, at this juncture these words are left untranslated.

[21]v. 4 represents the halakhah here provided for the series of events described at 1-3. Vv. 1-3 neither suggest nor command any activity. They merely describe what people have done and reflect probably

extant halakhah in pre-exilic Israel.

[22]See J. W. Wenham, Christ and the Bible (Downers Grove, Ill.: Intervarsity Press, 1973), p. 33f.

[23]Arndt-Gingrich, p. 119. Cf. Gen. 34:7 and all of Lev. 18 where the term has the signification of sexual immorality, whether rape, adultery or incest. It must be recognized that some forms of incest automatically include adultery, as for instance when one commits incest with the wife of a father, brother, son, etc. But not all cases of incest are adultery, e.g., if one commits incest with an unmarried aunt or sister.

[24]Jesus and the Law, pp. 146-159.

[25]Life, 2 (11).

[26]Ibid. (11-12).

[27]This arithmetic is based on the view that he was born before the year 1 and was crucified around 30. The details are not indispensible to our purpose and are therefore glossed over here.

[28]"Judea which is on the far side of the Jordan" at 19:1 is the area called Peraea.

[29]That the Torah was read every Sabbath in the pre-Christian period is attested by Lk. 4:16; Acts 13:15; 15:21. That Josephus understood it as an ancient custom is evident from Ag. Ap. II, 17 (175) where he attributes it to Moses. Cf. Ant. XVI, 2.4 (43). P. Meg. 75a attributes to Moses the reading of the Torah on Sabbath mornings, Festivals, New Moons and the Intermediate Days of Pesah and Sukot; and to Ezra the Torah reading on Sabbath afternoons, Monday and Thursday mornings. Philo, On Dreams II, 18 (127) reflects the Sabbath custom; cf. On Creation 43 (128); Spec. Laws II, 15 (62f.). At Mekh. to Ex. 15:22, II, 90 the Sabbath afternoon, Monday and Thursday readings are attributed to even greater antiquity than the era of Ezra, to that of the prophets. See Adolf Büchler, "The Reading of the Law and Prophets in a Triennial Cycle" JQR, 5 (1893), now conveniently available in Contributions to the Scientific Study of Jewish Litergy, ed. Jacob Petuchowski (New York: KTAV, 1970), 181-302.

30See Roger Le Déaut, "Targumic Literature and N. T. Interpretation," Biblical Theology Bulletin IV, (1974), 243-289; Daube, The New Testament, pp. 74, 368.

31See Chap. 3 on lifnim meshurat hadin. I will discuss the Qumran attitude toward divorce and polygamy below.

32Samuel Holdheim, Maamar Haishut (Hebrew) (Berlin: n.p., 1890), p. 28; Hummel, Die Auseinandersetzung, pp. 49-51; H. Merkel, "Jesus und der Pharisaer," NTS, 14 (1968), 194-208; p. 207.

33Similarly C. G. Montefiore, Synoptic Gospels I, 236; II, 689, also places the discussion within the parameters of a Hillel-Shammai debate, and thereby misses essential nuances in the controversy.

34Op. cit., p. 122f.

35D. R. Catchpole, "The Synoptic Divorce Material as a Traditio-Historical Problem," BJRL, 57 (1957), 92-127.

36A. Isaksson, Marriage and Ministry, pp. 27-34.

37T. V. Fleming, "Christ and Divorce," Theological Studies, 24 (1963), 106-120; p. 109.

38This dissertation, in basing itself upon the Aland text, does not concern itself with the problem of whether the exceptive clauses are original or Matthean redactions. T. W. Manson, Teachings, p. 200, n. 5, assumes that it is "as certain as anything can be in N. T. criticism" that there were no exceptions in the original teaching of Jesus. This implies that the Marcan and Lucan versions are more authentic and that Mark has priority over Mt. But I take the view that Matthew has priority, as do A. Schlatter, Der Evangelist Matthäus (Stuttgart: Caliver, 1948), p. 572; and more recently, A. Isaksson, op. cit., pp. 75-92. So too B. Vawter, op. cit., p. 165, concludes that Mt. 19:9 is the original version of Jesus' logion.

39Fleming, op. cit., p. 112.

40This is how Mt. 5:32 is taken by J. A. Fitzmyer, "The Matthew Divorce Texts and Some

New Palestinian Evidence," Theological Studies, 37 (1976), 197-226; p. 207.

[41]Ibid., p. 226.

[42]See D. F. Hauck and S. Schulz, "Pornē," TWNT VII, 579-595; Arndt-Gingrich, p. 699.

[43]Michael Goulder, Midrash and Lection, p. 291.

[44]Calvin long ago interpreted porneia as adultery. See A Harmony of the Gospels Mt. Mk. and Lk., trans.T. H. L. Parker (Grand Rapids, Mich.: Wm. B. Eerdmans, 1972), II, 246.

[45]"A Catholic View on Divorce," JES, 6 (1969), 53-67; p. 58, n. 22.

[46]The Masoretic Text reads vaēre̊, but Mss. provide evidence for vaterē̊, "she saw," the antecedent being Judah.

[47]Jerusalem Bible.

[48]Translation of Greek Bible, The Septuagint Version of the Old Testament and Apocrypha (London: Samuel Bagster and Sons, n.d.)

[49]The New Oxford Annotated Bible.

[50]Op. cit., 207, n. 39.

[51]Ibid., pp. 208-211.

[52]Test. Reub. 3:15 informs us Jacob never had sexual relations with Bilhah after Reuben's act of adultery with her. At Ben Sira 23:23 the faithless wife commits moikheia through an act of porneia. In other words, a wife's fornication is adultery and that is what we have at Mt. 5:32; 19:9. In reference to this, Banks, p. 154 reads into M. Sot. 5:1; Yeb. 2:8 the uncertain inference that under so-called "Jewish law" one would be "compelled" to divorce an adulterous wife. One cannot have sexual relations but one need not divorce.

[53]Freely rendered, the three clauses of the Mishnah are as follows: a) Bet Shammai says: a man should not divorce his wife except if he found in her some grossly indecent matter (basing the meaning of

érvat dabar on Deut. 23:15.). b) Bet Hillel says even if he only found something indecorous, such as her burning his food. c) R. Akiba says even if he found someone prettier, for the verse (Deut. 24:1) reads, "if she does not find favor in his eyes."

[54]R. C. H. Lenski, Interpretations of St. Matthew's Gospel (Columbus, Ohio: Wartburg Press, 1943), p. 232ff., pp. 732f.

[55]Jesus and the Law, p. 192, n. 1.

[56]Kilpatrick, Origins, pp. 59-60 argues for the lectionary purpose of the Gospel of Matthew. It is necessary to accept neither the rhetoric nor all the particulars of Goulder's argument concerning the Sermon on the Mount, Midrash and Lection, pp. 250-311 in order to agree with the probability that 5:31-32 represent a summary of a discourse presented for convenient lection or catechetical use by Matthew. For example, I do not agree with Goulder (p. 290), that "the main architecture of the sermon" derives "from the Marcan record of the teaching of Jesus" since I believe Mk. is later than Mt. But this does not negate the possibility that Mt. 5:31-32 is related to a discourse, if not as Goulder thinks, from Ex. 20-23, then from Deut. 24:1-4. Although, again, Goulder (p. 291), is correct that Mt. 19:3 appears to place Jesus into the framework of the Bet Hillel-Bet Shammai debate, he overlooks the obvious point that Jesus agrees with neither.

[57]Op. cit., p. 193.

[58]Ibid.

[59]Op. cit., p. 150.

[60]M. Sot. 9:9 mentions Yohanan b. Zakkai as one abrogator, and 9:10 provides the name of Yohanan Kohen Gadol, an enigmatic personality. But while there is much divergence of opinion as to who he was, and therefore when he lived, all views have him pre-Christian. Yohanan b. Zakkai, it will be remembered, was a contemporary of Jesus. Not relevant to this dissertation, but I believe worthy of mention for future research, is my conjecture that Jesus was a colleague-disciple of Yohanan's in Galilee sometime during 20-30 A.D.

[61]_Ant._ IV, 8. 23 (253). At _Ant._ XV.7.10 (259), Josephus errs concerning the halakhah of divorce, stating that a divorced woman requires her husband's consent to remarry.

[62]Stendahl, _The School_, p. 137; Gundry, _The Use of the O.T._, pp. 37f.

[63]Gundry, ibid.

[64]I. Schmid, _Das Evangelium nach Matthäus_ (Regensburg: Pustet, 1965), p. 104.

[65]"Die Unzuchtsklausel," pp. 125ff.

[66]M. Kid. 2:7; B. Yeb. 10b, 44b; 52b; 69a, 92b; Ket. 29b; Kid, 64a, 67b, 68a; Sot. 18b; San. 53a; Tem. 29b.

[67]"The Synoptic Divorce Material," p. 127.

[68]See also on this W. D. Davies, _The Setting_, p. 104f. where he calls Matthew's treatment of the divorce halakhah a "radical departure." Where I disagree with Davies is in his equating Jesus' halakhah with that of "Shammai" (sic). The Bet Shammai did not limit divorce to adultery.

[69]Chap. 3 above.

[70]See, for example, on _prozbol_ above.

[71]See above, the principle _ain kiddushin tofsin_, and n. 66.

[72]Judaism, I, 124. None of his references at n. 3 bear this out. But see on Ben Sira below.

[73]See _Aramaic Papyri of the Fifth Century B.C._, ed. A. Cowley (Oxford: Clarendon, 1923), pp. 44-50; Papyrus 15, lines 22-23, p. 49; cf. Papyrus 9, pp. 25-29, lines 8-9; _Brooklyn Museum Aramaic Papyri_, ed. Emil G. Kraeling (New Haven, Conn.: Yale University Press, 1953), p. 143, Papyrus 2, line 9; Reuven Yaron, _Introduction to the Law of the Aramaic Papyri_ (Oxford: Clarendon, 1961), pp. 53-64.

[74]B. Porten, _Archives From Elephantine_ (Berkeley and Los Angeles: University of California Press, 1968), pp. 209f., 223, 268f.

[75]See Tcherikover, Hellenistic Civilization, pp. 269ff. If Elephantine was indeed founded before the destruction of Jerusalem in 587 B.C., it is conceivable that the Jews there did not yet live under the absolute discipline of the Pentateuch. As we will see below, even in Philonic times, Jews of Egypt did not necessarily follow the Torahitic and Palestinian halakhah. See also Daube, New Testament, p. 366.

[76]M. Ket. 7, throughout, offers a concentrated set of texts for this term as a technical one for "divorce."

[77]Both the Ezra and Nehemiah texts can be conveniently studied in the Anchor Bible, Ezra-Nehemiah, pp. 80-88; 211-219. The question of divorce as such is not discussed.

[78]Ibid., 87f. That mixed marriage remained a grave issue is witnessed by the space given it at Jub. 30. The author of Jubilees appears to favor the Ezraic policy of compulsory separation, in order to restore ritual purity to the community.

[79]Ralph Marcus, Law in the Apocrypha (New York: AMS Press, 1966).

[80]According to the translation of Box and Oesterley "Sirach," in Apocrypha and Pseudepigrapha, 2 vols., ed. R. H. Charles (Oxford: Clarendon Press, 1913) II, 268-517.

[81]The critical note of Box and Oesterley calls attention to the original Greek, "according to thy hand." For the Hebrew text see The Hebrew Text of theBook of Ecclesiasticus, ed. Israel Levi, 3rd ed. (Leiden: E. J. Brill, 1969). There is no Hebrew for 23:22ff. and 25:26. The Greek at 25:26 is clearly a reference to divorce for the husband is advised that if the wife does not behave under his authority apo tōn sarkōn sou, apoteme autēn, "from your body (flesh) cut her away." This is clearly alluding to the right to sever the "one flesh" of Gen. 2:24. At Ben Sira 42:9, the Greek text has misēthē, "hated" as does the Hebrew, and thereby matching the usual term for divorce.

[82]See Louis Finkelstein, "The Book of Jubilees and Rabbinic Halakhah," HTR, 16 (1928), 39-61, now

republished in his Pharisaism in the Making, pp. 199-221; Solomon Zeitlin, "The Book of Jubilees, Its Character and Its Significance," "The Book of Jubilees and the Pentateuch," both now in Studies in the Early History of Judaism II, 116-164.

[83]As it stands, Jubilees is a midrashic re-write of Genesis and Exodus (until Chapter 14), and based upon its many divergences from the Pentateuch it is thought by some scholars to have been produced in opposition to the Torah. See Zeitlin, op. cit., pp. 148f. The weight of opinion, however, tends to see the book as teaching a conservative program for anti-hellenists, seeking to further the consolidation of Ezra and Nehemiah. See my Emergence I, Chap. 5. Whether a version of Lev., Num. and Deut. and the rest of Ex. ever existed we cannot presently determine.

[84]There is indeed the tendency in some quarters to see the targumists as prone to limit divorce to adultery on the basis of the term aberah (sin) as denoting sexual immorality. It is so used at Gen. R. 90:3 and B. San. 70a. But while it has the sexual connotation it does not necessarily mean adultery. Sexual exhibitionism and flirtation do not technically constitute adultery. In any event Ben Sira apparently favored easier divorce for the husband.

[85]Chap. 2, notes 22-26.

[86]B. Ritter, Philo und die Halacha: Einevergleichende Studie unter steter Berüchsichtigung des Josephus (Leipzig: J. C. Hinrichs, 1879) emphasizes the contrasts between Philonic and rabbinic halakhah and argues that Philo reflects Jewish law in Alexandria and not the Palestinian tradition. See also Erwin J. Goodenough, The Jurisprudence of the Jewish Courts in Egypt (Amsterdam: Philo Press, 1968).

[87]Emergence of Contemporary Judaism I, Chap. 6, and notes, especially 139-144, 153, 169.

[88]S. Belkin, Philo and the Oral Law (Cambridge, Mass.: Harvard University Press, 1940).

[89]H. A. Wolfson, Philo, 2 vols. (Cambridge, Mass.: Harvard University Press, 1962).

[90]Belkin, op. cit., pp. 29-48.

[91]Spec. Laws III, 5 (30); 14 (80-82).

[92]Ibid., 5 (30).

[93]Ibid., Translation by F. H. Colson.

[94]See Belkin's discussion, op. cit., p. 229f.

[95]Op. cit. III, 14 (79f.).

[96]Belkin, p. 230.

[97]This translation is Belkin's, p. 229.

[98]Ibid., p. 230.

[99]This source merely limits the right of a man to take a vow of sexual abstention from his wife to two weeks. The Mishnah does not specify what is to be done if he vows to abstain, or actually abstains longer.

[100]Op. cit., III, 14 (82).

[101]Mekh., ed. Lauterbach, III, 30.

[102]Strack, Introduction to Talmud, pp. 114, 311, notes 2-3. R. Yonatan is cited in several trustworthy Mss. of Abot at 4:11.

[103]See n. 74 above; and Cowley, Aramaic Papyri, p. 46. On the other hand a divorce document given by a woman to her husband came to light at Wady Murabbaat, dated to about 134. See Millar Burrows, More Light on the Dead Sea Scrolls (New York: Viking Press, 1958), p. 33.

[104]Josephus, Ant. XV. 7.10 (259f.). In his section on the customs and halakhah pertaining to Jewish marriage, Josephus, ibid. IV, 8.23 (253) refers to divorce as being on any grounds, reflecting the Hillelite position which is also alluded to at Mt. 19:3. But see n. 61.

[105]P. Ket. 30b, 31c. See Porten, op. cit., p. 261, n. 55.

[106]See above, Chap. 3.

[107]Op. cit., p. 231. See also Colson's note on Philo's text at Spec. Laws III, 5 (30) and the Appendix, p. 633.

[108]See CDC 5:9f.: "The law of arayot (sexual immorality) written for the men, are similar for the women."

[109]The text as rendered here is from MegilotMidbar Yehudah, ed. A. M. Habermann (Israel: Machberoth Lesifruth, 1959), p. 79. See also the texts in Documents of Jewish Sectaries I Fragments of a Zadokite Work, ed. Solomon Schechter, (rpt. New York: KTAV, 1970). The Zadokite Document, ed. Chaim Rabin (Oxford: Clarendon Press, 1954).

[110]Gen. 1:27.

[111]Gen. 7:9, minus the words "to Noah."

[112]Deut. 17:17.

[113]This word is left untranslated, as its meaning will have to be decided upon in the course of the discussion. The second fault in which they are trapped is given at 5:7f., men marrying their nieces.

[114]See the notes of Schechter and Rabin, pp. 16-19; A. Dupont-Sommer, The Essene Writings From Qumran (Oxford: Basil Blackwell, 1961), pp. 128f.; Cf. Geza Vermes, Post-Biblical Jewish Studies (Leiden: E. J. Brill, 1975), 50-56.

[115]R. H. Charles, The Apocrypha II, 796; S. Schechter, op. cit., pp. xvii, 68, n. 3.

[116]Louis Ginzberg, An Unknown Jewish Sect, pp. 19f., 131f., 306f.; Catchpole, op. cit. p. 124; Chaim Rabin, op. cit., p. 17; Geza Vermes, op. cit., p. 51; The Dead Sea Scrolls in English (Harmondsworth, Eng.: Penguin, 1975), pp. 36f.; Daube, New Testament, p. 85. Ginzberg astutely connects this prohibition with Lev. 18:18 believing that the Qumran author interpreted the first three words of that verse, veishah él ábotah (lo tikah) (usually translated, as the Oxford Bible does, "you shall not take a woman to her sister" (as wife) as meaning "one woman together with another"); cf. Ex. 26:5, 6, 17. See Ginzberg, p. 19 for a full discussion of the exegesis involved.

117See Vermes, Post-Biblical, pp. 51ff.

118Op. cit., p. 129, n. 1. Where Dupont-Sommer fails, however, is in his acceptance of this as a prohibition on divorce as well as on remarriage. Daube, p. 85 also suggests the passage is against divorce. But this passage says nothing about divorce; it only condemns polygamy.

119See n. 118.

120Rabin, p. 17, n. 3 to line 20 indicates "the Rabbis" take zonah to be one who violates the incest laws of Lev. 18 and cites L. Ginzberg as viewing this rule as anti-incest. This has no warrant. Zenut may refer to incest in the opinion of some rabbis, but during the first century as we see at Sifra 9 4a various rabbis expressed themselves differently in attempting to define zonah, and none of these mention incest. At Spec. Laws I, 19, (102) Philo uses pornē for the Hebrew zonah of Lev. 21:7 where it is sexual promiscuity, and not incest, which he has in mind. Adultery is the extreme form of sexual promiscuity, and zenut as well as porneia in these contexts refers to adultery. As noted earlier there would be no need for a divorce when a marriage is incestuous and therefore retroactively invalid. Cf. M. Yeb. 6:5, B. Yeb. 61a for a rabbinic discussion of zonah. There the zonah is variously defined as a woman one marries though knowing she is unable to procreate, a woman who has had intercourse in her past life as a gentile and is now a proselyte, or as slave and is now free, or one who is generally promiscuous. Incest is not mentioned.

121p. 17, n. 4 to line 21.

122p. 67; his translation (p. 66) indicates he takes CDC 13:17 to refer to divorce. See also Ginzberg, Unknown Sect, p. 306.

123The Hebrew text is entirely undecipherable, so much so that only two Hebrew words relevant to the question are in evidence. These are למגרש וכן which may be taken as Rabin does, "and so for one who divorces." The context may imply that one who divorces must receive permission from the overseer, as Rabin argues, at n. 1 to line 17. But there can be no certainty. Cf. Schechter, p. 85, n. 22.

223

[124]"Matthean Texts," p. 215.

[125]Translated by Vermes, _Post-Biblical_, p. 53.

[126]Op. cit., p. 158.

[127]While Dupont-Sommer does not clarify, I assume he reads the Hebrew consonants (n. 123 above) as _megorash_, (expelled) rather than _megaresh_ (divorces). On the other hand, some support for a prohibition of divorce at Qumran is offered by the Karaite historian who maintains that the Zadokites forbade divorce. See Schechter, op. cit., p. xix; _Karaite Anthology_, ed. Leon Nemoy (New Haven, Conn.: Yale University Press, 1955), pp. 50, 333.

[128]Daube also makes a telling point, that Deut. 17:17 directed to the king is applied to all members of the community since "the king" is taken to be "the congregation" at CDC 7:16f.

[129]See n. 127.

[130]"Matthean Texts," p. 215.

[131]Note 128.

[132]See also Vermes, _Post-Biblical_, pp. 53ff.

[133]Op. cit., p. 220, and see n. 84.

[134]Ibid., p. 221.

[135]For interesting study of the anti-divorce attitude as related to a theology that saw the creation of the human race in androgynous terms, see Paul Winter, "Sadoqite Fragments IV 20, 21 and the Exegesis of Genesis 1:27 in Late Judaism," _ZAW_, 68 (1956), 71-84; 70 (1958), 260-261. See also J. Abrahams, _Studies in Pharisaism and the Gospels_ 2 vols. (rpt. New York: KTAV, 1967), pp. 68ff.

[136]The wife's assent to the divorce was not required, as we see at M. Yeb. 14:1.

[137]Victor Tcherikover, _Hellenistic Civilization and the Jews_, pp. 349f.

[138]I am not unmindful that one can place another

construction upon the Qumran material: a) that the Zadokite Fragment does not at all refer to divorce either at 4:20f. or 13:17; b) that the Temple Scroll refers only to the king and that one is not justified in midrashically equating the "king" and the "congregation" for the halakhah of divorce; c) that CDC and Temple Scroll represent two differing views at Qumran, not to be taken in tandem. The conclusion would then be possible: CDC proves nothing; the Temple Scroll has only a no-divorce halakhah that applies to the king.

139See Ginzberg, Unknown Sect, p. 307, n. 4, where he says that L. Blau, Jüdische Ehescheidung und der jüdische Scheidebrief (Strassburg: K. J. Trübner, 1911) I, 31-40 proved "irrefutably" that Mt. held the Shammaitic view which was the earlier halakhah. This is based on the common interpretation of Bet Shammai as having limited the grounds for divorce to adultery, which I have rejected, as is clear throughout. The earlier halakhah cannot be singled out with certainty. There appears to have been the anti-divorce sentiment co-existing with easy divorce (Elephantine) and more stringent interpretations of Deut. 24:1 by the targumists. But it is possible that the perushite rejection of divorce is prior to Bet Shammai, although Bet Shammai may represent an earlier halakhah than that of Bet Hillel. See n. 72.

140Ginzberg, pp. 23f.

141Actually we have no explicit early halakhic statement for proto-rabbinic permission to marry a niece. The permission must be adduced from the absence of a prohibition in the Torah and in the earlier tannaitic sources, as well as from the testimony of the Zadokite Document against the "opponents" of the group. These inferences are also reinforced by indirect evidence, statements approving such a marriage: at T. Kid. 1:4 ("A person should not marry until his sister's daughter grows up," implying that he wait lest she remain unbetrothed); beraitot at B. Yeb. 62b-63a and San. 76b; P. Yeb. 13c. Perhaps the oldest source is the hermeneutical use of kelal and perat at Lev. 18:6f. to explain the permission to marry a niece, at Sifra 86a.

142Op. cit., pp. 23f.

143At M. Kid. 2:7, combined in the same pericope,

we find polygamy taken for granted, but that there is
no marriage transacted in an incestuous case.   See
also a <u>beraita</u> at B. Git. 34b; T. Git. 8:5.

V. Notes

[1]Gen. 2:14a; Ex. 16:4-5, 22-30; 20:8-11; 23:12; 31:12-17; 34:21; 35:2-3; Lev. 16:31; 19:3, 30; 23:3; Num. 15:32-36; Deut. 5:12-15; II Ki. 4:23; Is. 1:13; 56:1-8; 58:12; Jer. 17:19-27; Ez. 20:12-13, 16, 20-21, 24; 22:8, 26; 23:38; 44:24; 46:1-4, Amos 8:5; Neh. 10:32; 13:15-22; I Chron. 23:31; II Chron. 2:3; 8:13; 31:3. These references do not exhaust all the references to the Sabbath in the O.T. They cover the basic sources that refer to Sabbath halakhah or point to the cult as customarily conducted on the Sabbath as referred to by Jesus at Mt. 12:5. See Niels-Erik A. Andreasen, The Old Testament Sabbath, A Tradition-Historical Investigation (Missoula, Mont.: Society of Biblical Literature, 1972).

[2]Chap. 1.

[3]Mot yumat in the Hebrew means "will assuredly be put to death." Here it is parallel to "that person will be cut off from its people" thus leading to the possible definition of the enigmatic O.T. term karet, as originally signifying either a judicial death penalty or a parallel divine annihilation of the soul. This, of course, raises other problems concerning the nature of the concept of the Afterlife in biblical times. Something of the nature of ostracism and expulsion was practiced at Qumran, and this might have been a later way of interpreting karet. For this reason we might be constrained to see the parallel term mot yumat also viewed as a literary formula in later times, designed to press the heavy moral obligation entailed in the observance of the miẓvah. Hence the death penalty might have been abandoned at Qumran. See below, section D, 6.

[4]The scope of this dissertation does not call for a critical discussion of the dating of this or any other Old Testament passage. Whether the passages are dated to the monarchical period or to the post-exilic period is of no substantive importance to us in terms of their application in proto-rabbinic and New Testament sources.

[5]Ex. 35:2-3; Num. 15:32-36; Is. 58:13; Jer. 17:19-27; Neh. 13:15-22.

[6]Spec. Laws II, 45 (250-251). Philo does not indicate that such a practice is no longer in vogue as

he would have done for apologetic purposes if indeed it was no longer in vogue. As a matter of fact, Philo appears to approve of the death sentence. As for the implication of a threat of death to Jesus at Mt. 12:14, see below.

[7]This is evident in the above-cited passages of Isaiah which are all from the hand of an Anonymous Prophet; Neh. 13:15-22; Judith 8:6; I. Macc. 1:39; 2:29-41; 10:34; II Macc. 5:25ff.; 6:6ff.; 8:25-28; 12:38; 15:1-5; Jub. 1:10; 2:23, 27, 29-30; 50:6-13; the Qumran references will be dealth with separately below.

[8]See n. 7.

[9]The references listed here are the major ones alluding to actual halakhah. a) Philo: Dec. 20 (96-101); Spec. Laws II, 15 (56-64) 16 (65-70); 45 (249-251); Moses II, 4 (21-22); 39 (209-216); 40 (217-220); On Creation 43 (128); Hyp. 7:12f.; Mig. Ab. 16 (91); Every Good Man 12 (81f.); b) Josephus: War I, 7; 3 (146); II, 17, 10 (456); 19, 2 (517); Ant. III, 10.1 (237); XII, 6.2. (274f.; 276ff.); XIV. 4.2 (63), 4.3 (64); Ag. Ap. I, 22 (209-212); II.17 (175).

[10]Marcus, Law in the Apocrypha, pp. 75f. However, Marcus refers to Jub. 1:12 on p. 76.

[11]See n. 7.

[12]Josephus, Ant. XIII, 12:4 (337); War VII, 8.7 (362f.).

[13]Finkelstein, Pharisaism, pp. 101-106, dates the book to a time between 175 and 167 B.C. See also Gene L. Davenport, The Eschatology of the Book of Jubilees (Leiden: E. J. Brill, 1971), pp. 10-18, where he dates the first stage of the book's composition to ca. 200 B.C. and its final redaction to 140-104 B.C.

[14]James C. Vander Kam, Textual and Historical Studies in the Book of Jubilees (Missoula, Mont.: Scholar Press, 1977), pp. 217-238 arrives at a date just after 163 B.C. for its final form.

[15]I have dealt with this in Emergence I, Chap. 5 where I adopt a date of about 190-160 B.C. See n. 77 there.

[16]See below concerning the Qumran halakhah as it relates to both the pericope at Mt. 12:1-8, 9-14 and to proto-rabbinic halakhah.

[17]"The Book of Jubilees and the Rabbinic Halakhah," p. 51, Pharisaism, p. 211.

[18]Mekh. III, 197f. At B. Yom. 35b, is indicated the pre-Christian provenance of this concept in its attribution to Shemâya and Abtalion, 1st cent. B.C. It could well have come from Yosi b. Yoezer, "the permitter."

[19]Op. cit., p. 114.

[20]Ibid.

[21]See Chap. 2.

[22]See Chap. 3.

[23]Judaism I, 3.

[24]Op. cit., p. 114.

[25]Judaism and Christianity I, 167.

[26]Ibid., p. 171.

[27]Yohanan b. Zakkai uses Hos. 6:6 to stress that not the cult, but loving deeds, is the source of salvation. See Ab. de R. N. A., 4; B, 8. On the meaning of Hosea's term hesed see Nelson Glueck, Hesed in the Bible, trans. Alfred Gottschalk (Cincinnati: Hebrew Union College Press, 1967), pp. 56-69. Cf. PRE 12, "More Beloved is the service of loving-kindness than the sacrifices and burnt-offerings which Israel will bring in the future upon the altar. . . ," citing Hos. 6:6 See Pirke de Rabbi Eliezer, trans. G. Friedlander (New York: Bloch, 1916), pp. 89, 107. Cf. Jacob Neusner, A Life of Yohanan ben Zakkai, 2nd ed. (Leiden: E. J. Brill, 1970), p. 189f.

[28]Sayings of Jesus, pp. 189f.

[29]Tradition, p. 76, n. 2; "Überlieferung," p. 71, n. 2. So too Klausner, Jesus of Nazareth, trans. Herbert Danby (New York: Macmillan, 1946), p. 279 errs on this point.

[30]It is not clear that apolesōsin, "destroy" must be taken in the most literal sense as "to kill." See below, C.

[31]Severino Pancaro, The Law in the Fourth Gospel (Leiden: E. J. Brill, 1975), p. 8.

[32]Josephus, Ag. Ap. II, 21 (184-185).

[33]Jesus and the Law, p. 113.

[34]See K. Bornhäuser, "Zur Pericope vom Bruch des Sabbats," NKZ, 33 (1922), p. 326.

[35]Op. cit., pp. 120-122.

[36]Op. cit., pp. 79-83 (English), pp. 73-78 (German).

[37]Auseinandersetzung, p. 45.

[38]See also G. Strecker, Der Weg, p. 135.

[39]Op. cit., p. 130.

[40]David Flusser, Jesus, trans. Ronald Walls (New York: Herder and Herder, 1969), pp. 46-50.

[41]Ibid., p. 46. See also S. Pines, "The Jewish Christians of the Early Centuries of Christianity According to a New Source," Proceedings, The Israel Academy of Sciences and Humanities, II (1966), 63.

[42]Ibid.

[43]Ibid., p. 50.

[44]This along with circumcision are doheh shabbat, supersede the Sabbath. See M. Sabh. 19; Pes. 6:1-2; Er. 10:13; B. M. K. 3b; Mak. 8b; Men. 72a; R. H. 9a; Shab. 132b.

[45]Pikuah nefesh doheh shabbat, the need to save life supersedes the Sabbath. See: Mekh. III, 197f.; B. Shab. 57a; M. Yom. 8:6; Shab. 14:4; 22:6; T. Shab. 15:11, 15, 16. The word pikuah, from pakah, to break through, open, means to remove a person from under debris. See B. Ket. 5a, 19a.

[46]Even during the middle ages when the peculiar relationship between the feudal, and later, the national states and the Jewish community, provided the latter with absolute power over its population, it was impossible to suppress halakhic diversity. See my discussion of this in Emergence II, passim.

[47]See for example the unpublished Dissertation of R. Guelich, Not to Annul the Law Rather to Fulfill the Law and the Prophets. An Exegetical Study of Jesus and the Law in Matthew with Emphasis on 5:17-48, for University of Hamburg, 1967, pp. 34-38. Guelich relies for this judgment entirely upon secondary sources.

[48]These errors are espoused by Guelich, ibid., p. 35.

[49]Ibid., pp. 45f.

[50]Der Weg, p. 32ff., n. 4.

[51]Zekhariah Frankel, Mavờ Hayerushalmi, p. 1.

[52]Chap. 3 above.

[53]This Sabbath pericope is discussed by numerous scholars. The following is a brief selection of sources in addition to those found throughout the notes. Banks, pp. 113-131; Guelich, Not to Annul, pp. 46-64; Barth, "Das Gesetzesverständnis" in Überlieferung, pp. 75-78; G. Strecker, Der Weg. p. 32f.; Hummel, Auseinandersetzung, pp. 40-44; F. W. Beare, "The Sabbath Was Made For Man?" JBL, 79 (1960), 130-136; Strack-Billerbeck, Kommentar I, 610-622; T. W. Manson, The Sayings, pp. 187-190; Abrahams, Studies, I, 129-135; C. Hinz, 'Jesus und der Sabbat," Kerygma und Dogma, 19 (1973), 91-108; E. Lohse, "Jesu Worte über den Sabbat," Judentum, Urchristentum, Kirche (1960), 79-89.

[54]Davies, The Setting, pp. 103f.; Doeve, Jewish Hermeneutics, pp. 106f.; Daube, New Testament, pp. 67-71.

[55]This verse has no textual problem connected with it. See Metzger, op. cit., p. 31. My translation follows: "At that time on the Sabbath, Jesus passed through the grain fields. His disciples, being hungry, proceeded to strip ears and eat."

Manson, Sayings, p. 190 anticipates my view that Jesus and his disciples are on a journey, not a mere pleasure stroll. The translation of tillein as "to strip" instead of the usual "pluck" (or "pick," in the Jerusalem Bible) is based upon an argument by J. D. M. Derrett, "Judaica in St. Mark," Studies in the New Testament (Leiden: E. J. Brill, 1977), p. 90, and notes 24, 26. The meaning "pick" by Arndt-Gingrich, p. 825, may also fit the idea expressed by Derrett, to strip or take off grains from the head or ear of the standing wheat.

56See n. 55, Derrett references.

57Contra David Hill, The Gospel of Matthew, New Century Bible (Greenwood, S.C.: Attic Press, 1975), p. 210. Hill lacks precision for his statement as well as overlooking the question of dating primary and secondary works. A "derivative activity" or toladah such as tolesh was not yet as serious a matter as it became in later literature. Little tannaitic evidence is available, and what there is points to a difference of opinion concerning the status of toladah. See e.g., B. B. K. 2a, Shab. 70b.

58I see 12:1 "at that time" as linking this event to the mission of Chapters 10-11. Chapter 10 contains Jesus' instructions concerning the mission. Chapter 11 contains material that relates to the period between 11:1 and 12:1.

59M. Peah. 8:7 indicates one should prepare food on Friday to suffice for three Sabbath meals for a traveller. It is possible that the nearby villages had no idea Jesus and his disciples would turn up there, this mishnaic suggestion is post-Jesus, or the villagers were opposed to him and his disciples, for which reason they proceeded through a grain field. Fields commonly had private or public pathways running through them (M. B. B. 6:7), and one could avoid violating the rule against travelling more than 2000 cubits (M. Er. 4:7; Sot. 5:3) between villages by strolling through the field on the Sabbath. See also P. Targ. to Ex. 16:29 upon which is based the halakhah of 2000 cubits, in tandem with Num. 35:5.

60See Thesaurus Talmudis, ed. Chaim J. Kosowski (Jerusalem: Israel Ministry of Education and Culture, 1971), XXVII, 304-318 for numerous references that indicate the differences of opinion regarding halakhot in instances where there is doubt and double doubt.

61See Lawrence H. Schiffman, The Halakhah at
Qumran (Leiden: E. J. Brill, 1975), pp. 109ff.
Schiffman translates the halakhah at CDC 11:4-5 as
prohibiting entering a partnership. The Hebrew is ạl
yitạreb. Rabin, Zadokite Document, p. 54f.,
translates "let no man starve himself," following
Jub. 50:"12. S. Hoenig took the Hebrew to mean one
must not "mingle" or "socialize" on the Sabbath; in
"An Interdict Against Socializing on the Sabbath,"
JQR, 62 (1971), 78f. Schechter, Documents, p. 81
translates as "mingle," but at n. 19 points to the
reading yitạneh, not to fast. Ginzberg, Unknown Sect,
p. 64, errs in reporting Schechter but seems to prefer
yitraẹv, that one should not "starve himself" on the
analogy of a mishnaic phrase, reported in a beraitạ at
B. San. 65b.

62See B. R. H. 19a; Taan. 17b; P. Taan. 67a;
Ned. 40d; Sabbath festivity with food and drink was
favored at B. Shab. 117b-119a, referring back to
Is. 58:13. See also Josephus, Life, 54 (279).

63B. Shab. 11a; Taan. 12b.

64Mekh. III, 206. See note 57.

65See n. 59. Klausner, Jesus, p. 278 sees
"plucking" as a universal prohibition of the
Pharisees, by whom he means the rabbis.

66The translation of this phrase is open to much
discussion. It is generally taken in one of two ways:
1) the "bread of the Presence" the twelve lehem
hapanim, of Lev. 24:5, which is on display from
Sabbath to Sabbath when new ones are brought in and
the old ones are eaten by the priests (ibid., 8f.);
2) the two "loaves of offering" at Lev. 23:17, at the
Shabuot festival. M. Men. 11:2 informs us that
neither of these types of loaves may be baked on the
Sabbath. Therefore, one must reject the usual
understanding, e.g., that of Strack-Billerbeck,
Kommentar I, 611 who call it the Schaubrote
("Shewbread," or the lehem hapanim); Barth, op. cit.
(German ed.) p. 76, n. 4. But M. Men. 11:3 refers to
the high priests' cakes of Lev. 6:12-16 and says the
baking of these supersedes the Sabbath. See Kommentar
I, 610-622; 622-630; B. Men. 95b-96a.

[67]The word _protheseōs_ at Mt. 12:4 merely signifies that the loaves were set out. This could just as well refer to the priests' daily meal-offering of Lev. 6:12-16, as to the _lehem hapanim_. The logic, however, in the light of M.'Men. 11:2-3 (see n. 66) weighs on the side of these being the priests' loaves. Where the evangelist says the loaves are _tois hiereusin monois_ he might not mean as food. At I Sam. 22:10 Doeg reports that David received "provision" at Nob, not the bread of Presence.

[68]Schlatter, _Matthäus_, pp. 394-5; cf. Hill, _Matthew_, p. 210, citing D. E. Nineham, _St. Mark_, p. 105.

[69]This is almost seen by Doeve, op. cit., p. 106f. but he calls it a _gezerah shavah_.

[70]The biblical allusions here are Num. 28:9-10; Ez. 46:1-4, 12; I Chron. 23:31; II Chron. 2:3; 8:13; 31:3.

[71]See n. 44. At B. Yom. 85a-b we find a parallel passage that leads us through a series of _kal vehomer_ arguments: saving life supersedes the cult, the cult supersedes the Sabbath, saving life therefore certainly supersedes the Sabbath.

[72]See n. 70.

[73]It is not necessary to cite the numerous references here to a very commonly held position. See F. W. Beare, "The Sabbath Was Made for Man?"

[74]The entire question of the meaning of _kyrios_ and _ho huios tou anthrōpou_ in this verse is not germane to our discussion and is threrefore omitted here. It is all the same for our purpose if Jesus is represented as saying that _he_ determines the halakhah as the messianic Son of Man, for this does not change any of the substance of 1-7, or if Jesus is merely climaxing his arguments with another philosophic observation of how halakhah is determined (such as "go and see what the people are doing," at B. Ber. 45a). I agree with Rudolf Bultmann, _Theology_, I, 18: Klausner, _Jesus_, 278, and others who see v. 8 as referring to humans, not as a Christological reference to Jesus as the Danielic figure.

[75]David Hill, "On the Use and Meaning of Hosea

234

vi. 6 in Matthew's Gospel," NTS, 24 (1977), 107-119.

[76]Ibid., p. 107.

[77]Op. cit., p. 43.

[78]Op. cit., p. 76 (German version).

[79]Op. cit., p. 116.

[80]Safek nefashot, a reasonable doubt that life may be at stake, is adequate to supersede the Sabbath: B. Shab. 57a; M. Yom. 8:6; T. Shab. 15:11, 15, 16. See notes 44-45.

[81]Sheliah mizvah doheh shabbat.

[82]Although Numbers Rabbah is a collection of late date, this statement is given as an anonymous halakhah in the context of older proto-rabbinic material. Cf. a beraita at B. Shab. 19a.

[83]The Origins of the Gospel of Matthew, p. 116.

[84]Contra Kilpatrick, ibid.; and Jack Dean Kingsbury, Matthew: Structure, Christology, Kingdom (Philadelphia: Fortress Press, 1975), pp. 106, 116.

[85]F. F. Bruce, "The Davidic Messiah in Luke-Acts," Biblical And Near Eastern Studies, ed. Gary A. Tuttle (Grand Rapids, Mich.: Wm. B. Eerdmans, 1978), p. 7.

[86]See M. Shab. 19; Pes. 6:1-2; Er. 10:13; Shebi. 1:4; B. M. K. 3b-4a; Mak. 8b; Men. 65a, 72a; R. H. 9a, and notes 44, 45, 80 and 81.

[87]The Diatessaron, 7:37 preserves aspects of all the Synoptics, from Mk. 2:23, Mt. 12:1, and Lk. 6:1 by reading "When Jesus was walking through the cornfields on the Sabbath day, (Mark, omitting Matthew's "at that time") his disciples were hungry (Mt.), and rubbing the ears of the corn with their hands (Lk.), they were eating." The translation is from The Diatessaron of Tatian, trans. J. Hamlyn Hill (Edinburgh: T. and T. Clark, 1894). This edition is a translation from Latin and Arabic, based upon a 14th cent. Arabic Ms. with a Latin translation published in Rome in 1888 by Agostino Ciasca of the Vatican's Guild of Writers.

[88]See Pines, The Jewish Christians, p. 63, notes 256-257 on this. While his point has merit, its significance for the Mt. pericope is reduced in the light of my approach. Furthermore, Pines, n. 257, is too sanguinary in his view that R. Judah at B. Shab. 128a permitted plucking. See n. 55 above.

[89]The article by Etan Levine, "The Sabbath Controversy According to Mt.," NTS, 22 (1976), 480-483, is irrelevant. The ómer is one of the several elements of the cult in addition to Sabbath sacrifice that superseded the Sabbath when the cult was in operation before 70 A.D., as is clear at M. Men. 10:1, 3, 9. See n. 86 above. Levine sees the cutting of the ómer as the analogue for the disciples plucking grain. But this is superfluous, since all cultic activity is permitted and that is precisely the point behind Mt. 12:5. One does not need a specific cultic activity as an analogy. The Sadducees opposed cutting the ómer on the Sabbath, but they are not involved in this pericope, so Jesus is not arguing against them. Everything Jesus allowed we find solidly embedded in rabbinic literature. With whom is Jesus quarrelling? Obviously he can only be opposing the stringent halakhah of the perushim who did not provide any waiver for the Sabbath halakhah, as is clear in both Jubilees and the Zadokite Document.

[90]Studies, I, 134.

[91]For contrasing views on the use of autōn here see Kilpatrick, pp. 109-11; Hummel, pp. 28ff. Perhaps W. C. Allen, The Gospel According to St. Matthew, 3rd ed. (Edinburgh: T. and T. Clark, 1912), p. 129, does best by making no comment at all. Davies, The Setting, pp. 296f. believes the Matthean use of autōn here, at 4:23, 13:54 and elsewhere, points to the Jamnian move to expel the Christians from the synogogues. While I am in full agreement that post-Yoḥanan Jamnia probably made every effort to expel Christian Jews from the synogogues, I do not believe there is any pointed significance to the use of autōn. Moderns speaking of people within their own religious denominations will often use the third person pronoun in colloquialisms. I asked a Presbyterian a question about the use of palm leaves on Easter in the Presbyterian church, and his reply opened not with "We," but with "They." It is also natural when writing that a person will speak of "the Jews" rather than "We," and most especially if a

Conservative Jew speaks of Reform Jews he will refer to "their Temples." But both are Jews and pray in one another's houses of worship. The perushim probably had synagogues of their own as many groups had, whether based upon geographic origin, or social, economic, and liturgical differences. Each group frequented a synogogue of its preference, but that did not mean "radical separation" as Davies felicitously phrases it for a very large proportion of modern scholars (p. 297). See Salo Baron, A Social and Religious History II, 199f., 403f., n. 33. One hyperbolic report at B. Ket. 105 informs us that there were 394 synagogues in Jerusalem in 70 A.D., and another at P. Meg. 73d that there were 480. The sources are quite prolific on synagogues organized on the basis of geographic origins, and are corroborated by Acts 6:9. That separate synagogues based on liturgical and socio-economic differences existed is clear from the negative reference to the first-century synagogues of the ámmei haárez at M. Ab. 3:14.

92This pericope is discussed by Barth, Überlieferung, pp. 73f.; Banks, pp. 123-131; Strack-Billerbeck, I, 622-630; H. Loewe, "Pharisaism" I, 166ff.; R. Hummel, pp. 44f.; Strecker, Der Weg, p. 33. When reading what scholars have written on the healing pericope one must be wary not to take at face value the often-made generalization that the rabbis allowed relief to a sufferer on the Sabbath only if his life was in danger. See Hill, Matthew, p. 212. See n. 80 above.

93Op. cit., p. 166.

94It is not strictly pertinent to this dissertation, but it is appropriate to recall that Jn. 9:6, 11, 14f., emphasizes the making of a compound which Jesus used as a salve or medicine. The criticism of Jesus at Jn. 9:16 seems indeed to be for making the compound (v. 15) rather than for the act of healing.

95Here I rely for my translation of hen as "one" rather than taking it as an indefinite article, on the use of hen on the model of Hebrew or Aramaic in accord with F. Blass, and a. DeBrunner, A Greek Grammar of the New Testament and Other Early Christian Literature, trans. Robert W. Funk, (Chicago: University of Chicago, 1961), p. 129. An analogy may be found at Mt. 21:24.

[96]Severino Pancaro, The Law in the Fourth Gospel (Leiden: E. J. Brill, 1975), pp. 8-17.

[97]Raymond Brown, The Gospel According to John Anchor Bible, 2nd ed. (New York: Doubleday, 1977), I, 210. Brown is over-enthusiastic, however, when he states, "that Jesus violated the rules of the scribes for the observance of the Sabbath is one of the most certain of all the historical facts of his ministry." This is about as accurate as it would be today to argue that a Conservative or Reform rabbi who uses electricity on the Sabbath is in violation of the Sacred day because the Orthodox prohibit its use.

[98]Saving a life.

[99]The possibility of the later loss of life.

[100]See for example M. Shab. 8:1; 9:7; 10:1; T. Shab. 12:8ff. Of special interst is T. Shab. 12:12 where R. Meir is said to refuse a healing process which he permits because he does not wish to act contrary to his colleague's view.

[101]See also T. Shab. 7:23; 15:11, 15f.; M. Ed. 2:5.

[102]Claude G. Montifiore, Rabbinic Literature and Gospel Teaching, p. 244.

[103]Activity no. 9 at M. Shab. 7:2. See n. 57.

[104]M. Shab. 18:3; T. Shab. 14:3; B. Shab. 128b. It is clear from the sources that there were differences over the extent of the help one can offer, but at Qumran, none was allowed.

[105]zaár baálei hayyim, B. Shab. 128b; B. M. 32a-b.

[106]English Authorized Version, Revised Standard Version, Jerusalem Bible.

[107]Today's English Version.

[108]"To destroy," Deut. 2:34; 20:17; etc.

[109]Jastrow, I, 504, herem, 3) A Grammatical Analysis of The Greek New Testament,

p. 37, selects an easier meaning, and perhaps closer to the truth: "do away with." This need not imply the physical destruction as do the other translations. Cf. the pertinent remarks concerning early first-century excommunication by Douglas R. A. Hare, The Theme of Jewish Persecution, pp. 48-56. Although Hare (p. 51) did not recognize that the New Testament Pharisees had a halakhah similar to that of Qumran, he pointed out that they used a form of excommunication upon their own people. I would take this further to argue that the pietists would also use herem and nidui against outsiders, in order to keep their own followers isolated from their influence.

110See Hare, ibid., p. 54. Hare correctly distinguishes between formal expulsion from the synagogue and the practice of social ostracism which was basically socio-economic, and one might add "academic," insofar as one could not study under a banned scholar.

111Gen. 2:1-4a; Ex. 16:4-5, 22-30; 20:8-11; 23:12; 31:12-17; 34:21; 35:2-3; Lev. 19:3, 30; 23:3; 24:8; 26:2; Num. 15:32-36; 28:9-10; Deut. 5:12-15. For a discussion of various aspects of the Old Testament Sabbath, its origins and its nature as a social and cultic institution as well as the covenantal aspects attached to it, see Andreasen, The O.T. Sabbath.

112Philo, Spec. Laws II, (250-251).

113Andreasen, op. cit., p. 62. Early Jewish commentators, beginning with the Aramaic targum to Amos, took this to be a reference to the fallow year in which prices go up steeply and enable the grain merchant to profiteer.

114II Ki. 4:23; I Chron. 9:32; 23:30-31; II Chron. 2:3; 8:13; 31:3.

115Ez. 20:12-13; 16, 20-21, 24; 22:8, 26; 23:38; 44:24; 45:17; 46:1-4.

116According to the Judaic Canon, Nehamiah is in Writings.

117Neh. 9:14; 10:32, 34; 13:15-22.

118Ag. Ap., I, 22 (208-211). See also Finkel,

The Pharisees and The Teacher of Nazareth Concerning the Sabbath, pp. 75f., 170ff.

[119]Josephus, ibid., 210.

[120]Michel Testuz, Les idées religieuses de Livre des Jubilés (Geneva and Paris: Droz and Minard, 1960), pp. 140-143, sees properly this emphasis upon the Sabbath: "La charactéristique du Livre des Jubilés est de faire du jour du Sabbat 'une fête de joie'" (p. 143).

[121]This interpretation of the biblical mot yumat at Ex. 31:14 is also alluded to by Philo, QG. I, (16) where he translates Gen. 2:17 mot tamoot ("you will surely die") as "you will die by the death" (English translation by Ralph Marcus). He indicates there is a two-fold life: that of the corruptible body and that which is without body. The evil person is dead even while he lives, for true life is excellence of character. The good man, even when his body dies, does not die, but is borne to eternal life. Again at QG. I (70) to Gen. 4:10, Philo says God hears the good even after their bodily death for they live an incorporeal life, while the wicked are not even heard when alive because they are dead to the true life and their bodies are like tombs. Cf. Alleg. Int. I, 33 (105-108). From the latter source, at 108, it appears that Philo does not agree with Jubilees that immortality or the eternal life of the soul is lost. The soul is dead during the life of the body, but when the natural death of the body takes place, the soul is liberated to its proper life.

[122]All sixteen items may be found at Jub. 2:29-30; 50:8, 12. The first six items are from Chap. 2, the other ten from Chap. 50. Some items from 2 appear duplicated at 50 (e.g., items 3 and 4). But R. H. Charles comments at 2:29 that this text is corrupt and that the passage with these two items should probably be omitted. Item 2 may be rooted in Ex. 16:23, but perhaps, as I have earlier indicated, the manna halakhah may not have applied as permanent halakhah, and the prohibition on cooking is the logical result of item 10. In rabbinic literature the discussion related to cooking is complex and yields a diversity of indecisive halakhah. See B. Shab. 37a-40b. M. Bez. 5:2 implies a tannaitic prohibition on preparing food on the Sabbath. The prohibition of sexual relations is not maintained in

later times, and is referred to as a practice of the
early hasidim or pietists, at B. Nid. 38a; Ket. 62b.
At M. Ned. 3:10 (cf. 8:6) the "eaters of garlic"
refers to the notion that among ten enactments
instituted by Ezra was the eating of garlic on Fridays
as an aphrodisiac which increases the production of
semen and makes sexual relations more productive. See
B. B. K. 82a and the beraita at B. Ket. 62b; at the
latter source we find the application of Ps. 1:3 to
Sabbath sexuality. Various items are found in earlier
or almost contemporary sources: Isaiah (1), Nehemiah
(4, 5), the Pentateuch (possibly 2, 9, 10, 11), Judith
(15), Maccabees (16). Item 3 is new. It is
ameliorated in rabbinic literature (M. Shab. 17:6); it
is permitted to draw water and fill a trough with it
for animals to drink (B. Er. 20b). Item 6 is new and
rejected in rabbinic literature as noted above. Item
7 is not found as "planning" at Nehemiah 13:16-21;
10:32, but as actual trade and commerce. Jub. 50:8 is
therefore more severe, actually seeking to regulate
human thought to prohibiting even discussing and
planning a trip or business, or taking a business
trip, depending upon the reading. See Charles, loc.
cit. Items 8 and 12 are new and may be derived from
Ex. 16:29. But both items are ameliorated in rabbinic
literature. Item 8 is softened by the institution of
the ᶜerub for the right to travel beyond Sabbath limits
(M. Er. 4:3, 7; 5:7; Sot. 5:3); item 12 is alleviated
at M. Shab. 16:8, reporting on Gamaliel's arrival by
ship on a Sabbath which points to the permissibility
of sailing on a vessel on the Sabbath.
Cf. B. Shab. 19a. Items 13 and 14 are retained at
M. Shab. 7:2. Item 15, no fasting, is encouraged in
the rabbinic literature but there are options
(B. Shab. 11a; Er. 41a). At item 16 R. H. Charles
misinterprets M. Shab. 6:2, 4 as prohibiting war, when
these passages prohibit the wearing of war gear on the
Sabbath as mere ornament (Cf. B. Shab. 19a). The
prohibition against war signifies either that we have
here a pre-Maccabean halakhah or an objection to the
Maccabean innovation. Both possibilities can be
affirmed. It is possible that an older halakhah is
republished in opposition to the Hasmoneans.
Proto-rabbinic halakhah permitted even a siege of a
city to continue on a Sabbath and not only
self-defense (B. Shab. 19a a beraita citing Shammai).

[123]See also Finkelstein, "The Book of Jubilees
and Rabbinic Halakhah," Pharisaism, pp. 45ff.

[124]The question of authorship of the various sections of our present Book of Isaiah is not deemed of substantive pertinence to our theme and is therefore not examined.

[125]On Creation 43 (128); Moses II, 39 (216); Dec. 20 (96-100f.); Spec. Laws II, 15 (60-63).

[126]Miq. Ab. 16 (91). See Wolfson, Philo, I, 55-73; 115-140.

[127]On The Creation 43 (128). Cf. Moses II, 39 (211). While this is not specific it is relatively so even in its generality, for it certainly prohibits any and every activity involved in gainful employment. The question would arise: What of the priest and the teacher who function on the Sabbath? Philo does not take up such halakhic questions.

[128]Items 2-7 are found at Miq. Ab. 16 (91). The prohibition on lighting a fire is also at Spec. Laws, II, 16 (65).

[129]Items 8-9 are found at Moses, II, 4 (22); 10-11 at 39 (211, 213, 219, 220). Spec. Laws, II, 45 (250-251); cf. Sifre Num. 113, 132.

[130]A comparative table would show the following: Jubilees items 1-3, 6, 8, 11-16 are not found in Philo. One would have to use hermeneutical rules to discover them in Philo, or infer from some of Philo's more general comments that these items would be prohibited. For example, the fact that fire is prohibited may imply that cooking is prohibited. But Jubilees (item 2) prohibits all food preparation, not only cooking or baking that requires fire. Would Philo permit the preparation of a tossed green salad? Jubilees item 7 is paralleled in Philo's items 3, 8, 9. Jubilees, item 1 and Philo, item 2 are parallel. Philo's items 5, 6, and 11 are not found in Jubilees. Does this imply that Jubilees allowed court cases on the Sabbath, or to conduct preliminary activities on the Sabbath even for such acts as are forbidden? Undoubtedly the general statements in both Jubilees and Philo for complete rest, to do no work, like those of the Pentateuch, were open to continued questioning and ongoing interpretation. Cf. The comparative table offered by S. T. Kimbrough, "The Concept of Sabbath at Qumran," Revue de Qumran, 5 (1964-1966), 483-502; see pp. 487-498. An article that treats

Qumran Sabbath halakhah as more stringent is that of Baruch Sharvit, "The Sabbath of the Sect of the Wilderness of Judah" (Hebrew), Beth Mikra, 21 (1976), 507-516.

[131]Moses II, 4 (22).

[132]Chap. 3, above; n. 40.

[133]The humanitarian objectives of the Torah are found at On the Virtues, 81, 97, 99, 121, 140 and elsewhere. There is some ambiguity as to whether Philo would permit superseding the Sabbath in a case of great natural or communal calamity at On Dreams II, 18 (123-132). Cf. Mt. 24:20.

[134]Ex. 31:14f.; Jub. 2:25, 27; Philo, Spec. Laws II, 45 (249).

[135]Ibid.; translation by F. H. Colson.

[136]In modern times those who adhere to what they term "orthodox" Judaism do not allow the needs of Sabbath worship to supersede the Sabbath. Other Jews allow certain activities in the course of worship which some would not allow elsewhere, e.g., the use of instrumental music or an amplifying system. Others will permit the use of such instruments and technology whether or not it is related to worship.

[137]Items 5-6.

[138]Philo, Mig. Ab. 16 (91).

[139]The major document recording the Sabbath halakhah among the published texts of the Dead Sea Scrolls is the Zadokite Document (CDC). The Sabbath halakhah is found at CDC 10:14-11; 18. See Lawrence Schiffman, The Halakhah at Qumran, pp. 77-135; Ginzberg, An Unknown Jewish Sect, pp. 55-70; see also his index entry "Sabbath" for extensive references throughout the work; see C. Rabin The Zadokite Documents, S. Schechter, Documents of Jewish Sectaries; Habermann, Megilot Midbar Yehudah for the texts and their respective textual notes.

[140]Fire is not specified at Qumran. The obvious reason for this is that any member of the sect takes an oath to observe the Torah of Moses (CDC 15:9, 12). For this reason too, interestingly enough, CDC does

not specify a prohibition to engage in agriculture, nor riding an animal (Ex. 20:10). The two prohibitions of Jubilees that are neither in the Torah nor mentioned in CDC are sailing and the conduct of war. CDC includes Philo's items 5, 6 and 11 which are not in Jubilees.

[141]Kimbrough, op. cit., p. 498, citing D. Howlett, The Essenes and Christianity (New York: Harper, 1957), p. 159.

[142]Ibid., p. 502.

[143]Erubin (plural), erub (singular), refers to the prescribed ritual forms required to relax some of the restrictions on free movement on the Sabbath, e.g., to enable one to walk beyond the distance of 2000 cubits, or to change the status of a domain from public to private in order to be able to move things about within its boundaries. The actual meaning of the term is "mixture" or "fusion," signifying that separate abodes or domains are fused. The erub consists of food. It is symbolically placed at a specific junction to become a "residence" and thereby establish legal continuity between the domains. A comprehensive explanation of this complex halakhic institution is found at the Introduction to tractate Erubin of Mishnayoth, Order Moed, ed. Phillip Blackman (Gatewhead, Eng.: Judaica Press, 1973), II, 99ff.

[144]Op. cit., pp. 109ff.

[145]Documents, p. 81; text at p. 108.

[146]P. 81, n. 19 to line 4f.

[147]Unknown Sect, p. 64.

[148]Life, 54 (279).

[149]See n. 145.

[150]Zadokite Documents, p. 54. Habermann, op. cit., p. 85 retains the reading yitareb and suggests in his note, p. 195 that it means one is not to engage in taharut, "contention," a far-fetched idea.

[151]Schechter reads tipol. See his text, op. cit., p. 108, and his translation and notes, p. 81. Rabin, op. cit., p. 57, reads tapil. Schiffman, op.

cit., pp. 121f., prints tapil but translates as tipol.
Rabin, p. viii, concedes that he is not "able to
distinguish with confidence between yod and vav" and
undoubtedly this is a case in point. Habermann,
p. 85, reads tipol. As tipol it makes sense. As
tapil we have a rather curious situation of an animal
off away from its barn at a time so close to giving
birth and doing so in a peculiar state of gymnastics
that cause the foetus to fall into a convenient pit.

152In some Toseftā texts this is at 15:3. Cf.
B. Shab. 128b. Some texts read that the animal falls
into a well, and then the danger to life is even
clearer. See variant reading provided by Saul
Lieberman, The Toseftā, The Order of Mo'ed (New York:
Jewish Theological Seminary, 1962), p. 65. Mt. 12:11
clearly reads "pit" as does CDC 11:13f. But the
Hebrew beêr ("well") can also mean "pit" and bor
("pit") can also means "cistern" where water might be
present. No significance can attach to the reading.

153At B. Shab. 128b this interpretation is given
in the name of Rab, a second-third century scholar,
disciple of Judah haNasi, editor of the Mishnah. How
early the tradition is we cannot tell.

154Op. cit., p. 122.

155Jastrow, II, 1231.

156Op. cit., p. 57, line 17, notes 1, 2, 3.

157Op. cit., pp. 68f.

158Op. cit., p. 497.

159Essene Writings, p. 153, and n. 5.

160Theodore Gaster, The Dead Sea Scriptures
(3rd ed. Garden City, N.Y.: 1976), translation at
p. 84, n. 54, pp. 111f.

161Jean Daniélou, The Dead Sea Scrolls
andPrimitive Christianity, trans. Salvator Attanasio
(Baltimore, Md.: Helicon Press, 1958), p. 35f.

162The principle of pikuah nefesh is at B. Yom.
84b, 85a-b; San. 74a; M. Shab. 18:3; Mekh. III,
197ff.: T. Shab. 15:16f; M. Yom. 8:6; B. Ket. 5a, 15b,
19a; Habermann, p. 195 states that al, "do not" (save

the person) is no grounds for this. R. H. Charles, "Fragments of a Zadokite Work," Apocrypha II, 828, correctly sees this Qumran halakhah as contrary to rabbinic halakhah. In the text used by Charles, the halakhah is at 13:26.

[163]Ginzberg, pp. 74ff. He reads yatĕh, that anyone who "causes to stray," that is, the one who misleads others, is not subject to the death penalty for his sinful teachings, but that the person who actually commits the sinful act is culpable as in the Pentateuch and Jubilees.

[164]Op. cit., p. 60, n. 3 to line 3.

[165]Op. cit., p. 78.

[166]Num. 28:10 allows the daily tamid as well. It is evident from proto-rabbinic sources that other offerings were also permitted on the Sabbath, e.g., the paschal lamb, B. Pes. 66a.

[167]See Jacob Milgrom, "The Temple Scroll," BA, 41 (1978), 105-120. It has not been possible for me to gain access to The Temple Scroll, but it appears from Milgrom's summary that there is no additional Sabbath halakhah in it.

[168]The statement of Joachim Jeremias, New Testament Theology, p. 208, that Jesus ". . . rejected it [the halakhah] in a radical way. In particular, he fought against the Rabbinic Halakhah on the Sabbath," is typical of much modern scholarship and is the summary position which must be rejected. See his discussion, pp. 208f. One of the many errors in his presentation is the statement "The only [my emphasis] thing that could release a man from his obligation to observe the Sabbath Halakhah was danger to his life. . . ." But Jeremias correctly does not view Mt. 12:8 as Christological. While he looks at Mk. 3:4 to find the love command as vital to Sabbath halakhah, he could have more aptly cited the use of Hos. 6:6 at Mt. 12:7.

VI. Notes

[1] I use this term as a possible translation of both hē basileia tōn ouranōn and hē basileia tou theou. The Hebrew malkhut shamayim, as used e.g., at B. Ber. 13b, signifies the "kingship" of God, as affirmed by the recital of the Shemá. This talmudic source is second century and must, of course, be taken with caution.

[2] Philo's Therapeutae. See his On the Contemplative Life.

[3] Chapter Three above.

[4] Translation by H. St. J. Thackeray, War I, 5.2 (110).

[5] Morton Smith, "Jesus' Attitude Towards the Law," Fourth World Congress of Jewish Studies Papers (Jerusalem: World Union of Jewish Studies, 1967) I, 241-244; p. 242.

[6] Teaching of Jesus, pp. 296f.

[7] M. Sot. 3:3; beraitá, B. Sot. 22b; P. Sot. 20c; B. B. B. 60b; Pes. 70b; T. Ber. 3:25; T. Sot. 15:11-12; M. Hag. 2:7; M. Yad. 4:6. There are references where perushite halakhah seems more "liberal" than that of the Sadducees, e.g., M. Yad. 4:7 on the question of one's liability for a servant's damage to another's property. But this and many other references must each be studied against the total complex of halakhah. Regretfully, Elias Rivkin, A Hidden Revolution (Nashville: Abingdon, 1978), pp. 125-179, has made many unwarranted assumptions and drawn insupportable conclusions concerning this material. Nevertheless, his study is important for its provocative contribution toward a new comprehensive monograph on the subject of perushite halakhah in comparison to the halakhah that goes by the name of "rabbinic." One of the issues involved is to decide when a proto-rabbi is "perushitic," but not a real parush, and what Sadducees and Boethusians really mean in juxtaposition with perushim, hakhamim and sofrim. Rivkin raises a legitimate question as to why perushim is sometimes translated as Pharisees, and at other times is not, and whether each translation is necessarily correct. See also his useful notes at pp. 312-329, which must be read, however, with

caution.

[8]G. R. Driver, The Judaean Scrolls (Oxford: Basil Blackwell, 1965), pp. 45f., 69. See CDC 16:10f.; IQM 7:3.

[9]Philo, The Contemplative Life 3 (32f.).

[10]See, for example, most recently, Robert H. Stein, The Method and Message of Jesus' Teachings (Philadelphia: The Westminster Press, 1978), p. 120.

[11]Dissertation, pp. 43ff.

[12]Ibid., pp. 51f.

[13]Third-fourth century Palestinian Amora. See Strack, Introduction, p. 125.

[14]Note 13.

[15]"The Gospel of Thomas," Introduction, Helmut Koester, trans. Thomas O. Lambdin, The Nag Hammadi Library in English, General Ed. James M. Robinson (New York; etc.: Harper and Row, 1977), pp. 117-130. Koester, p. 117, thinks there are preserved Greek fragments that may be dated to ca. 200 and that the earliest Greek, Syriac or Aramaic collection may be 1st cent., in some instances possibly older than synoptic material. Of the thirteen codices found at Nag Hammadi Thomas is given as Codex II, Tractate 2, and the reference at n. 16 is according to the pagination of the codices.

[16]P. 38 of the codex, line 19f.; p. 121 of Nag Hammadi Library. See also The Secret Sayings of Jesus, ed. Robert M. Grant and David Noel Freedman, trans. William R. Schoedel (Garden City, N.Y.: Doubleday and Co., 1960), listed as logion 28, p. 147.

[17]Mig. Ab. 16 (91).

[18]A concomitant of this which requires further investigation as part of a separate monograph on the "rabbinism" of Jesus, is that during the 20 years or so between his visit to the Temple (Lk. 2:42-47), and his appearance before John the Baptist (Lk. 3:21; Mt. 3:13; Mk. 1:9), Jesus was first a disciple and then a colleague of proto-rabbis in Galilee. The most celebrated of those was Yohanan b. Zakkai. My

conjecture is that Jesus and Yoḥanan were the same age and ultimately were colleagues in Galilee. Jesus would have been a mature disciple and colleague of proto-rabbis during the decade 20-30 when Yoḥanan b. Zakkai was in Galilee and Jesus was in his formative period. Both probably studied at both the schools of Hillel and Shammai and both took independent directions. While Yoḥanan remained a strict constructionist for some Sabbath matters, Jesus was lenient. Both taught cooperation with Rome, and during Yoḥanan's period of leadership at Yabneh, no action was taken against Christians.

[19]One is entitled to assume that the tradition at M. Ab. 5:24 is much older than its attribution to the undatable Judah b. Tema. For example, it is also attributed to the first-century scholar Samuel the Small who was a contemporary of Jesus and died at an advanced age after being with Gamaliel II at Yabneh and authoring the birkhat haminim. See Herford, Aboth, pp. 143f., 118f.; 119, n. 1; Sayings of the Jewish Fathers, ed. Charles Taylor, Hebrew section, p. 43. Taylor indicates that M. Ab. 5:24 (Herford ed.) is an appendix that did not belong to the original Abot, and he cites a variant text that attributes it to Samuel the Small.

[20]Mekh. III, 198.

BIBLIOGRAPHY

Albeck, C. Einführung in die Mishchna. Trans. Tamar and Pessach Galewski. Berlin and New York: De Gruyter, 1971.

Albeck, C. Mavo LaMishnah. Jerusalem: Mosad Bialek, 1959.

Albeck, C. Untersuchunger über die Redaktion der Mischna. Berlin: C. A. Schwetschke, 1923.

Allen, W. C. The Gospel According to S. Matthew. The International Critical Commentary. 3rd ed. Edinburgh: T. and T. Clark, rpt. 1972.

Alon, Gedalyahu. Jews, Judaism and the Classical World. Jerusalem: The Magnes Press, 1977.

Alon, Gedalyahu. Mehkarim Betoledot Yisrael. 2 vols. Tel Aviv: Hakibutz Hameuhad, 1957-1958.

Alon, Gedalyahu. Toledot Hayehudim be Eretz Yisrael Bitekufat Hamishnah Vehatalmud. Tel-Aviv: Hakibutz Hameuhad, 1952-1955.

Ancient Near Eastern Texts Related to the Old Testament. Ed. James B. Pritchard. 2nd Ed. Princeton, N.J.: Princeton University Press, 1955.

Andreasen Neils-Erik A. The Old Testament Sabbath, A Tradition-Historical Investigation. Missoula, Mont.: Society of Biblical Literature, 1972.

Apocrypha and Pseudepigrapha of the O.T. Ed. R. H. Charles. 2 vols. Oxford: Clarendon Press, 1913.

Aramaic Papyri of the Fifth Century B.C. Ed. A. Cowley. Oxford: Clarendon Press, 1923.

The Authorized Daily Prayerbook. Ed. J. H. Hertz. New York: Bloch, 1948.

Bacher, W. Agadot Hatannaim. Trans. A. Z. Rabinowitz. Jerusalem: Devir, 1921.

Bacon, B. W. "Jesus and The Law." JBL, 47 (1928), 203-231.

Bacon, B. W. Studies in Matthew. New York: Holt and
Co., 1930.

Baltensweiler, H. Die Ehe im Neuen Testament.
Zurich: Zwingli-Verlag, 1967.

Banks, R. J. Jesus and the Law in the Synoptic
Tradition. Cambridge: Cambridge University
Press, 1975.

Baron, Salo. A Social and Religious History of the
Jews. 16 vols. New York and Philadelphia:
Jewish Publication Society, 1952-1976.

Barth, G. "Das Gesetzesverständnis des Evangelisten
Matthäus," in Bornkamm, Barth and Held,
Überlieferung und Auslegung im Matthäusevangelium.
5th ed. Neukirchen: Buchhandlung des
Erzieungsvereins, 1960.

Baur, F. C. Vorlesungen uber neutestamentliche
Theologie. Leipzig: Fues, 1864.

Beare, F. W. "The Sabbath Was Made For Man?" JBL, 79
(1960), 130-136.

Belkin, S. Philo and the Oral Law. Cambridge, Mass.:
Harvard University Press, 1940.

Berger, K. Die Gesetzesauslegung Jesu. Teil I:
Markus und Parallelen. Neukirchen-Vluyn:
Neukirchener Verlag, 1972.

Berman, Saul J. "Lifnim Mishurat Hadin." JJS, 26
(1975), 86-104; 28 (1977) 181-193.

Biblia Hebraica. Ed. Rudolf Kittel, Paul Kahle.
Stuttgart: American Bible Society, 1952.

Black, Matthew. An Aramaic Approach to the Gospels
and Acts. 3rd ed. Oxford: Clarendon Press,
1967.

Bläser, Peter. Das Gesetz bei Paulus. Munster:
I. W. Aschendorff, 1941.

Blau, Ludwig. Jüdische Ehescheidung und der jüdische
Scheidebrief. Strassburg: K. J. Trübner, 1911.

Bornkamm, G. "Die Auferstandene und der Irdische." in Überlieferung und Aulegung im Matthäus-evangelium. Neukirchen: Buchhandlung des Erzieungsvereins, 1960.

Bornkamm, G. "Endwartung und Kirche im Matthäus-evangelium." in Überlieferung und Auslegung im Matthäusevangelium. Neukirchen: Buchhandlung des Erzieungvereins, 1960.

Bornkamm, G. Jesus of Nazareth. Trans. Irene and Fraser Mcluskey with James M. Robinson. New York: Harper and Row, 1975.

Bornkamm, G.; Barth, G.; Held, H. J. Tradition and Interpretation in Matthew. Trans. Percy Scott, London: SCM Press, 1963.

Bornkamm, G.; Barth, G.; Held, H. J. Überlieferung und Auslegung im Matthäusevangelium. 5th ed. Neukirchen: Buchhandlung des Erziehungsvereins, 1968.

Bousset, W. Die Religion des Judentums im Neutestamentlichen Zeitalter. Berlin: Reuther and Reichard, 1903.

Box, G. H. Judaism in the Greek Period. rpt. Westport, Conn.: Greenwood Press, 1971.

Brandon, S. G. F. The Fall of Jerusalem and the Christian Church. London: S.P.C.K., 1951.

Brandon, S. G. F. Jesus and the Zealots. New York: Charles Scribner's Sons, 1967.

Branscomb, B. H. Jesus and the Law of Moses. New York: Smith, 1930.

Brooklyn Museum Aramaic Papyri. ed. Emil G. Kraeling. New Haven, Conn.: Yale University Press, 1953.

Brown, Raymond. The Gospel According to John. The Anchor Bible. 2nd ed. New York: Doubleday, 1977.

Bruce, F. F. Biblical Exegesis in the Qumran Texts. London: Tyndale; Grand Rapids, Mich.: Wm. Eerdmans, 1960.

Büchler, A. Die Priester under der Cultus im
LetztenJahrzehnte des Jerusalemishchen Tempels.
Vienna: Israel Theological Lehranstalt, 1895.

Büchler, A. Types of Palestinian Jewish Piety From 70
B.C.E. To 70 C.E. London: Jews' College, 1922.

Bultmann, R. The History of the Synoptic Tradition.
Trans. John Marsh. Oxford: Basil Blackwell,
1963.

Bultmann, R. Primitive Christianity in its
Contemporary Setting. Trans. R. H. Fuller.
London and New York: Meridian Books, 1956.

Bultmann, R. Theology of the New Testament. 2 Vols.
in 1. Trans. K. Grobel. New York: Charles
Scribner's Sons, 1951-1955.

Catchpole, D. R. "The Synoptic Divorce Material As a
Traditio-Historical Problem." Bulletin of John
Rylands University Library of Manchester 57
(1974) 92-127.

Christianity, Judaism and Other Graeco-Roman Cults.
Ed. Jacob Neusner. 4 parts. Leiden: E. J.
Brill, 1975.

Cody, Aelred. A History of the Old Testament
Priesthood. Rome: Pontifical Biblical
Institute, 1969.

Cohen, Boaz. Jewish and Roman Law. New York: Jewish
Theological Seminary, 1966.

Contributions to the Scientific Study of Jewish
Liturgy. Ed. Jakob Petuchowski. New York:
KTAV, 1970.

Cope, O. Lamar. Matthew, A Scribe Trained For
the Kingdom of Heaven. The Catholic Biblical
Quarterly Monograph Series 5. Washington, D.C.:
Catholic Biblical Association, 1976.

Cullman, Oscar. "The Significance of the Qumran Texts
For Research Into the Beginnings of Christianity."
JBL, 74 (1955), 213-226.

Daniel-Rops, Henri. Jesus and His Times. Trans. Ruby
Millar. New York: Dutton, 1958.

Daniélou, Jean. The Dead Sea Scrolls and Primitive Christianity. Trans. Salvator Attanasio. Baltimore, Md.: Helicon Press, 1958.

Daube, David. The New Testament and Rabbinic Judaism. London: Athlone Press, 1952.

Daube, David. "Rabbinic Methods of Interpretation and Hellenistic Rhetoric." HUCA, 22 (1949), 239-264.

Davenport, Gene L. The Eschatology of the Book of Jubilees. Leiden: E. J. Brill, 1971.

Davies, W. D. Paul and Rabbinic Judaism. rpt. New York: Harper and Row, 1967.

Davies, W. D. "Reflections on A Scandinavian Approach to 'The Gospel Tradition.'" The Setting of the Sermon on the Mount. rpt. Cambridge: Cambridge University Press, 1977, 464-480.

Davies, W. D. The Setting of the Sermon on the Mount. rpt. Cambridge: Cambridge University Press, 1977.

Derrett, J. Duncan M. Law in the New Testament. London: Darton, Longman and Todd, 1970.

Derrett, J. Duncan M. Studies in the New Testament. Leiden: E. J. Brill, 1977.

The Diatessaron of Tatian. Trans. J. Hamlyn Hill. Edinburgh: T. and T. Clark, 1894.

Dibelius, M. From Tradition to Gospel. Trans. from Rev. 2nd Ed. Bertram Lee Woolf, New York: Scribner, 1965.

von Dobschütz. "Matthäus als Rabbi und Katechet." ZNW, 27 (1928), 338-348.

Documents of Jewish Sectaries. I, Fragments of a Zadokite Work. Ed. Solomon Schechter. rpt. New York: KTAV, 1970.

Dodd, C. H. According To The Scriptures. New York: Charles Scribner's Sons, 1953.

Doeve, J. W. Jewish Hermeneutics in the

Synoptic Gospels and Acts. Assen: Van Goraim, 1954.

Driver, G. R. The Judean Scrolls. Oxford: Basil Blackwell, 1965.

Driver, S. R. Deuteronomy. A Critical and Exegetical Commentary. International Critical Commentary. New York: Charles Scribner's Sons, 1895.

Dupont-Summer, A. The Essene Writings From Qumran. Oxford: Basil Blackwell, 1961.

Encyclopedia Judaica, 16 Vols. Ed. Cecil Roth and Geoffrey Wigoder et. al. Jerusalem: Macmillan Co., 1971.

Enelow, Hyman G. "The Modern Reconstruction of the Pharisees," in Selected Works of Hyman G. Enelow. Kingsport, Tenn.: Kingsport Press, 1935.

Englander, Henry. "The Men of the Great Synagogue." HUCA, Jubilee Volume (1925), 145-169.

Epstein, J. N. Mavò Lenusah Hamishnah, Jerusalem: n. p., 1948.

Epstein, J. N. Mavo-ot Lesifrut Hatannaim. ed. Ezra Melamed. Tel Aviv: Devir, 1957.

Eusebius. The Ecclesiastical History. Trans. Kirsopp Lake. 2 Vols. Cambridge, Mass.: Harvard University Press, 1953.

Finkel, Asher. The Pharisees and the Teacher of Nazareth. Leiden: E. J. Brill, 1964.

Finkelstein, Louis. "The Book of Jubilees and Rabbinic Halakhah." HTR, 16 (1928), 39-61; Pharisaism in the Making. 199-221.

Finkelstein, Louis. Haperushim VeAnshei Keneset Hagedolah. New York: Jewish Theological Seminary, 1950.

Finkelstein, Louis. "Introductory Study to Pirke Abot." JBL, 57 (1938), 13-50.

Finkelstein, Louis. "The Maxim of the Anshe Keneset Hagedolah." JBL, 59 (1940), 455-469.

Finkelstein, Louis. New Light From The Prophets. New York: Basic Books, 1969.

Finkelstein, Louis. Pharisaism in the Making. New York: KTAV, 1972.

Finkelstein, Louis. The Pharisees: The Sociological Background of Their Faith. 2 Vols. 2nd Ed. Philadelphia: Jewish Publication Society, 1940.

Fishbane, Michael. "The Qumran Pesher and Traits of Ancient Hermeneutics." Proceedings of the Sixth World Congress of Jewish Studies. Jerusalem: Magnes Press, 1977.

Fitzmyer, J. A. "The Matthean Divorce Texts and Some New Palestinian Evidence." Theological Studies, 37 (1976), 197-226.

Fleming, T. V. "Christ and Divorce." Theological Studies, 24 (1963), 106-120.

Frankel, Zekhariah. Darkhe Hamishnah. Lipsiae: H. Hunger, 1859.

Frankel, Zekhariah. Mabo Hayerushalmi. Breslau: Schletter, 1870.

Frazer, Sir James George. Folklore in the Old Testament. 3 Vols. London: Macmillan, 1918.

Gaster, Theodore. The Dead Sea Scriptures. 3rd ed. Garden City, N.Y.: 1976.

Gerhardsson, B. Memory and Manuscript. Trans. Eric J. Sharpe. Uppsala: C. W. K. Gleerup, 1961.

Gesenius' Hebrew and Chaldee Lexicon to the Old Testament. Trans. Samuel P. Tregelles. Grand Rapids, Mich.: Wm. B. Eerdmans, 1952.

Ginzberg, Louis. A Commentary on the Palestinian Talmud. 4 Vols. New York: KTAV, 1971. (Hebrew).

Ginzberg, Louis. An Unknown Jewish Sect. New York: Jewish Theological Seminary, 1976.

256

Ginzberg, Louis. "The Mishnah Tamid." Journal of Jewish Lore and Philosophy 1. (1919) 33-34; 197-209; 265-295.

Ginzberg, Louis. On Jewish Law and Lore. Philadelphia: Jewish Publication Society, 1955.

Ginzberg, Louis. Legends of the Jews. 7 Vols. Philadelphia: JPS, 1946.

Gluck, Nelson. Hesed in the Bible. Trans. Alfred Gottschalk. Cincinnati: Hebrew Union College Press, 1967.

Goodenough, E. R. The Jurisprudence of the Jewish Courts in Egypt. Amsterdam: Philo Press, 1968.

Goppelt, L. Typos, Die typologische Deutung des Alten Testaments in Neuen. Darmstadt: Wissenschaftliche Buchgesellschaft, 1969.

Goulder, M. Midrash and Lection in MT. London: SPCK, 1974.

A Grammatical Analysis of the Greek New Testament. Ed. Max Zerwick and Mary Grosvenor. Rome: Biblical Institute Press, 1974.

Gray, Barbara C. "Movements of the Jerusalem Church During the First Jewish War." The Journal of Ecclesiastical History, 24 (Jan. 1973), 1-7.

A Greek-English Lexicon of the New Testament and Other Early Christian Literature. Ed. W. Bauer. Trans. W. F. Arndt and F. W. Gingrich. Chicago: University of Chicago Press, 1974.

The Greek New Testament. Ed. Kurt Aland, M. Black, Bruce M. Metzger, Allen Wikgren. Stuttgart: Württemberg Bible Society, 1966.

The Greek Versions of the Testaments of the Twelve Patriarchs. Ed. R. H. Charles. Oxford: Clarendon Press, 1908.

Guelich, R. "The Antithesis of Mt. 5:21-48: Traditional and/or Redactional?" NTS, 22 (1976), 444-457.

Guelich, R. A. "Not to Annul the Law Rather to

Fulfill the Law and the Prophets." Dissertation, University of Hamburg, 1967.

Gundry, R. H. The Use of the Old Testament in St. Matthew's Gospel. Leiden: E. J. Brill, 1967.

Guttmann, A. "The Problem of the Anonymous Mishnah." HUCA, 16 (1941), 137-155.

Guttmann, Alexander. Rabbinic Judaism in the Making. Detroit: Wayne State University Press, 1970.

Hadas, Moses. Hellenistic Culture. New York: Columbia University Press, 1959.

Hare, D. R. A. The Theme of Jewish Persecution of Christians in the Gospel According to St. Matthew. Cambridge: Cambridge University Press, 1967.

von Harnack, A. Aus Wissenschaft unds Leben II. Giessen: Töpelmann, 1911.

von Harnack, A. "Hat Jesus das alt Testamentliche Gesetz abgeschaft?" in Aus Wissenschaft und Leben II. Giessen: Töpelmann, 1911.

Herbert, G. "The Problem of the Gospel According to Matthew." Scottish Journal of Theology, 14 (1961), 403-413.

The Hebrew Text of the Book of Ecclesiasticus. Ed. Israel Levi. 3rd ed. Leiden: E. J. Brill, 1969.

The Hellenistic Age. J. B. Bury et. al. Cambridge: University Press, 1925. rpt. New York: Kraus Co., 1968.

Hengel, Martin. Hellenism and Judaism. Trans. John Bowden. 2 Vols. Philadelphia: Fortress Press, 1974.

Herford, Travers. The Pharisees. Boston: Beacon Press, 1962.

Herzog, Issac. The Main Institutions of Jewish Law. 2 Vols. 2nd ed. London: Soncino Press, 1967.

Hill, David. The Gospel of Matthew. New Century

Bible. Greenwood, S.C.: Attic Press, 1975.

Hill, David. "On the Use and Meaning of Hosea 6:6 in Matthew's Gospel." NTS, 24 (October 1977), 107-119.

Hinz, C. "Jesus und der Sabbat." Kerygma und Dogma, 19 (1973), 91-108.

Hoenig, S. "An Interdict Against Socializing on the Sabbath." JQR, 62 (1971), 77-83.

Hoffman, D. Die erste Mischna. Berlin: H. Itzkowski, 1881.

Hoffman, D. The First Mishna and the Controversies of the Tannaim. trans. Paul Forchheimer. New York: Maurosho Publications, 1977.

Holdheim, Samuel. Ma'amar Haishut (Hebrew) Berlin: n.p. 1860.

Holzmeister, U. "Die Streitfrage über die Ehescheidungstexte bei Matthäus 5:32, 19:9." Biblica, 26 (1945), 133-146.

Hummel, R. Die Auseinandersetzung zwischen Kirche und Judentum im Matthäusevangelium. Munich: Chr. Kaiser Verlag, 1963.

Isaksson. Marriage and Ministry in the New Temple. Trans. N. Tomkinson. Lund: C. W. K. Gleerup, 1965.

Jastrow, Marcus. A Dictionary of the Targumim, The Talmud Babli and Yerushalmi and the Midrashic Literature. 2 Vols. New York: Pardes, 1950.

Jeremias, Joachim. The Eucharistic Words of Jesus. Trans. Norman Perrin. Philadelphia: Fortress Press, 1977.

Jeremias, Joachim. Jerusalem in the Time of Jesus. Trans. F. H. and C. H. Cave. Philadelphia: Fortress Press, 1969.

Jeremias, Joachim. New Testament Theology. Trans. John Bowden. New York: Scribner, 1971.

Jeremias, Joachim. The Prayers of Jesus. Studies in

Biblical Theology. Second Series.
6. Naperville, Ill.: Alec R. Allenson, 1967.

Josephus. With an English Translation by
H. St. J. Thackeray, R. Marcus, A. Wikgren and
L. H. Feldman. 9 Vols. Loeb Classical Library.
London, New York and Cambridge, Mass.: William
Heinemann and Harvard University Press,
1926-1965.

Judaism and Christianity. Ed. W. O. E. Oesterley,
London: The Sheldon Press, 1937.

Kahler, M. Jesus und das Alte Testament. Leipzig:
A. Deichert, 1896.

Kaplan, Julius. The Redaction of the Babylonian
Talmud. Jerusalem: Makor, 1973.

Katz, B. Z. Perushim, Zedukim, Kannaim, Nozrim.
Tel-Aviv: N. Twersky, 1947.

Kilpatrick, G. The Origins of the Gospel According
to St. Matthew. Oxford: Clarendon Press, 1946.

Kimbrough, S. T. "The Concept of Sabbath at Qumran."
Revue de Qumran, 5 (1964-1966), 483-502.

Kingsbury, Jack Dean. Matthew: Structure,
Christology, Kingdom. Philadelphia: Fortress
Press, 1975.

Klausner, Joseph. Jesus of Nazareth. Trans. Herbert
Danby. New York: Macmillan, 1946.

Klostermann, Erich. Jesu Stelling zum Alten Testament.
Kiel: R. Cordes, 1904.

Knight, G. F. Law and Grace: Must a Christian Keep
the Law of Moses? Philadelphia: Westminster
Press, 1962.

Koch, K. The Growth of the Biblical Tradition.
Trans. from 2nd ed. S. M. Cupitt. New York:
Scribner, 1969.

Landman, Leo. Jewish Law in the Diaspora.
Philadelphia: JPS, 1968.

Lauterbach, J. Z. "Ordination." Jewish Encylopedia.

New York and London: Funk and Wagnalls, 1912, Vol. IX. 428-430.

Lauterbach, J. Z. Rabbinic Essays. Cincinnati: Hebrew Union College Press, 1951.

Lenski, R. C. H. Interpretation of St. Matthew's Gospel. Columbus: Wartburg Press, 1943.

Levine, Etan. "The Sabbath Controversy According to Mt." NTS, 22 (1976), 480-483.

Lieberman, Saul. Greek in Jewish Palestine. New York: The Jewish Theological Seminary, 1942.

Lieberman, Saul. Hellenism in Jewish Palestine. New York: The Jewish Theological Seminary, 1950.

Lindblom, Johannes. Prophecy in Ancient Israel. Philadelphia: Fortress Press, 1962.

The Lives of the Prophets. Trans. C. C. Torrey. Philadelphia: Society of Biblical Literature, 1946.

Loewe, Herbert. "Pharisaism." Judaism and Christianity. Vol. I. The Age of Transition. Ed. W. O. E. Oesterley. London: The Sheldon Press, 1937.

Loewe, R. "The 'Plain' Meaning of Scripture in Early Jewish Exegesis." PIJSL I. Ed. J. G. Weiss. Jerusalem: Hebrew University, 1964.

Lohse, E. "Jesu Worte über den Sabbat." Judentum, Urchristentum. Kirche (1960) 79-89.

Longenecker, R. N. Biblical Exegesis in the Apostolic Period. n.p.: William B. Eerdman's Pub. Co., 1975.

Manson, T. W. Ethics and the Gospel. London: SCM Press, 1960.

Manson, T. W. "Jesus, Paul and the Law." Judaism and Christianity III. Ed. E. I. J. Rosenthal. rpt. London: KTAV, 1969, 125-141.

Manson, T. W. "The O. T. in the Teaching of Jesus." Bulletin of the John Rylands Library, 34 (1952),

312-332.

Manson, T. W. The Sayings of Jesus. London: SCM Press, 1949.

Manson, T. W. The Teachings of Jesus. Cambridge: University Press, 1931.

Mantel, Hugo. Studies in the History of the Sanhedrin. Cambridge, Mass.: Harvard University Press, 1965.

Marcus, Ralph. Law in the Apocrypha. New York: AMS Press, 1966.

Megilot Midbar Yehudah. Ed. A. M. Habermann. Israel: Machberoth Lesifruth, 1959.

Meier, J. P. Law and History in Matthew's Gospel. Rome: Biblical Institute Press, 1976.

Mekhilta de R. Ishmael. Trans. Jacob Z. Lauterbach. Philadelphia: Jewish Publication Society, 1949.

Merkel, H. "Jesus und der Pharisäer." NTS, 14 (1968), 194-208.

Metzger, Bruce M. A Textual Commentary on the Greek New Testament. n.p.: United Bible Societies, 1971.

Midrash Rabbah. New York: Grossman, 1951.

Mielziner, Moses. Introduction to the Talmud. 4th Ed. New York: Bloch Publishing Co., 1968.

Mishnayoth. Ed. Philip Blackman. 6 Vols. 3rd Ed. Gateshead, England: Judaica Press, 1973.

Montefiore, Claude G. Rabbinic Literature and Gospel Teaching. London: Macmillan, 1930.

Moore, G. F. "Christian Writers on Judaism." HTR, 14 (1921), 197-254.

Moore, G. F. Judaism in the First Centuries of the Christian Era: The Age of the Tannaim. 3 Vols. Cambridge, Mass.: Harvard University Press, 1950.

The Nag Hammadi Library in English. General Ed.
James M. Robinson. New York: Harper and Row,
1977.

Neufeld, E. Ancient Hebrew Marriage Laws. London:
Longman's Green and Co., 1944.

Neusner, Jacob. Development of a Legend. Leiden:
E. J. Brill, 1970.

Neusner, Jacob. Eliezer Ben Hyrcanus. 2 Vols.
Leiden: E. J. Brill, 1970.

Neusner, Jacob. A Life of Rabban Yohanan Ben Zakkai.
2nd ed. Leiden: E. J. Brill, 1970.

Neusner, Jacob. The Rabbinic Traditions About the
Pharisees Before 70. 3 Vols. Leiden:
E. J. Brill, 1971.

Newman, J. Halakhic Sources. Lieden: E. J. Brill,
1969.

Pancaro, Severino. The Law in the Fourth Gospel.
Leiden: E. J. Brill, 1975.

Patte, Daniel. Early Jewish Hermeneutic in Palestine.
Missoula, Mont.: Scholars Press, 1975.

Percy, E. Die Botschaft Jesu. Lund: Gleerup, 1953.

Pfeiffer, Robert H. History of New Testament Times.
New York: Harper & Row, 1949.

Philo. The Greek Text of Cohn and Wendland; Trans.
F. H. Colson, Ralph Marcus and G. H. Whitaker.
12 Vols. The Loeb Classical Library. Cambridge,
Mass.: Harvard University Press; London:
William Heinemann, 1949-1962.

Pines, Schlomo. "The Jewish Christians of the Early
Centuries of Christianity According to a New
Source." Proceedings of the Israel Academy of
Sciences and Humanities. Vol. II. No. 13.
1966.

Pirke Aboth. Ed. R. Travers Herford. New York:
Jewish Institute of Religion. 1945.

Porten, B. Archives from Elephantine. Berkeley and

Los Angeles: University of California Press, 1968.

Rabin, C. Qumran Studies. New York: Schocken, 1975.

von Rad, Gerhard. Deuteronomy. A Commentary. Philadelphia: The Westminster Press, 1966.

Rankin, O. S. Israel's Wisdom Literature. New York: Schocken, 1969.

Reimarus, H. S. The Goal of Jesus and His Disciples. Trans. G. W. Buchanan. Leiden: E. J. Brill, 1970.

Riesenfeld, H. The Gospel Tradition and Its Beginnings: A Study in the Limits of 'Formgeschichte'. London: A. R. Mowbray, 1957.

Ritter, Bernhard. Philo und die Halacha: Eine vergleichende Studie unter steter Berücksichtigung des Josephus. Leipzig: J. C. Hinrichs, 1879.

Rivkin, E. "Defining the Pharisees: The Tannaitic Sources." HUCA, 40-41 (1969-70), 205-249.

Rivkin, Ellis. A Hidden Revolution. Nashville: Abingdon, 1978.

Robinson, J. A. T. Redating the New Testament. Philadelphia: The Westminster Press, 1976.

Rössler, D. Gesetz und Geschichte. Neukirchen: Neukirchener Verlag, 1960.

Sand, A. Das Gestez und die Propheten. Regensburg: F. Pustet, 1974.

Sand, A. "Die Unzuchtsklausel in Mt. 5:31-32 und 19:3-9." Münchener Theologische Zeitschrift 20 (1969) 118-129.

Sanders, E. P. Paul and Palestinian Judaism. Philadelphia: Fortress Press, 1977.

Sayings of the Jewish Fathers. Ed. Charles Taylor. "Prolegomenon." Judah Goldin, 2nd Ed. New York: KTAV, 1969.

Schachter, M. The Babylonian and Jerusalem Mishnah
Textually Compared. Jerusalem: Mosad Harav
Kook, 1959.

Schiffman, Lawrence H. The Halakhah at Qumran.
Leiden: E. J. Brill, 1975.

Schlatter, A. Der Evangelist Matthäus. Stuttgart:
Caliver, 1948.

Schmid, I. Das Evangelium nach Matthäus. Regensburg:
Pustet, 1965.

Schmidt, K. L. Der Rahmen der Geschichte Jesu. 2nd ed.
Darmstadt: Wissenschaftliche Buchgesellschaft,
1964.

Schoeps, H. J. Aus frühchristlicher Zeit,
religionsgeschichtliche Untersuchungen.
Tubingen: Mohr, 1950.

Schürer, E. A History of the Jewish People in the
Time of Jesus Christ. 5 Vols. Trans.
John Macpherson et. al. New York: Scribner,
1897-1898.

Schürer, E. A History of the Jewish People in the
Time of Jesus. Ed. Nahum Glatzer. New York:
Schocken, 1975.

Schweizer, E. Des Evangelium nach Matthäus.
Gottingen: Vanderhoeck and Ruprecht, 1973.

Schweizer, E. "Observance of the Law and Charismatic
Activity in Matthew." NTS, 16 (1969-70),
213-230.

The Secret Sayings of Jesus. Ed. Robert M. Grant,
David Noel Freedman. Trans. William R. Schoedel.
Garden City, New York: Doubleday and Co., 1960.

Septuaginta. Ed. Alfred Rahlfs. 2 Vols. 3rd ed.
New York: American Bible Society, 1949.

Sifra. Ed. J. H. Weiss. Vienna: 1861.

Sifre Debe Rab. Ed. Meir Friedman. Vienna: n.p.,
1863. rpt. Jerusalem, 1967.

Sifre on Deuteronomy. Ed. Louis Finkelstein. 2nd ed.

New York: Jewish Theological Seminary, 1969.

Sigal, Phillip. The Emergence of Contemporary Judaism. 2 Vols. Pittsburgh, Pa.: Pickwick Press, 1977.

Sigal, Phillip. New Dimensions in Judaism. Jericho, N.Y.: Exposition Press, 1972.

Smith, Morton. "A Comparison of Early Christian and Early Rabbinic Tradition." JBL, 82 (1963), 169-176.

Smith, Morton. "Jesus' Attitude Towards the Law." Fourth World Congress of Jewish Studies Papers. Jerusalem: World Union of Jewish Studies, 1967. I. 241-244.

Smith, Morton. "Palestinian Judaism in the First Century." in Israel: Its Role in Civilization. Ed. Moshe Davies. New York: Jewish Theological Seminary, 1956. 67-81.

Smith, Morton. Palestinian Parties and Politics That Shaped the Old Testament. New York and London: Columbia University Press, 1971.

Socrates, Scholasticus. A History of the Church. London: Samuel Bagster and Sons, 1844.

Sowers, S. G. The Hermeneutics of Philo and Hebrews. Richmond, Va.: John Knox, 1965.

Stein, Robert H. The Method and Message of Jesus' Teachings. Philadelphia: The Westminster Press, 1978.

Stendahl, K. The School of St. Matthew. Uppsala: Gleerup, 1954.

Strack, H. Introduction to the Talmud and Midrash. Trans. from 5th ed. New York: Meridian Books, 1959.

Strack, H. L., Billerbeck, P. Kommentar zum Neuen Testament aus Talmud und Midrasch. 5 Vols. Munich: C. H. Becksche, 1965.

Strauss, D. F. Das Leben Jesu. 4th ed. Bonn: n.p., 1877.

Strecker, G. Der Weg der Gerechtigkeit. 2nd ed. Munich: Kosel-Verlag, 1946.

Streeter, B. H. The Four Gospels. A Study of Origins. London: Macmillan & Co., 1953.

Suggs, J. M. Wisdom, Christology and Law in Matthew's Gospel. Cambridge, Mass.: Harvard University Press, 1970.

The Synoptic Gospels. ed. C. G. Montefiore. 3 Vols. London: Macmillan, 1909.

Talmud Babli. (The Babylonian Talmud). New York: Shulsinger Bros., 1947.

Talmud Yerushalmi. (The Palestinian Talmud). New York: Shulsinger Bros., 1948.

Tarn, W. W. and G. T. Griffith. Hellenistic Civilization. 3rd rev. ed. London: Edward Arnold and Co., 1952.

Taylor, V. The Formation of the Gospel Tradition. London: Macmillan and Co., 1933.

Tcherikover, Victor. Hellenistic Civilization and the Jews. Trans. S. Applebaum. Philadelphia: Jewish Publication Society, 1969.

Testuz, Michael. Les ideés religieuses du Livre des Jubilés. Geneva: E. Droz; Paris: Minard, 1960.

Theological Dictionary of the New Testament. 10 Vols. Eds. Gerhard Kittel and G. Friedrich. Trans. G. Bromiley. Grand Rapdis, Mich.: Eerdmans, 1964-1979.

Theologisches Wörterbuch zum Neuen Testament. Ed. Gerhard Kittel, 9 Vols. Stuttgart: W. Kohlhammer, 1935.

Thesaurus Talmudis. Ed. Chaim J. Kosowski. Jerusalem: Israel Ministry of Education and Culture and Jewish Theological Seminary, 1971.

Thompson, T. L. "A Catholic View on Divorce." Journal of Ecumenical Studies, 6 (1969), 53-67.

The Tosefta. Ed. Saul Lieberman. 4 Vols. New York:

The Jewish Theological Seminary, 1955-1973.

The Tosefta. Ed. Moshe S. Zuckermandel. Jerusalem: Wahrmann Books, 1963.

Vander Kam, James C. Textual and Historical Studies in the Book of Jubilees. Missoula, Mont.: Scholars Press, 1977.

Vawter, Bruce. "The Divorce Clauses in Mt. 5:32 and 19:9." Catholic Biblical Quarterly 16 (1954) 155-167.

Vermes, Geza. The Dead Sea Scrolls in English. Harmondsworth, Eng.: Penguin Books, 1975.

Vermes, Geza. Jesus the Jew. New York: Macmillan, 1973.

Vermes, Geza. Post-Biblical Jewish Studies. Leiden: E. J. Brill, 1975.

Vermes, Geza. Scripture and Tradition in Judaism. Leiden: E. J. Brill, 1961.

Weber, F. Jüdische Theologie auf Grund des Talmud und verwandter Schriften. Leipzig: Dorffling, 1897.

Weiss, I. H. Dor Dor Vedorshav. 5 Vols. Wilna: Joseph Zawadzki, 1911.

Wenham, J. W. Christ and the Bible. Downers Grove, Ill.: Intervarsity Press, 1973.

Wenham, J. W. Our Lord's View of the O. T. London: Tyndale Press, 1953.

Wilken, Robert L. Judaism and the Early Christian Mind. New Haven: Yale University Press, 1971.

Williamson, R. Philo and the Epistle to the Hebrews. Leiden: E. J. Brill, 1970.

Winter, Paul. "Sadoqite Fragments IV 20, 21 and the Exegesis of Genesis 1:27 in Late Judaism." ZAW, 68 (1956), 71-84; 70 (1958), 260-261.

Wolfson, H. A. Philo. 2 Vols. Cambridge, Mass.: Harvard University Press, 1962.

Yaron, Reuven. Introduction to the Law of the Aramaic
    Papyri. Oxford: Clarendon Press, 1961.

The Zadokite Documents. Ed. Chaim Rabin. Oxford:
    Clarendon Press, 1954.

Zeitlin, Solomon. "The Book of Jubilees. Its
    Character and Its Significance." Studies in the
    Early History of Judaism. Vol. II.

Zeitlin, Solomon. "The Book of Jubilees and the
    Pentateuch." Studies in the Early History of
    Judaism. Vol. II.

Zeitlin, Solomon. The Rise and Fall of the Judean
    State. 3 Vols. Philadelphia: Jewish
    Publication Society, 1968-78.

Zeitlin, Solomon. "Studies in Tannaitic
    Jurisprudence." Journal of Jewish Lore and
    Philosophy I (1919) rpt. New York: KTAV, 1969.

Zeitlin, Solomon. Studies in Early History of Judaism.
    IV Vols. New York: KTAV, 1973-1978.